The Echo of Ancient Civilizations

The Dawn of Civilization

Doug Richardson

Shadowplay Communications, LLC

Shadowplay.com
FREE BONUS

The Greatest Mystery of the American Southwest is yours for the taking. Get the Amazon Best Seller "*Anasazi of Chaco Canyon*" free, as well as the Mac and PC Video Game and Simulation!

Additionally, you'll be eligible for FREE promotional copies of our books and audiobooks, plus exciting bonuses:

Shadowplay.com/bonus

Copyright © 2023 by Doug Richardson and Shadowplay Communications, LLC

All rights reserved. No portion of this book may be reproduced in any form without written permission from the publisher or author, except as permitted by U.S. copyright law.

Contents

1. Revealing the Dawn of Civilization — 1
2. Oral and Written Records — 9
3. Ancient History of the East — 13
4. The Assyrians and the Babylonians: Chaldea — 23
5. The Caucasians of India — 31
6. The Persians and Zoroaster — 41
7. The Phoenicians — 49
8. The Origin of The Hebrews — 55
9. Greece and the Greeks — 63
10. Greek Religion — 72
11. Sparta — 84
12. Athens — 90
13. The Greeks and the Persian Wars — 97
14. The Arts in Greece — 105
15. The Greeks in Asia Before Alexander — 113
16. The Last, Decadent Years of Greece — 121
17. Rome and the Ancient People of Italy — 128
18. Roman Religion — 134
19. The Reign of the Kings — 142
20. Roman Conquest and the Roman Army — 150

21.	The Peoples of the Conquered Lands	161
22.	Greek and Oriental Influence	169
23.	The Peasants	177
24.	The Emperors	187
25.	Greek Influence on Roman Art	203
26.	The Appearance of Jesus	213
27.	The Conclusion: The Fall	223
Thank You!		234

Chapter 1

Revealing the Dawn of Civilization

Prehistoric Discoveries

In the depths of the earth, archaeologists have uncovered weapons, tools, human remains, and artifacts left by people who lived long before written history. These discoveries can be found all over the world, from France and Switzerland to England, Asia, and Africa. These remains are considered prehistoric because they date back to a time before written records. For the past one hundred and fifty years, scientists and scholars have been studying, interpreting, and collecting these relics. Today, many museums have entire halls dedicated to prehistoric artifacts. In Saint-Germain-en-Laye, near Paris, there is a museum entirely devoted to prehistoric remains. In Denmark, there is a collection of over 75,000 objects. As people continue to dig, build, and excavate, new discoveries are made every day. These artifacts are not found on the surface but buried deep, where they have been preserved over time. They are usually found in layers of gravel or clay that have gradually accumulated. The Science of Prehistory. Scientists study these artifacts to learn more about the people who left them behind. By examining their skeletons and tools, they can reconstruct their physical appearance and way of life. This study has given rise to a new field of science, known as Prehistoric Archaeology. Add in carbon dating, which can accurately determine the age of objects and some organic matter, and we can learn much about our furthest ancestors. The Four Ages. Prehistoric remains come from a variety of different cultures and time periods. These artifacts have been buried for thousands of years, dating back to a time when giant woolly mammoths roamed the earth. This long period of time can be divided into four distinct periods, known as the Rough Stone Age, the Polished Stone Age, the Bronze Age, and the Iron Age.

The epochs of human history are named after the materials utilized in crafting tools, such as stone, bronze, and iron. However, these periods are vastly dissimilar in length. The Rough Stone Age was ten times longer than the Age of Iron.

The Stone Ages

The earliest remnants of the Stone Age have been discovered in gravel deposits. In the Somme Valley, a French scholar discovered sharp flint tools between 1841 and 1853. These tools were buried six feet deep in gravel beneath three layers of clay, gravel, and marl, which is a loose or crumbling earthy deposit, that had never been disturbed. Bones of cattle, deer, and even elephants were also found in the same location. Initially, scholars dismissed this discovery, attributing the flint chipping to chance. However, in 1860, several scholars studied the remains in the Somme Valley and acknowledged that the flints were undoubtedly fashioned by humans. Since then, over 6,000 similar flints have been found in strata of the same order in the Seine Valley or in England, some alongside human bones. There is no longer any doubt that humans lived during the formation of the gravel deposits. If the strata covering these remains have always accumulated as gradually as they do today, then the humans whose bones and tools we unearthed must have lived more than 200,000 years ago. This was confirmed when carbon dating technology became available.

The Cave Men

Remains have also been discovered in rock-cut caverns, often above a river. The most prominent of these are located on the banks of the Vezere river in Southwest France, but they are present in many other places. Sometimes, they were utilized as dwellings and even as burial sites for humans. Skeletons, weapons, and tools are found together in these caves. There are flint axes, knives, scrapers, and lance points, as well as bone arrows, harpoon points, and needles similar to those used by certain indigenous peoples to this day.

The earth is littered with the remains of animals, discarded by these men who, like all indigenous peoples, were not particularly tidy. After consuming the meat, they tossed the bones into a corner, often splitting them open to extract the marrow. Among the animal remains, one can find not only the hare, deer, ox, horse, and salmon, but also extinct creatures such as the rhinoceros, cave bear, mammoth, elk, bison, and reindeer. Some of these bones have been discovered with intricate designs engraved upon them, depicting scenes such as combat, a reindeer hunt, or a mammoth with woolly hide and curved tusks. These men were undoubtedly contemporaries of the mammoth and the reindeer, and like the Eskimos of today, were hunters and fishermen who knew how to work with flint and kindle fires. The polished Stone Age was a time of great innovation, as evidenced by the discovery of Lake Villages in Switzerland. In 1854, during an unusually dry summer, the low water level of Lake Zurich revealed wooden piles that had been driven into the lake bottom, along with rudimentary utensils. These were the remains of an ancient village built over the water, and since then, over 200 similar villages have been discovered in Swiss lakes. The piles, which were trunks of trees sharpened to points and driven into the lake bottom, were required by the tens of thousands to support each village. The wooden platform supported by the pile work served as the foundation for wooden houses covered with turf. Artifacts found among the piles reveal the lifestyle of the former inhabitants who hunted and consumed animals such as deer, boar, and elk, but were also tended domesticated animals such as oxen, goats, sheep, and dogs. They were skilled in agriculture, able to till the ground, reap, and grind their grain. In the ruins of their villages, grains of wheat and even fragments of unleavened bread have been found. They wore rough hemp cloths and sewed them into garments with bone needles.

They crafted rudimentary pottery, but their technique was clumsy. Their vases were poorly fired, turned by hand, and adorned with few decorations. Like their cave-dwelling ancestors, they fashioned knives and arrows from flint, but they also learned to polish a very hard stone to make axes. This is why we call their era the Polished Stone Age. They lived much later than the cave dwellers and did not know of mammoths or rhinoceroses, but they were familiar with elk and reindeer.

Monuments of Massive Stone

Megaliths are massive stone structures made of enormous blocks of rough stone. Sometimes the rocks are exposed, while other times, they are covered with a layer of earth. Buried megaliths are called tumuli because they resemble hills. When opened, they reveal a chamber of rock, sometimes paved with flagstones. Above-ground megaliths come in various forms. The dolmen, or rock table, is a long stone laid flat over other stones set into the ground. The cromlech, or stone circle, consists of massive rocks arranged in a circle. The menhir is a block of stone standing on its end, often with several arranged in a line. In Carnac, Brittany, four thousand menhirs in eleven rows still stand, though there were once ten thousand in the area. Megalithic monuments are abundant in western France, especially in Brittany. Nearly every hill in England has them; the Orkney Islands, an archipelago off the northeastern coast of Scotland, contain more than two thousand. Denmark and North Germany are also dotted with these structures, and the locals refer to the tumuli as tombs of the giants. Megaliths are not exclusive to Europe, they can be found in India and along the African coast. It remains a mystery which people possessed the knowledge and ability to quarry, transport, and erect such massive stones. For a long time, it was believed that the ancient Gauls or Celts were responsible, hence the name Celtic Monuments. However, the presence of similar structures in Africa and India challenges this theory.

THE ECHO OF ANCIENT CIVILIZATIONS

When one of these mounds still intact is opened, one always sees a skeleton, often several, either sitting or reclining; these monuments, therefore, were used as tombs. Arms, vases, and ornaments are placed at the side of the dead. In the oldest of these tombs. The weapons are axes of polished stone; the ornaments are shells, pearls, and necklaces of bone or ivory. The vases are very simple, without a handle or neck, decorated only with lines or points. Calcified bones of animals lie about on the ground, the relics of a funeral feast laid in the tomb by the friends of the dead. Amidst these bones, we no longer find those of the reindeer, a fact which proves that these monuments were constructed after the disappearance of this animal from Western Europe, and, therefore, at a time subsequent to that of the lake villages.

The Age of Bronze

As soon as men learned to smelt metals, this technology became dominant in the manufacture of weapons. The first metal to be used was copper, easier to extract because it was easy to find and easier to manipulate since it is malleable without the application of heat. Pure copper, however, was not used as much, as weapons made of it were too fragile, but a little tin was mixed with it to give it more resistance. It is this alloy of copper and tin that we call bronze. Bronze Utensils. Bronze was used in the manufacture of ordinary tools such as knives, hammers, saws, needles, and fish hooks; in the fabrication of ornamental bracelets, brooches, and earrings; and especially in the making of daggers, lance points, axes, and swords. These objects are found by thousands throughout Europe in mounds, under the more recent dolmens, in the turf pits of Denmark, and in rock tombs. Near these objects of bronze, ornaments of gold are often seen and, now and then, the remains of a woolen garment. It cannot be due to chance that all implements of bronze are similar and all are made with the same alloy. What people invented bronze? Nobody knows.

The Iron Age

Iron, a metal harder to smelt and work than bronze, was not widely used until men learned how to use it. Once it was discovered that iron was harder and cut better than bronze, men preferred it in the manufacture of arms. In the time of Homer, iron was still a precious metal reserved for swords, while bronze was retained for other purposes. As a result, many tombs contain confused remains of utensils of bronze and weapons of iron. Iron weapons, including axes, swords, daggers, and bucklers, were ordinarily found by the side of a skeleton in a coffin made of stone or wood, as warriors had their arms buried with them. However, they were also found scattered on ancient battlefields or lost at the bottom of a marsh which later became a turf pit. In one day, 100 swords, 500 lances, 30 axes, 460 daggers, 80 knives, and 40 stilettos, all made of iron, were found in a turf pit in Schleswig. Not far from there, in the bed of an ancient lake, a great boat 66 feet long was discovered, fully equipped with axes, swords, lances, and knives. It is impossible to enumerate all the iron implements that were found. They have not been as well preserved as bronze, as iron is rapidly eaten away by rust. Thus, at first glance, they appear older, but in reality, they are more recent. The inhabitants of northern Europe knew iron before the coming of the Romans in the first century before Christ. In an old cemetery near the salt mines of Hallstadt in Austria, 980 tombs filled with instruments of iron and bronze were opened without finding a single Roman-era artifact. However, the Iron Age continued under the Romans. Almost always, iron objects are found accompanied by ornaments of gold and silver, Roman pottery, funeral urns, inscriptions, and Roman coins bearing the effigy of the emperor.

The Ages of Humanity

The story of humanity is one of progress, of moving from one age to another. The people of every country used rough stone, polished stone, bronze, and iron, but not all at the same time. The Egyptians used iron while the Greeks were still in the Bronze Age, and the Danes used stone while others used bronze. The arrival of Europeans marked the end of the polished stone age in America, while the natives of Australia still use rough stone tools. The four ages do not mark periods in the life of humanity, but rather epochs in the civilization of each country. The study of prehistoric archaeology is still a young science, but we have learned much about primitive humans through the remains they left behind. Discoveries can be made at any time, and the finds are already innumerable. However, they rarely tell us what we want to know. We still do not know how long each of the four ages lasted, when they began and ended in different parts of the world, or who built the caverns, lake villages, mounds, and dolmens. When a country moves from one age to another, is it the same people with new tools, or new people altogether? Even when we think we have found the answer, a new discovery can confound us. Despite these uncertainties, three conclusions seem certain: First, humans have lived on Earth for a long time, at least as early as the geological period known as the Quaternary. Second, humans have progressed from the savage state to civilized life, gradually improving their tools and ornaments from rough stone axes and bear tooth necklaces, to iron swords and gold jewelry. Third, human progress has accelerated over time, with each age being shorter than the one before it. The story of humanity is a long and complex one, and we have much more to learn. But with each new discovery, we come closer to understanding our past and our place in the world.

Chapter 2

Oral and Written Records

Legends, the tales passed down through generations by oral tradition, are the most ancient records of people and their doings. These stories were recited long before they were ever written down and are often mixed with fable. The Greeks, for example, told of their heroes from the oldest times who had exterminated monsters, fought giants, and even battled against the gods themselves. The Romans had their own legends, like the story of Romulus who was said to have been nourished by a wolf and raised up to heaven. Almost all peoples have such stories from their infancy, but one should not place too much confidence in these legends. True history, on the other hand, has its beginning only with authentic accounts written by well-informed individuals. This moment, however, is not the same for all peoples. The history of Egypt, for instance, dates back well over 3,000 years before Christ, while the history of the Greeks only goes back to around 800 years before Christ. Germany has a written history since the first century of our era, while Russia's history dates back only to the ninth century. Certain indigenous tribes still have no history at all. The history of civilization itself begins with the oldest civilized peoples and continues up to the present day. Antiquity is the most remote period, while Modern Times is the era in which we currently live. Ancient History, which begins with the oldest known nations like the Egyptians and Chaldeans from the period around 3,000 years before our era, surveys the peoples of the Orient, including the Hindus, Persians, Phoenicians, Jews, Greeks, and finally, the Romans. This period ends around the fifth century A.D. when the Roman Empire of the West finally collapsed. Modern History, on the other hand, starts at the end of the fifteenth century with the invention of printing, the discovery of America and the Indies, and the Renaissance of the sciences and arts. It concerns itself, especially, with the peoples of the West, including Spain, Italy, France, Germany, Russia, and America. Between Antiquity and Modern Times, there is a period of about ten centuries that belongs to neither ancient times, since the civilization of Antiquity has perished, nor modern times, since modern civilization does not yet exist. This period is commonly referred to as the Middle Ages.

The ancient civilizations of the Assyrians, Greeks, and Romans have long vanished from the earth, leaving behind only remnants of their religion, customs, and arts. These remnants, which include books, monuments, inscriptions, and languages, are what we call sources, as they provide us with knowledge of ancient history. Books were one of the written records left behind by ancient peoples. While some had sacred books such as the Hindus, Persians, and Jews, the Greeks and Romans passed down histories, poems, speeches, and philosophical treatises. However, books alone do not provide us with all the information we need. We have no Assyrian or Phoenician books, and many other peoples left very few books. The ancients wrote less than we do, resulting in a smaller body of literature to pass down. Additionally, the need to transcribe everything by hand resulted in only a small number of copies of books, most of which have been destroyed or lost. The art of deciphering these manuscripts is called Palaeography. Monuments were also built by ancient peoples such as palaces for their kings, tombs for the dead, fortresses, bridges, aqueducts, and triumphal arches. Many of these monuments have fallen into ruin or have been destroyed. Some still stand however, such as the pyramids, the temples of Thebes and Philae, the palace of Persepolis in Persia, the Parthenon in Greece, the Colosseum in Rome, and the Maison Carree and Pont du Gard in France. While some monuments are visible to the traveler, the majority have been recovered from the earth, sand, river deposits, and debris, requiring excavation to reach them. Assyrian palaces, for example, can only be reached by cutting into the hills.

For instance, a trench of forty feet was required to reach the tombs of the kings of Mycenae. The passage of time is not the only force responsible for covering these ruins, men have also played a part. In ancient times, builders did not bother to level off the ground or clear the site before constructing. Instead of removing debris, they piled it up and built on top of it. When the new structure eventually fell into disrepair, its remains were added to those of earlier times, creating several layers of ruins. When Schliemann excavated the site of Troy, he had to dig through five layers of debris which were actually five ruined villages, one on top of the other, with the oldest one buried fifty feet deep. By chance, one town has been preserved in its entirety. In 79 A.D., Mount Vesuvius erupted, spewing out a river of lava and a hail of ashes that suddenly buried two Roman cities, Herculaneum under lava and Pompeii under ashes. The lava burned everything it touched, while the ashes covered and preserved the objects, protecting them from the air and leaving them intact. As we remove the ashes, Pompeii emerges before us exactly as it was eighteen centuries ago. We can still see the wheel ruts in the pavement, the designs drawn on the walls with charcoal, the paintings, utensils, furniture, bread, nuts, olives, and even the skeletons of people caught in the disaster. Monuments teach us a great deal about ancient peoples. The study of monuments is called Archaeology. Inscriptions refer to all forms of writing other than books. Most inscriptions are carved in stone, but some are on bronze plates. At Pompeii, they have been found drawn on walls in colors or charcoal. Some have the character of commemorative inscriptions, similar to those attached to our statues and buildings today. In the monument of Ancyra, for example, Emperor Augustus tells the story of his life. The majority of inscriptions are epitaphs engraved on tombs. Others serve as public notices, containing laws or regulations that were to be made known to the people. The study of inscriptions is called Epigraphy.

The languages spoken by ancient peoples offer insight into their history. By comparing the words of two different languages, we can see that they share a common origin, indicating that the people who spoke them were descended from the same ancestors. This field of study is known as linguistics.

Missing Pieces

In spite of all the exciting discoveries of modern archeology, it would be a mistake to assume that books, monuments, inscriptions, and languages alone can provide a complete understanding of ancient history. While they offer many details, often the most important information eludes us. Scholars continue to excavate and decipher, and each year brings new discoveries of inscriptions and monuments. Yet, there will always be gaps in our knowledge, and some of these may never be filled.

Chapter 3

Ancient History of the East

The Egyptians

In the Land of Egypt, the Nile reigns supreme. It is a slender yet fertile strip of land that stretches along both banks of the river, enclosed by towering mountains on either side. The Nile is approximately 700 miles long and 15 miles wide. The Delta begins where the hills recede, a vast plain cut by the Nile's arms and canals. As Herodotus once said, "Egypt is entirely the Nile's gift." Every year, at the summer solstice, the Nile swells with melted snow from Abyssinia, flooding the parched soil of Egypt. It rises to a height of 26 or 27 feet, and sometimes even as high as 33 feet. The entire country becomes a lake, with villages perched on eminences emerging like little islands. The water recedes in September, and by December, it has returned to its proper channel. The Nile leaves behind a fertile, alluvial bed that serves as a natural fertilizer. The peasant sows his crop with almost no labor on the softened earth. The Nile brings both water and soil to Egypt, without it, Egypt would revert to a desert of sterile sand where rain never falls. The Egyptians are aware of their dependence on the Nile. A song in its honor goes like this: "Greetings to thee, O Nile, who hast revealed thyself throughout the land, who comest in peace to give life to Egypt. Does it rise? The land is filled with joy, every heart exults, every being receives its food, every mouth is full. It brings bounties that are full of delight, it creates all good things, it makes the grass to spring up for the beasts." Egypt is an oasis in the midst of the African desert. It produces an abundance of wheat, beans, lentils, and all leguminous foods. Palms grow in forests, and herds of cattle and goats graze on pastures irrigated by the Nile, along with flocks of geese.

Despite having a territory hardly equal to that of Belgium, Egypt still supports 5.5 million inhabitants. No country in Europe is as densely populated as Egypt, and in antiquity, it was even more crowded than it is today.

In the fifth century B.C., Egypt was well known to the Greeks, more so than any other land in the Orient. Herodotus, a Greek historian, visited Egypt during this time and chronicled its people, customs, religion, and history. He even relayed stories he had heard from his guides. Other Greek scholars such as Diodorus and Strabo also wrote about Egypt, but they only saw the country during its decline and had no knowledge of ancient Egypt. It wasn't until the French expedition to Egypt from 1798 to 1801 that scholars were able to examine the Pyramids and the ruins of Thebes and collect drawings and inscriptions. However, they were unable to decipher the hieroglyphs or Egyptian picture writings. It was believed that each sign represented a word, but this was incorrect. In 1821, a French scholar named Champollion experimented with a different system. He discovered an inscription at Rosetta in three forms of writing, including hieroglyphs and a Greek translation. Champollion found the letters P, T, O, L, M, I, and S in the name of King Ptolemy, which allowed him to find the entire alphabet. He then deciphered the hieroglyphs and found they were written in a language similar to Coptic, which was already known to scholars. Since Champollion's breakthrough, many scholars have traveled to Egypt and studied its history and culture. These students of Egyptology, as they are known, can be found all over Europe. A French Egyptologist named Mariette conducted excavations for the Viceroy of Egypt and established the Museum of Boulak. France also established a school of Egyptology in Cairo, which is currently directed by Maspero.

Discoveries

Egypt is a land of great discoveries. The Egyptians built their tombs like houses and filled them with all kinds of objects for the use of the dead: furniture, clothing, weapons, and food. The entire country was filled with tombs that were similarly furnished. Under this extremely dry climate, everything has been preserved, and objects come to light intact after being buried for 4,000 or 5,000 years. No people of antiquity have left so many traces of themselves as the Egyptians, and none are better known to us. The Egyptian Empire. Antiquity of the Egyptian People. An Egyptian priest once said to Herodotus, "You Greeks are only children." The Egyptians considered themselves the oldest people in the world. Down to the Persian conquest in 520 B.C., there were twenty-six dynasties of kings. The first dynasty dates back 4,000 years, and during these forty centuries, Egypt had been an empire. The capital was at Memphis in Lower Egypt until the tenth dynasty, which was the period of the Old Empire. Later, in the New Empire, it was at Thebes in Upper Egypt. Memphis and the Pyramids. Memphis was built by the first king of Egypt and was protected by an enormous dike. The village has existed for more than five thousand years, but since the thirteenth century, the inhabitants have taken the stones of its ruins to build houses in Cairo. What these people left, the Nile recaptured. The Pyramids, not far from Memphis, are contemporaneous with the Old Empire. They are the tombs of three kings of the fourth dynasty. The greatest of the pyramids which is 480 feet high, required the labor of 100,000 men for thirty years. To raise the stones for it, the Egyptians constructed gradually ascending platforms that were later removed when the structure was completed.

Egyptian Civilization

The statues, paintings, and instruments discovered in the tombs of this epoch provide evidence of a highly civilized people. While other prominent nations of antiquity, such as the Hindus, Persians, Jews, Greeks, and Romans remained in a savage state 3,500 years before our era, the Egyptians had already mastered the art of cultivating the soil, weaving cloths, working metals, painting, sculpting, and writing. They had an organized religion, a king, and an administration. Thebes. In the eleventh dynasty, Thebes replaced Memphis as the capital. The ruins of Thebes still stand today and are truly remarkable, spanning both banks of the Nile with a circumference of approximately seven miles. On the left bank, there is a series of palaces and temples that lead to vast cemeteries. On the right bank, two villages, Luxor and Karnak, are built in the midst of the ruins, separated by a double row of sphinxes which once numbered over 1,000 monuments. Among the ruined temples, the most magnificent was the temple of Ammon at Karnak, surrounded by a wall over one and one-third miles long. The famous Hall of Columns, the greatest in the world, measured 334 feet in length, 174 feet in width, and was supported by 134 columns, twelve of which were over 65 feet high. Thebes was the capital and sacred city for 1,500 years, serving as the residence of kings and the dwelling place of priests. The Pharaoh. The king of Egypt, known as Pharaoh, was considered the son of the Sun god and his incarnation on earth, with divinity ascribed to him. In one picture, King Rameses the Second is shown standing in adoration before the divine Rameses who is sitting between two gods. The king, as a man, adores himself as a god. As a god, the Pharaoh had absolute power over men, giving orders to his great nobles at court, warriors, and all his subjects. However, while the priests adored him, they also surrounded and watched him. The high priest of the god Ammon, their leader, eventually became more powerful than the king, often governing under the king's name and in his place.

The Pharaoh's Subjects

In ancient Egypt, the king, priests, warriors, and nobles owned everything, including the people. The rest of the population were simply peasants who worked the land for their rulers. Scribes in the king's service watched over the peasants and collected the farm dues, often using force. One of these scribes wrote to a friend, "Have you ever thought about the life of a peasant who tills the soil? The tax collector is on the platform, busy taking the tithe of the harvest. He has armed men with strips of palm. They all cry, 'Come, give us grain!' If the peasant doesn't have any, they throw him to the ground, bind him, drag him to the canal, and throw him in headfirst." Despotism. Like infants, the Egyptian people have always been carefree, gentle, and docile, always willing to submit to tyranny. In Egypt, the cudgel was the tool of education and government.

"The young man," said the scribes, "has a back to be beaten; he hears when he is struck." One day, a French traveler visiting the ruins of Thebes asked his guide, "But how did they do all this?" The guide laughed, touched him on the arm, and showed him a palm. "This is what they used to accomplish all this," he said. "You know, sir, with 100,000 branches of palms split on the backs of those who always have their shoulders bare, you can build many a palace and some temples too." Isolation of the Egyptians. The Egyptians rarely traveled beyond their borders. They feared the sea and did not engage in trade with other nations. They were not a military people although their kings often led expeditions with mercenaries against the warriors of Ethiopia or the tribes of Syria. They won battles which they depicted on the walls of their palaces, and brought back captives to build monuments. However, they never made great conquests. More foreigners came to Egypt than Egyptians went abroad.

The Egyptians, as Herodotus said, were the most religious of all people. Their devotion was unmatched, with paintings depicting men in prayer before their gods and religious manuscripts filling their libraries. The principal deity of the Egyptians was the Sun god, a creator who knew all things and existed from the beginning. This god had a divine wife and son. The Egyptians adored this trinity, although they gave it different names depending on the region. For example, at Memphis, they called the father Phtah, the mother Sekhet, and the son Imouthes. At Abydos, they were known as Osiris, Isis, and Horus; at Thebes they were called Ammon, Mouth, and Chons. The people of one province even adopted the gods of other provinces, leading to a complicated religion with many gods emanating from each god of the trinity. These gods had their history which was that of the sun. Osiris, the sun, was slain by Set, the god of the night. Isis, the moon and Osiris', wife bewailed and buried him. Horus, their son and the rising sun, avenged his father's death by killing his murderer. Ammon-ra, the god of Thebes, was represented as traversing heaven each day in a bark called "the good bark of millions of years." The shades of the dead propelled it with long oars, while the god stood at the prow, ready to strike his enemies with his lance. The hymn they chanted in his honor, praised him as the master of the two horizons and the one who treads the heavens on high. Heaven and earth were glad and joyful when they saw him rising in his bark after he had overwhelmed his enemies. The Egyptians prayed for Pharaoh's abounding life, bread for his hunger, water for his throat, and perfumes for his hair.

Animal-headed Gods were a common representation of the Egyptian gods. While some were depicted as human, many were portrayed as beasts. Each god had its own animal form such as Ptah as a beetle, Horus as a hawk, and Osiris as a bull. Often, these figures were combined creating a man with the head of an animal or an animal with the head of a man. Each god could be depicted in four forms such as Horus as a man, a hawk, a man with the head of a hawk, and a hawk with the head of a man. The meaning behind these symbols is unclear, but the Egyptians themselves began to view the animals that represented their gods as sacred. The bull, beetle, ibis, hawk, cat, and crocodile were among the animals that were cared for and protected. In fact, during the first century B.C., a Roman citizen killed a cat in Alexandria which caused the people to rise up in a riot. They seized him and despite the king's pleas, murdered him. At the same time, they feared the Romans greatly. Each temple had a sacred animal that was worshipped. The traveler Strabo visited a sacred crocodile in Thebes and observed the priests feeding it cakes, grilled fish, and a drink made with meal. The most revered of these animal gods was the bull Apis which represented both Osiris and Ptah. It resided in a chapel in Memphis and was served by the priests. After its death, it was embalmed and became an Osiris, known as Asar-hapi. Its mummy was then placed in a vault. The sepulchres of the Asar-hapi formed the massive Serapeum monument which was discovered by Marietta in 1851.

The Cult of the Dead was a central part of Egyptian religion. They believed that every person had a "double" or "Ka", which survived even after death. This belief is still held by many primitive societies today. During the Old Empire, the Egyptian tomb was known as the "House of the Double." It was a small room that was set up like a chamber with everything the double might need such as chairs, tables, beds, chests, linen, closets, garments, toilet utensils, weapons, and sometimes even a war chariot. Statues, paintings, and books were also placed there for the entertainment of the double. Grain and food were provided for the sustenance of the double. A statue in the likeness of the deceased was placed in the tomb as a double of the dead. Once the opening to the vault was sealed, the living still provided for the double by bringing food or beseeching a god to supply the spirit with what it needed. An inscription might read, "An offering to Osiris that he may confer on the Ka of the deceased some bread, drinks, meat, geese, milk, wine, beer, clothing, perfumes all good things and pure on which the god or the Ka subsists." Later, during the eleventh dynasty, the Egyptians believed that the soul flew away from the body and sought Osiris under the earth, the realm into which the sun seemed to sink every day. There, Osiris sat on his tribunal surrounded by forty-two judges. The soul appeared before them to give an account of its past life. Its actions were weighed in the balance of truth, and its "heart" was called to witness. The dead cried out, "O heart, the issue of my mother, my heart when I was on earth, offer not thyself as witness, charge me not before the great god." If the soul was found to be bad, it was tormented for centuries and then annihilated. If the soul was good, it sprang up across the firmament. After many tests, it rejoined the company of the gods and was absorbed into them.

Mummies were an essential part of Egyptian culture. During the pilgrimage, the soul may want to return to the body for rest, therefore the body must remain intact. The Egyptians learned to embalm the corpse by filling it with spices, bathing it in natron, and wrapping it in bandages thus creating a mummy. The mummy was then placed in a wooden or plaster coffin and buried in a tomb with all the necessities for its afterlife. Along with the mummy, a book called the "Book of the Dead" was deposited. This book provided guidance on what the soul should say when defending itself before the tribunal of Osiris. The soul must declare its innocence of fraud, vexing the widow, forbidden acts, idleness, and stealing from the temples. The soul must also claim to have never taken a slave from their master, removed provisions or bandages from the dead, altered the grain measure, hunted sacred beasts, or caught sacred fish. The soul must profess its purity and declare that it has given bread to the hungry, water to the thirsty, clothing to the naked, and has made sacrifices to the gods while offering funeral feasts to the dead. This book reveals the morality of the Egyptians which included the observance of ceremonies, respect for everything pertaining to the gods, sincerity, honesty, and beneficence. The Egyptians were also pioneers in the arts necessary for civilized people. As early as the first dynasty, 3,000 years before Christ, paintings on tombs exhibited men working, sowing, harvesting, and processing grain. They also depicted herds of cattle, sheep, geese, and swine, as well as people dressed in rich clothing, processions, and feasts where the harp was played. The Egyptians knew how to manipulate gold, silver, and bronze, and manufacture arms and jewelry, glass, pottery, and enamel. They also wove garments of linen and wool, as well as cloths that were transparent or embroidered with gold.

The architects of ancient times were the most venerable artisans in the world. They constructed colossal monuments that seem to last forever. Even after all this time, they remain impervious to destruction. They didn't build for the living, but for the gods and the dead, namely temples and tombs. Only a small amount of their houses' debris remains, and even the palaces of their kings, when compared to their tombs, seem like mere inns in the language of the Greeks. The house was meant to serve only for a lifetime, while the tomb was for eternity. The Great Pyramid is an example of a royal tomb and most ancient tombs had this form. In Lower Egypt, rows of pyramids still remain scattered around, some larger, others smaller, serving as the tombs of kings and nobles. Later on, tombs were constructed underground, some under the earth while others were cut into the granite of the hills. Each generation needed new tombs which was the reason why Necropolis, the richer and greater city of the dead, was built near the town of living people. The gods also required eternal and splendid dwellings. Their temples included a magnificent sanctuary, the dwelling of the god. These structures were surrounded by courts, gardens, chambers where the priests lodged, and wardrobes for their jewels, utensils, and vestments. This combination of edifices, the work of many generations, was encircled by a wall.

The temple of Ammon at Thebes was the result of the combined labor kings of all the dynasties beginning from the twelfth to the last. Ordinarily, in front of the temple, was a great gateway that consisted of two pyramidal towers with inclined faces called pylons. On either side of the entrance stood an obelisk, a needle of rock with a gilded point, or perhaps a colossus in stone representing a sitting giant. The long avenue leading to the temple entrance was often lined with sphinxes. Pyramids, pylons, colossi, sphinxes, and obelisks characterize this architecture. Everything is massive, compact, and, above all, immense. Hence, these monuments appear clumsy but indestructible.

Sculpture

The ancient Egyptian sculptors began their craft by imitating nature. The oldest statues are striking for their lifelike quality and are likely portraits of the deceased. One such example is the famous squatting scribe of the Louvre. However, starting with the eleventh dynasty, sculptors were no longer free to represent the human body as they saw fit. They were required to follow conventional rules dictated by religion. As a result, all statues began to resemble one another, with parallel legs, joined feet, crossed arms on the chest, and a motionless figure. Although often majestic, the statues became stiff and monotonous. Art had ceased to reproduce nature and had become a conventional symbol. Painting. The Egyptians used very solid colors in their paintings which remain fresh and bright even after 5,000 years. However, they were not skilled in coloring designs and knew neither tints, shadows, nor perspective. Like the works of sculpture, paintings were subject to religious rules and were therefore monotonous. If fifty people were to be represented, the artist made them all look alike. Literature. The literature of the Egyptians is found in the tombs. It includes not only books on medicine, magic, and piety, but also poems, letters, accounts of travels, and even romances. Destiny of the Egyptian Civilization. Even after the fall of their empire, the Egyptians conserved their customs, religion, and arts. As subjects of the Persians, then the Greeks, and finally the Romans, they maintained their old usages, hieroglyphics, mummies, and sacred animals. However, between the third and second centuries A.D., Egyptian civilization slowly faded away.

Chapter 4

The Assyrians and the Babylonians: Chaldea

From the lofty and snow-capped mountains of Armenia flow two swift and deep rivers, the Tigris to the east, and the Euphrates to the west. At first, they run parallel to each other, but as they reach the plain, they diverge. The Tigris flows straight, while the Euphrates takes a great detour towards the sandy deserts before they converge again and empty into the sea. The land they encircle is known as Chaldea, a vast plain with remarkably fertile soil. Although rainfall is scarce, the streams provide water, and when the clayey soil is irrigated by canals, it becomes the most productive land in the world. Wheat and barley yield up to 200-fold, and in good years, the returns are 300-fold. Palms cover the land, and from them, the people make their wine, meal, and flour. For many centuries, Chaldea was home to civilized peoples, perhaps as long as Egypt. Many races from different lands have converged on these great plains. Turanians of the yellow race, akin to the Chinese, came from the northeast; Cushites, deep brown in color and related to the Egyptians, came from the east; Semites, of the white race and of the same stock as Arabs, descended from the north. The Chaldean people emerged from this melting pot of races. Chaldean priests claimed that their kings had ruled for 150,000 years. Although this is a myth, they were not wrong in attributing great antiquity to the Chaldean empire. The land of Chaldea is dotted with hills, each of which is a mass of debris, the remnants of a ruined city. Many of these have been excavated and numerous cities have been uncovered such as Our, Larsam, and Bal-ilou. Some inscriptions have been recovered as well. De Sarsec, a Frenchman, discovered the ruins of an entire city destroyed by invaders with its palace burnt to the ground. These ancient peoples are still shrouded in mystery, and many sites remain to be excavated where new inscriptions may be found. Their empire was destroyed around 2300 B.C. and it may have been already ancient by then.

The Assyrians

The land beyond Chaldea, along the Tigris River, is known as Assyria. It is a fertile land, but also filled with hills and rocks. Due to its proximity to the mountains, it experiences snow in the winter and severe storms in the summer. For a long time, the Assyrians lived an obscure life in their mountainous region, while Chaldea was covered in towns. However, in the thirteenth century B.C., the Assyrian kings led great armies to invade the plains and founded a mighty empire with Nineveh as its capital. Until about forty years ago, we knew very little about the Assyrians aside from a legend recounted by the Greek historian Diodorus Siculus. According to the story, Ninus founded Nineveh and conquered all of Asia Minor. His wife Semiramis, daughter of a goddess, subjected Egypt before being transformed into a dove. However, this tale is entirely untrue. In 1843, the French consul at Mosul, Botta discovered the palace of an Assyrian king under a hillock near the Tigris at Khorsabad. This discovery marked the first time that people could view the artwork produced by the Assyrians. The winged bulls carved in stone and placed at the palace gate were found intact and later moved to the Louvre Museum in Paris. Botta's excavations drew the attention of Europe, leading to many expeditions being sent out, particularly by the English. Place and Layard investigated other mounds and discovered other palaces. These ruins had been well preserved, protected by the dry climate and a covering of earth. They found walls adorned with bas-reliefs and paintings, as well as statues and inscriptions in great numbers. It was now possible to study the structures on the ground, and publish reproductions of the monuments and inscriptions.

The discovery of the palace of Khorsabad, built by King Sargon at Nineveh the capital of the Assyrian kings, revealed a city built on several hills and surrounded by a quadrilateral wall 25 to 30 miles long. The exterior of the wall was made of bricks, while the interior was made of earth. Although the dwellings of the city have vanished, we have found many palaces built by various Assyrian kings. Nineveh was the royal residence until the fall of the Assyrian empire at the hands of the Medes and Chaldeans. The inscriptions on the bricks are formed by a combination of arrow or wedge-shaped signs, giving rise to the term cuneiform from the Latin words cuneus and forma. The writer used a stylus with a triangular point to make impressions on soft clay tablets, which were then baked to harden them and preserve the writing. The palace of Assurbanipal yielded a complete library of brick tablets serving as paper. Cuneiform writing has challenged scholars for many years, as it was used for five different languages namely Assyrian, Susian, Mede, Chaldean, and Armenian, and the signs were complex. The writing was comprised of symbolic signs, each representing a word such as sun, god, and fish, and syllabic signs each representing a syllable. There were almost 200 syllabic signs which were similar and easy to confuse. The same sign could represent a word and a syllable, and sometimes different syllables. The difficulty of the writing was such that even its creators struggled with it. Half of the cuneiform monuments we have are guides such as grammar rules, dictionaries, and pictures, that help us decipher the other half, just as Assyrian scholars did 2,500 years ago.

Cuneiform inscriptions have been deciphered in the same manner as Egyptian hieroglyphics. There was an inscription in three languages: Assyrian, Mede, and Persian. The last language provided the key to the other two. The Assyrians were a race of hunters and soldiers. Their bas-reliefs often depict them armed with bows and lances, frequently on horseback. They were skilled knights: vigilant, courageous, and clever in skirmishes and battles. However, they were also pompous, deceitful, and bloodthirsty. For six centuries, they terrorized Asia, emerging from the mountains to attack their neighbors and returning with entire populations reduced to slavery. They appeared to make war for the sheer joy of killing, ravaging, and pillaging. No people had ever displayed greater ferocity. Following the Asiatic custom, the Assyrians regarded their king as the representative of God on earth and obeyed him blindly. He was the absolute ruler of all his subjects, leading them into battle and fighting head-on against other Asian peoples. Upon his return, he recorded his exploits on the walls of his palace in a lengthy inscription. He recounted his victories, the spoils he had taken, the cities he had burned, and the captives he had beheaded or flayed alive. Here are some excerpts from these campaign stories: Assurnazir Halal in 882 writes, "I built a wall before the great gates of the city. I flayed the chiefs of the revolt and covered this wall with their skins. Some were entombed alive in the masonry, others were crucified or impaled along the wall. I had some of them flayed in my presence and had the wall adorned with their skins. I arranged their heads like crowns and their transfixed bodies in the form of garlands." In 745, Tiglath Pilezer the Second writes, "I imprisoned the king in his royal city. I erected mountains of bodies before his gates. I destroyed, devastated, and burned all his villages. I turned the land into a desert, transforming it into hills and heaps of debris."

In the seventh century B.C., Sennacherib boasted, "I swept through like a hurricane of destruction. On the soaked earth, the armor and weapons floated in the blood of my enemies like a river. I piled up their corpses like trophies and cut off their limbs. I mutilated those I captured like blades of straw, and as punishment, I cut off their hands." A bas-relief depicting the surrender of Susa to Assurbanipal shows the conquered chiefs being tortured by the Assyrians. Some had their ears cut off, others had their eyes gouged out, and some were flayed alive. Clearly, these kings took pleasure in burnings, massacres, and tortures. The Assyrian regime began with the capture of Babylon around 1270 B.C. From the ninth century B.C., the Assyrians who were always at war, conquered or ravaged Babylonia, Syria, Palestine, and even Egypt. The conquered peoples always revolted, and the massacres were repeated. Eventually, the Assyrians became exhausted. The Babylonians and Medes formed an alliance and destroyed the Assyrian empire. In 625 B.C., their capital Nineveh, which the Jewish referred to as, "the lair of lions, the bloody city, the city gorged with prey", was taken and destroyed forever. "Nineveh is laid waste," says the prophet Nahum, "who will mourn for her?" In place of the fallen Assyrian empire, a new power arose in ancient Chaldea. This empire is known as the Babylonian Empire or the Second Chaldean Empire. A Jewish prophet quotes one as saying to Jehovah, "I raise up the Chaldeans, that bitter and hasty nation which shall march through the breadth of the land to possess dwelling places that are not theirs. Their horses are swifter than leopards. Their horsemen spread themselves; their horsemen shall fly as the eagle that hasteth to eat." They were a people of knights, martial and victorious like the Assyrians. The Babylonian Empire was overthrown by the Persians in 538 B.C.

In the land of Babylon, ruled from 604 to 561 B.C. by the great Nebuchadrezzar also known as Nebuchadnezzar, the people worshipped many gods and built magnificent temples and palaces. The city of Babylon itself was a marvel, surrounded by a massive wall with a hundred gates of brass and a deep water-filled ditch. The city covered an area of 185 square miles, with fields for cultivation in case of a siege. The houses were tall and the streets intersected at right angles. One of the wonders of the world was the hanging gardens, a series of terraces planted with trees and supported by pillars and arches. Nearby, Nebuchadnezzar aimed to rebuild the town of Babel and created a magnificent temple dedicated to the seven planets. The temple comprised seven square towers, each painted with the color attributed to the planet it represented. The highest tower contained a chapel with a golden table and a priestess who kept watch continually. The Greek historian Herodotus visited Babylon in the fifth century B.C. and described the city in detail. Though the monuments of Babylon were made of crude brick and have decayed over time, inscriptions and plans of the city have been recovered. Babylon was less a city than a fortified camp, with thick walls and towers that could support a chariot. The people of Babylon were proud of their customs and religion, and their mighty king Nebuchadrezzar left a lasting legacy of magnificent architecture and engineering.

The customs of these ancient peoples are shrouded in mystery, known only through the monuments they left behind. These monuments almost exclusively celebrate the achievements of their kings, depicting the Assyrians in times of war, hunting, or performing ceremonies. Women are notably absent from these bas-reliefs, as they were confined to the harem and excluded from public life. In contrast, the Chaldeans were a people of laborers and merchants, but little is known about their daily lives. According to Herodotus, once a year in their towns the Chaldeans would gather all the girls for marriage. The prettiest were sold, and the profits from their sale became a dowry for the marriage of the plainest. Herodotus believed this to be the wisest of all their laws. The religion of the Assyrians and Chaldeans was intertwined as the former had adopted the beliefs of the latter. However, their religion is obscure to us today, having originated from a confusing mix of different religions. The Turanians, similar to the yellow race of Siberia today, believed in a world full of demons including plague, fever, phantoms, and vampires. Sorcerers were called upon to banish these demons using magical formulas. The Cushites worshipped a pair of gods, a male deity of force and a female deity of matter. The Chaldean priests, united in a powerful guild, merged these two religions into one. The supreme god in Babylon was Ilou, while in Assyria it was Assur. No temple was built in their honor. Three gods were said to have originated from Ilou: Anou the "lord of darkness", depicted as a man with the head of a fish and the tail of an eagle; Bel the "sovereign of spirits", represented as a king on a throne; and Nouah the "master of the visible world", depicted as a genius with four extended wings. Each of these gods had a female counterpart symbolizing fruitfulness. Below these gods were the Sun, the Moon, and the five planets. In the transparent atmosphere of Chaldea, the stars shone with a brilliance that is unfamiliar to us today. The Chaldeans built temples that served as observatories, where they could follow the movements of the celestial bodies they worshipped.

Astrology, the belief that the stars hold great power over the lives of men, was a deeply-rooted belief among the Chaldean priests. They believed that the moment of a man's birth, under the influence of a particular planet, determined his destiny. By observing the heavens, they believed they could predict future events. This led to the creation of the horoscope, where one's fortune could be foretold based on the star under which they were born. Comets were seen as harbingers of revolution, and the movements of the stars were believed to be indicative of what would come to pass on Earth. Thus, astrology was born. Sorcery too had its origins in Chaldea. The priests had magical words that could banish spirits or cause them to appear. This practice, a remnant of the Turanian religion, eventually gave rise to sorcery. Astrology and sorcery spread throughout the Roman Empire and later Europe, with corrupted Assyrian words still detectable in the formulas of sixteenth-century sorcery. On the other hand, Chaldea was also the birthplace of astronomy. The zodiac, the week of seven days in honor of the seven planets, the division of the year into twelve months, the day into twenty-four hours, the hour into sixty minutes, and the minute into sixty seconds, all originated in Chaldea. The system of weights and measures based on the unit of length was also adopted by all ancient peoples. As for the arts, we have no direct knowledge of Chaldean art as their monuments have fallen to ruin. However, the Assyrian artists whose works we possess imitated those of Chaldea, thus we can form a conclusion about the two countries. Both Chaldeans and Assyrians built with crude, sun-dried brick, but with the exterior wall faced with stone.

Built upon man-made mounds that were low and flat like great terraces, palaces were a grand spectacle in ancient Assyria. The crude brick used in construction was not suitable for broad and high arches, so the halls were straight and low but very long. An Assyrian palace was essentially a series of galleries, with flat terrace roofs equipped with battlements. At the entrance, one would find colossal winged bulls guarding the gate. Inside, the walls were adorned with precious woods, enamelled bricks, and sculptural alabaster plates. Sometimes the chambers were painted, and even richly encrusted marbles were used. The sculpture of the Assyrian palaces was particularly remarkable. Statues were rare and crude, so sculptors preferred to create bas-reliefs on large slabs of alabaster. These bas-reliefs depicted complex scenes such as battles, chases, sieges of towns, and ceremonies where the king appeared with a great retinue. Every detail was meticulously executed, including the files of servants in charge of the king's feast, the troops of workmen who built his palace, the gardens, fields, ponds, fish in the water, and birds perched over their nests or flitting from tree to tree. People were often depicted in profile, likely because the artist could not render their faces, but they still possessed dignity and life. Animals were also frequently depicted, especially in hunting scenes, and they were rendered with startling fidelity. The Assyrians closely observed nature and faithfully reproduced it, which is why their art was so meritorious. The Greeks themselves learned from the Assyrian school of art and imitated their bas-reliefs. While the Greeks excelled in their art, no other people, not even the Greeks, were better at representing animals than the Assyrians.

Chapter 5

The Caucasians of India

The Caucasian Languages

The various races that inhabit Europe today such as the Greeks and Italians in the south, the Slavs in Russia, the Teutons in Germany, and the Celts in Ireland, speak different languages. However, upon closer examination, it becomes clear that they all share a common stock of words, or at least certain roots. These same roots can be found in Sanskrit, the ancient language of the Hindus, and in Zend, the ancient tongue of the Persians. For example, the word "father" is "pere" in French, "pitar" in Sanskrit, and "pater" in Greek and Latin. It is the same word pronounced in various ways. From this, it has been concluded that the Hindus, Persians, Greeks, Latins, Celts, Germans, and Slavs all once spoke the same language and were therefore one people. The Caucasian People. These people called themselves Caucasians and lived in the northwest of India, either in the mountains of Pamir or in the steppes of Turkestan or Russia. From this center, they dispersed in all directions. The majority of the people, such as the Greeks, Latins, Germans, and Slavs, forgot their origin, but the sacred books of the Hindus and Persians preserve the tradition. Efforts have been made to reconstruct the life of our Caucasian ancestors in their mountain homes before the dispersion. They were a race of shepherds who did not till the soil. They subsisted on food coming from their herds of cattle and sheep, although they already had houses and even villages. It was a fighting race that knew the lance, the javelin, and the shield. The government was patriarchal, and a man had only one wife. As head of the family, he was at once priest, judge, and king, for his wife, children, and servants. In all the countries settled by the Caucasians, they followed this type of life: patriarchal, martial, and pastoral.

The tale of the Hindus begins with the arrival of the Caucasians in India, some 2,000 years before our time. These tribes crossed the Hindu-Kush passes and discovered the fertile plains of the Indus. There they found dark-skinned, flat-headed, and prosperous people whom they called Dasyous, or the enemy. The Caucasians waged war against them for centuries, ultimately subjecting or exterminating them, and gradually took over the entire Indus valley which they named after themselves: Hindus. The Hindus had a tradition of chanting hymns, or vedas, in honor of their gods during their ceremonies. These hymns were compiled into a vast collection that has survived to the present day. The Caucasians had not yet crossed the Indus when the hymns were collected, making them the oldest religion of the Hindus. The Hindu gods are called devas, which means resplendent. Anything that shines is considered a divinity, including the heavens, the dawn, the clouds, and the stars, but the sun and fire are especially revered. Indra, the sun, is the most powerful of the gods. He is known as the mighty one, the king of the world, and the master of creatures. Indra traverses the heavens on a chariot drawn by azure steeds, and he hurls thunderbolts, sends rain, and banishes clouds. India is a land of violent storms, and the Hindus explained this phenomenon in their own way. They saw the black cloud as an envelope containing the waters of heaven which they called the gleaming cows of Indra. When a storm gathers, an evil genius in the form of a three-headed serpent named Vritra drives away the cows and encloses them in a black cavern. The far-away rumblings of thunder are the bellowing of the cows. Indra then sets out to find them, striking the cavern with his club, which creates the thunderbolt, and the forked tongue of the serpent, which creates the lightning. Eventually, Indra vanquishes the serpent, the cave opens, and the waters fall on the earth, making Indra the victor, and he appears in glory.

Agni, the tireless, is considered by the Hindus to be another form of the sun. They produce it by rubbing two pieces of wood together, and believe that the fire comes from the wood and that the rain has placed it there. They conceive it as the fire of heaven descended to earth. When one places it on the hearth, it springs up as if it would ascend toward heaven. Agni dissipates darkness, warms mankind, and cooks their food; it is the benefactor and protector of the house. It is also the internal fire, the soul of the world; even the ancestor of the human race is the son of lightning. Thus heat and light, sources of all life, are the deities of the Hindus. To adore their gods, they strive to reproduce what they see in heaven. They ignite a terrestrial fire by rubbing sticks together and nourishing it by depositing butter, milk, and soma, a fermented drink, on the hearth. To delight the gods, they give cake and fruit offerings and animal sacrifices like cattle, rams, and horses. They then invoke them, chanting hymns to their praise. "When thou art bidden by us to quaff the soma, come with thy sombre steeds, thou deity whose darts are stones. Our celebrant is seated according to prescription, the sacred green is spread, in the morning stones have been gathered together. Take thy seat on the holy sward; taste, O hero, our offering to thee. Delight thyself in our libations and our chants, vanquisher of Vritra, thou who art honored in these ceremonies of ours, O Indra." The Hindus believe that the gods, delighted by their offerings and homage, will in turn make them happy. They say naively, "Give sacrifice to the gods for their profit, and they will requite you. Just as men traffic by the discussion of prices, let us exchange force and vigor, O Indra. Give to me and I will give to you; bring to me and I will bring to you." At the same time, the Hindus adore their ancestors who have become gods. This is perhaps the oldest cult of all. It is the basis of the family. The father, who has transmitted the fire of life to his children, makes offerings and sacrifices and utters prayers to gods and ancestors every day at his hearth fire, which must never be extinguished. Here it is seen that among Hindus, as among other Caucasians, the father is at once a priest and a sovereign.

The Brahmanic Society

The Hindus, crossing the Indus between the fourteenth and tenth centuries B.C., conquered the vast plains of the Ganges. Settling in this fertile land, amidst a people of slaves, they gradually changed their customs and religion, establishing the Brahmanic society. Many works in Sanskrit from this time, including the Vedas, form the sacred literature of the Hindus. The principal works are the great epic poems, the Mahabharata, with over 200,000 verses, the Ramayana with 50,000 verses, and the laws of Manu, the sacred code of India. In this new society, there were no longer poets who chanted hymns to the gods, as in the time of the Vedas. The men who knew the prayers and ceremonies became theologians by profession, and the people revered and obeyed them. Their conception of the structure of society was as follows: the supreme god, Brahma, produced four kinds of men, to each of whom he assigned a mission. From his mouth, he drew the Brahmans, who were the theologians, charged with studying, teaching the hymns, and performing the sacrifices. The Kshatriyas came from his arms; these were the warriors charged with protecting the people. The Vaishyas proceeded from the thigh; they raised cattle, tilled the earth, loaned money at interest, and engaged in commerce. The Shudras issued from his foot; their only mission was to serve all the others. There were already theologians, warriors, and artisans among the Caucasian people, with aborigines reduced to slavery below them. These were classes that one could enter and from which one could withdraw. But the Brahmans determined that every man should be attached to the condition in which he was born for all time. And the same holds true for his descendants. The son of a workman could never become a warrior, nor the son of a warrior a theologian. Thus, each is chained to his own state. Society is divided into four hereditary and closed castes.

The Unclean. In India, those who do not belong to one of the four castes are considered unclean and are excluded from society and religion. The Brahmans have classified forty-four grades of outcasts, with the lowest being the pariahs. Even their name is an insult. Outcasts cannot practice any honorable trade or approach other men. They can only possess dogs and donkeys, as these are unclean beasts. Outcasts must wear the garments of the dead, use broken pots as plates, and wear iron ornaments. They must constantly move from one place to another. The Brahmans. In the Indian caste system, the Brahmans hold the

THE ECHO OF ANCIENT CIVILIZATIONS   35

highest position. They are considered the first among men, higher than warriors and kings. Even a ten-year-old Brahman is considered more of a father than a hundred-year-old Kshatria. The Brahmans are not priests like those in Egypt and Chaldea, but they are knowledgeable about religion and spend their time reading and meditating on sacred books. They live off of presents given to them by others. Today, they remain the dominant class in India. Because they only marry among themselves, they have preserved the Caucasian type better than other Hindus and have a clearer resemblance to Europeans. The New Religion of Brahma. The Brahmans did not abandon the ancient gods of the Vedas; they continued to worship them. However, they created a new god through sheer ingenuity. When prayers are directed towards the gods, the deities are made to comply with the demands made on them, as if they believed that prayer was more powerful than the gods themselves. Thus, prayer or Brahma became the highest of all deities. Brahma is invoked with awe: "O god, I see in your body all the gods and the multitude of living beings. I am powerless to see you in your entirety, for you shine like the fire and the sun in your immensity."

Thou, the Invisible, art the supreme Intelligence, the sovereign treasure of the universe, without beginning, middle, or end, equipped with infinite might. Thine arms are limitless, thine eyes are as bright as the moon and sun, and thy mouth shines like the sacred fire. Thou alone fills all the space between heaven and earth, permeating the entire universe. Brahma, the soul of the universe, is not only the supreme god but also the very substance of the world. All beings are born from Brahma, naturally issuing from him like a tree from a seed or a spider's web. He did not create the world; he is the world. Every being has a soul, a part of Brahma's soul, including gods, men, animals, plants, and stones. These souls undergo transmigration or the passing from one body to another. When a person dies, their soul is tested. If it is good, it goes to the heaven of Indra to enjoy happiness. If it is bad, it falls into one of twenty-eight hells, where it is tormented by demons and forced to swallow burning cakes. Souls do not remain in heaven or hell forever but instead, begin a new life in another body. Good souls rise and enter the body of a saint or god, while evil souls descend and inhabit impure animals or plants. This journey continues until the soul reaches the highest sphere which takes twenty-four million years to achieve. Once perfect, the soul returns to the level of Brahma and is absorbed into it. The religion of the Caucasians was simple and happy, but this religion is complicated and barren. It takes shape among those who are not engaged in practical life and are weakened by life's heat and vexations.

Rites

The practice of religion is much more complex. Hymns and sacrifices are still offered to the gods, but the Brahmans have gradually invented thousands of minute customs so that one's life is completely engaged with them. For all the ceremonies of the religious life, there are prayers, offerings, vows, libations, and ablutions. Some of the religious requirements attach themselves to dress, ornaments, etiquette, drinking, eating, mode of walking, lying down, sleeping, dressing, undressing, and bathing. It is ordered that a Brahman shall not step over a rope to which a calf is attached, that he shall not run when it rains, that he shall not drink water in the hollow of his hand, and that he shall not scratch his head with both his hands. The man who breaks clods of earth, who cuts grass with his nails, or who bites his nails is, like the outcast, speedily hurried to his doom. An animal must not be killed, for a human soul may perhaps be dwelling in the body. One must not eat it on penalty of being devoured in another life by the animals which one has eaten. All these rites have a magical virtue; he who observes them all is a saint, and he who neglects any of them is impious and destined to pass into the body of an animal. Purity. The principal duty is keeping oneself pure, for every stain is a sin and opens one to the attack of evil spirits. But the Brahmans are very scrupulous concerning purity. Men outside of the castes, many animals, the soil, and even the utensils which one uses are so many impure things. Whoever touches these is polluted and must at once purify himself. Life is consumed in purification. Penances. For every defect in the rites, penance is necessary, often a terrible one. He who involuntarily kills a cow must clothe himself in its skin, and for three months, day and night, follow and tend a herd of cows. Whoever has drunk of arrack must swallow a boiling liquid which burns the internal organs until death results.

The Monks

To escape the perils of the world and maintain purity, it is best to depart from it. Often, a Brahmin who has reached certain age retreats to the desert, fasting, keeping watch, refraining from speech, exposing himself naked to the rain, standing erect amidst four fires under the scorching sun. After some years, the hermit becomes a "penitent"; then his only means of subsistence is through alms-giving. For whole days, he raises an arm in the air without uttering a word, holding his breath. Or perhaps, he cuts himself with razor blades. He may even keep his thumbs closed until the nails pierce his hands. Through these mortifications, he destroys passion, frees himself from this life, and through contemplation, ascends to Brahma. Yet, this path to salvation is only open to the Brahmin. Even he has the right to retreat to the desert only in old age, after having studied the Vedas throughout his life, practiced all the rites, and established a family. Buddhism. Buddha. Millions of men who were not Brahmins suffered through this life of minutiae and agony. A man then appeared who brought a doctrine of deliverance. He was not a Brahmin but of the Kshatriya caste, the son of a king from the north. Until the age of twenty-nine, he lived in his father's palace. One day, he met an old man with a bald head, wrinkled features, and trembling limbs. A second time, he met an incurable invalid, covered in ulcers, without a home. Again, he encountered a decaying corpse devoured by worms. And so, he thought, youth, health, and life are nothing, for they offer no resistance to old age, sickness, and death. He had compassion for men and sought a remedy. Then he met a religious mendicant with a grave and dignified air. Following his example, he decided to renounce the world. These four meetings had determined his calling.

Buddha, seeking enlightenment, fled to the desert, where he lived for seven years in penitence, enduring hunger, thirst, and rain. These mortifications brought him no peace. He ate, grew strong, and discovered the truth. He then returned to the world to preach it, gaining crowds of disciples who called him Buddha, the scholar. After forty-five years of preaching, Buddhism was established. According to Buddha, to live is to be unhappy. Every man suffers because he desires the goods of this world, such as youth, health, and life, but cannot keep them. All life is suffering, born of desire. To suppress suffering, one must root out desire and cease from wishing to live. The wise man is he who casts aside everything that attaches to this life and makes it unhappy. One must cease successively from feeling, wishing, and thinking. Then, freed from passion, volition, and even reflection, he no longer suffers and can come to the supreme good after his death, which consists of being delivered from all life and suffering. The aim of the wise man is the annihilation of personality, which the Buddhists call Nirvana. Buddha also preached the importance of charity, which was a new sentiment compared to the Brahmans, who considered life a place of suffering and annihilation as felicity.

The religion of the Brahmans was steeped in egoism, but Buddha was a man of compassion who preached love to his disciples and to all those who would listen. He knew that what despairing souls needed most was a word of sympathy, and he taught his followers to love even those who would do them harm. When Purna, one of his disciples, went out to preach to the barbarians, Buddha tested him by asking what he would do if they spoke angry words to him, or even struck him with a staff or sword. Purna replied that he would still think of them as good men, even if they did him harm, because he believed that all people were capable of goodness. Buddha's teachings were based on the principle of fraternity, which held that all men were equal in the eyes of God, regardless of their caste or social status. Unlike the Brahmans, who believed that they were purer than others, Buddha welcomed all men into his fold, including pariahs, beggars, cripples, and even murderers and thieves. He preached to them in simple language, using parables to illustrate his points, and he was not afraid to touch them or to be touched by them. Finally, Buddha was a man of great tolerance, who did not demand that his followers observe minute rites or exertions in order to achieve salvation. Instead, he taught them to be charitable, chaste, and beneficent, and to spread their goodness and mercy to all those around them. He believed that the perfect man was one who diffused himself in benefits over creatures, and who comforted the afflicted. His doctrine was one of mercy, and he knew that it was not always easy to follow, especially for those who were fortunate in the world.

Thus, five centuries before Christ, a new religion emerged, unlike any other. It lacked a god and elaborate rituals, instead emphasizing the importance of loving one's neighbor and striving for personal improvement. The ultimate reward was not eternal life, but rather annihilation. However, this religion also preached selflessness, equality, charity, and tolerance, concepts that had never been emphasized before. The Brahmins fiercely opposed it and eventually eradicated it from India, but Buddhist missionaries spread it to Ceylon, Indo-China, Tibet, China, and Japan. Today, it boasts millions of adherents. Over the past two millennia, Buddhism has evolved significantly. Buddha established communities of monks who renounced their families, took vows of poverty and chastity, and begged for their sustenance while wearing tattered clothing. These monks grew in number and established convents throughout Eastern Asia. They convened councils to establish doctrine and rules, and as they gained power, they began to view themselves as superior to other believers, much like the Brahmins. They preached that laypeople should support the religious and feel honored when the holy men accepted their offerings. In Tibet, the religious, including men and women, comprise a significant portion of the population, and their leader, the Grand Lama, is revered as a divine incarnation. As the Buddhist religion became more dominant, they also developed a complex theology filled with fantastical figures. They believe in an infinite number of worlds, each teeming with creatures like gods, humans, beasts, and demons who are born and die. Universes are destroyed and replaced, and the duration of each is called a "kalpa." To get a sense of a kalpa's length, imagine a rock twelve miles high, wide and long, and imagine that it is touched with a piece of fine linen once a century.

Before a quarter of a kalpa has passed, that rock would be worn down to the size of a mango kernel.

Buddhism Transformed into a Deity

The Buddhists of today no longer find it sufficient to honor their founder as a perfect man; instead, they have elevated him to the status of a god, erecting statues in his likeness and offering him worship. They also revere his disciples, constructing pyramids and shrines to house their bones, teeth, and cloaks. Devotees from all corners of the world come to pay homage to the impression of Buddha's foot. Mechanical Prayer. In modern times, Buddhists view prayer as a magical formula that acts on its own. They spend their days reciting prayers while they walk or eat, often in a language they do not comprehend. They have even invented prayer machines, which are revolving cylinders with papers attached to them on which the prayer is written. Each turn of the cylinder counts as the utterance of the prayer as many times as it is written on the paper. Amelioration of Manners. Despite these changes, Buddhism remains a religion of peace and charity. Wherever it is practiced, kings refrain from war and even hunting. They establish hospitals, caravansaries, and asylums for animals. Strangers, including Christian missionaries, are welcomed with hospitality. Women are allowed to go out and walk without veiling themselves, and fighting and quarreling are prohibited. In Bangkok, a city of over a million people, only one murder is known to occur each year.

Chapter 6

The Persians and Zoroaster

Iran rises between the Tigris and the Indus, the Caspian Sea and the Persian Gulf. It is a land five times the size of France, but only partially fertile. The terrain consists of scorching deserts and icy plateaus, with deep and wooded valleys. Mountains surround Iran, trapping the rivers, which either disappear into the sands or salt lakes. The climate is harsh, with extreme temperatures ranging from 104 degrees above zero to 40 degrees below zero, and violent winds that "cut like a sword." However, the valleys along the rivers are fertile, and the land is abundant with fruits and pastures. Iran was originally inhabited by Caucasian tribes, who were a race of shepherds. The Iranians were well-armed and warlike, fighting on horseback and drawing the bow. To protect themselves from the biting wind, they wore garments of skin sewn onto their bodies. The Iranians initially worshipped the forces of nature, particularly the sun or Mithra. However, between the tenth and seventh centuries before our era, their religion was reformed by a sage named Zarathustra or Zoroaster. Little is known about him except for his name. Zoroaster's doctrine was not written down by his own hand, but it was later recorded in the Zend-Avesta or law and reform, the sacred books of the Persians. The Zend-Avesta was written in an ancient language, the Zend, that was no longer understood by the faithful. The text was divided into twenty-one books, inscribed on 12,000 cow skins and bound by golden cords. The Mohammedans destroyed the Zend-Avesta when they invaded Persia, but some Persian families who were faithful to Zoroaster's teachings fled to India. Their descendants, known as Parsees, have maintained the old religion in India. Today, an entire book of the Zend-Avesta and fragments of two others have been found among the Parsees.

The sacred text of the Zoroastrian religion, the Zend-Avesta, tells the tale of two deities: Ahura Mazda, also known as Ormuzd, and Angra Manyou, also known as Ahriman. Ormuzd, the "omniscient sovereign," is the creator of the world, and is celebrated in prayer as "luminous, glorious, most intelligent and beautiful, eminent in purity, who possessest the good knowledge, source of joy, who hast treated us, hast fashioned us, and hast nourished us." As a perfect being, Ormuzd can only create good, while everything bad in the world is the creation of Ahriman, the "spirit of anguish." The armies of Ormuzd and Ahriman are made up of angels and demons, respectively. Ormuzd's soldiers, known as yazatas, are good angels, while Ahriman's troops are evil demons, called devs. The angels reside in the East, basking in the light of the rising sun, while the demons dwell in the West, shrouded in darkness. The two armies are in constant conflict, with the world serving as their battleground. Ormuzd and his angels seek to benefit humanity, making them good and happy, while Ahriman and his demons work to destroy them, making them miserable and wicked. All good things on Earth are the work of Ormuzd and serve a positive purpose. The sun and fire bring light and warmth, the stars guide us, fermented drinks quench our thirst, cultivated fields feed us, trees provide shade, and domestic animals, especially dogs, are loyal companions. Birds, particularly the rooster, are also revered for living in the air and announcing the arrival of a new day. Conversely, everything harmful is the work of Ahriman and serves a negative purpose. The night is dark and dangerous, drought and cold are harsh, the desert is unforgiving, poisonous plants and thorns harm us, and beasts of prey, serpents, and parasites like mosquitoes, fleas, and bugs cause us pain. Animals that live in dark holes, such as lizards, scorpions, toads, rats, and ants, are also considered to be the work of Ahriman. In the moral world, life, purity, truth, and work are considered good and come from Ormuzd, while death, filth, falsehood, and idleness are considered bad and come from Ahriman.

Worship stems from the belief in a good god and the need to fight for him. The Persians, unlike the Greeks, do not erect statues, temples, or altars to their gods. They believe that the gods do not have human forms and that Ormuzd, the god of light, only manifests himself under the form of fire or the sun. Therefore, the Persians perform their worship in the open air on the mountains, before a lighted fire. They sing hymns to Ormuzd's praise and sacrifice animals in his honor. Morality, for the Persians, involves fighting for Ormuzd by aiding his efforts and overcoming Ahriman's. They battle against darkness by supplying the fire with dry wood and perfumes and against the desert by tilling the soil and building houses. They also fight against impurity by keeping themselves clean and banishing everything that is dead, especially nails and hair, as demons and unclean animals assemble where they are. They fight against falsehood by always being truthful, as lying is considered shameful. They also fight against death by marrying and having many children, as the Zend-Avesta states that houses void of posterity are terrible. When a person dies, their body belongs to the evil spirit, and it must be removed from the house. However, burning, burying, or drowning the body would bring permanent pollution. Instead, the Persians expose the body with the face toward the sun in an elevated place and leave it uncovered, securely fixed with stones. The bearers then withdraw to escape the demons that assemble in places of sepulture. Dogs and birds, pure animals, come to purify the body by devouring it.

The destiny of the soul is a matter of great importance. When a person passes away, their soul separates from their body. On the third night after death, the soul crosses the Bridge of Assembling, also known as Schinvat. This bridge leads to paradise, which is located above the Gulf of Inferno. There, Ormuzd questions the soul about its past life. If the soul has lived a virtuous life, the pure spirits and spirits of dogs support it and help it cross the bridge. They grant the soul entrance into the abode of the blessed. The demons flee from the virtuous spirits, as they cannot bear their odor. However, if the soul has lived a wicked life, it comes to the dreadful bridge with no one to support it. Demons drag the soul to hell, where it is seized by the evil spirit and chained in the abyss of darkness. Mazdeism is a religion that originated in a country of violent contrasts. The Iranian people witnessed luxuriant valleys next to barren steppes, cool oases alongside burning deserts, and cultivated fields near stretches of sand. They saw the forces of nature engaged in eternal warfare, and they assumed that this combat was the law of the universe. Thus, a religion of great purity was developed, which urged people to work hard and practice virtue. However, this religion also introduced the belief in the devil and demons, which would later spread to the West and torment all the peoples of Europe. The Persian Empire was made up of many tribes living in Iran. Two of these tribes became notable in history: the Medes and the Persians. The Medes lived in the west, closer to the Assyrians. They destroyed Nineveh and its empire in 625 B.C. However, they soon adopted the flowing robes, indolent life, and superstitious religion of the degenerate Assyrians. Eventually, they were confused with them. On the other hand, the Persians lived in the East and preserved their manners, religion, and vigor. According to Herodotus, the Persians taught their children only three things for twenty years: to mount a horse, to draw the bow, and to tell the truth.

In the year 550 B.C., a man named Cyrus rose to power and became the leader of the Medes. He then went on to conquer and unite all the peoples of Iran. After that, he set his sights on Lydia, Babylon, and all of Asia Minor. According to the historian Herodotus, there was a legend that became attached to Cyrus. In his own words, Cyrus declared, "I am Cyrus, king of the legions, great king, mighty king, king of Babylon, king of Sumir and Akkad, king of the four regions, son of Cambyses, the great king of Susiana, grandson of Cyrus, king of Susiana." Cyrus' eldest son, Cambyses, killed his brother Smerdis and then conquered Egypt. The story of what happened next is told in an inscription that can still be seen today on the frontier of Persia. The inscription is carved into an enormous rock that stands about 1,500 feet high and is known as the rock of Behistun. On the rock, there is a bas-relief of a crowned king with his left hand on a bow. He tramples on one captive while nine other prisoners are presented before him in chains. The inscription, which is written in three languages, tells the story of the king's life. The inscription reads, "Darius the king declares, This is what I did before I became king. Cambyses, son of Cyrus, of our race, reigned here before me. This Cambyses had a brother Smerdis, of the same father and the same mother. One day Cambyses killed Smerdis. When Cambyses killed Smerdis, the people were ignorant that Smerdis was dead. After this, Cambyses made an expedition to Egypt. While he was there, the people became rebellious; falsehood was then rife in the country, in Persia, in Media and the other provinces. There was at that time, a magus named Gaumata; he deceived the people by saying that he was Smerdis, the son of Cyrus. Then the whole people rose in revolt, forsook Cambyses and went over to the pretender. After this, Cambyses died from a wound inflicted by himself. "After Gaumata had drawn away Persia, Media, and the other countries from Cambyses, he followed out his purpose: he became king. The people feared him on account of his cruelty: he would have killed the people so that no one might learn that he was not Smerdis, the son of Cyrus. Darius the king declares there was not a man in all Persia or in Media who dared to snatch the crown from this Gaumata, the magus. Then I presented myself, I prayed Ormuzd. Ormuzd accorded me his protection. Accompanied by faithful men, I killed this Gaumata and his principal accomplices. By the will of Ormuzd, I became king. The empire which had been stolen from our race I restored to it. The altars that Gaumata, the magus, had thrown down I rebuilt to the deliverance of the people; I received the chants and the sacred ceremonies." After overthrowing the usurper, Darius had to make war on many of the revolting princes. He declared, "I have won nineteen battles and overcome nine kings."

The Persian Empire rose to greatness under the leadership of Darius, who quelled rebellions and restored order to the land. He also expanded the empire's borders by conquering Thrace and a province of India. This vast empire brought together peoples from all over the Orient, including Medes, Persians, Assyrians, Chaldeans, Jews, Phoenicians, Syrians, Lydians, Egyptians, and Indians. It spanned from the Danube in the west to the Indus in the east, and from the Caspian Sea in the north to the Nile's cataracts in the south. It was the largest empire of its time, and it fell to a tribe of mountaineers who inherited the legacy of all the Asian empires. Oriental kings were not known for their involvement in their subjects' lives, and Darius was no exception. He allowed each people in his empire to govern itself according to its own customs, language, religion, laws, and even its ancient princes. However, he was careful to regulate the taxes his subjects paid. He divided the empire into twenty districts called satrapies, each with people who spoke different languages, and had different customs and beliefs. Still, each satrapy was to pay a fixed annual tribute, partly in gold and silver, and partly in natural products like wheat, horses, and ivory. The satrap, or governor, collected the tribute and sent it to the king. The king's total revenue amounted to sixteen million dollars, paid by weight, in addition to the tributes in kind. This sum, equivalent to one hundred and twenty million dollars in modern times, was used to support the satraps, the army, domestic servants, and an extravagant court. Despite this, the king still had enormous ingots of metal left over every year, which accumulated in his treasuries. Like all Orientals, the king of Persia took pride in possessing an immense treasure.

The ruler of Persia was a man of immense power and wealth, unmatched by any king before him. The Greeks referred to him as The Great King, a title befitting his absolute control over all his subjects, including the Persians and those who paid tribute to him. The writings of Herodotus reveal how Cambyses treated the great lords at his court. One day, he asked Prexaspes, whose son was his cupbearer, "What do the Persians think of me?" Prexaspes replied, "Master, they shower you with praises, but they believe that you have a little too strong a desire for wine." In anger, Cambyses commanded Prexaspes to find out if the Persians spoke the truth by shooting his son in the heart. The prince fell, and Cambyses had the body opened to see where the arrow had landed. It was found in the middle of the heart. The prince's joyous response to his father was, "You see that it is the Persians who are out of their senses; tell me if you have seen anybody strike the mark with so great accuracy." Prexaspes replied, "Master, I do not believe that even a god could shoot so surely." The Persians provided a significant service to the peoples of Asia. While conquerors demanded tribute and despots demanded allegiance, the Persians subjected all these peoples to one master, preventing them from fighting among themselves. Under Persian domination, there was no ceaseless burning of cities, the devastation of fields, massacre, or wholesale enslavement of inhabitants. It was a period of peace. The kings of the Medes and Persians followed the example of the lords of Assyria by building palaces for themselves. The most famous of these palaces were those at Susa and Persepolis. The ruins of Susa have been excavated by a French engineer, who discovered sculptures, capitals, and friezes in enameled bricks that demonstrate an advanced stage of art. The palace of Persepolis left ruins of considerable mass. The rock of the hill had been fashioned into an enormous platform on which the palace was built. The approach to it was by a gently rising staircase so broad that ten horsemen could ascend, riding side by side.

Persian architects, in their quest for beauty, looked to the Assyrians for inspiration. At Persepolis and Susa, much like in Assyria, we see flat-roofed buildings with terraces, gates guarded by stone-carved monsters, and intricate bas-reliefs and enameled bricks depicting hunting scenes and ceremonies. However, the Persians improved upon their models in three ways. Firstly, they opted for marble instead of brick. Secondly, they installed painted wooden floors in the halls. And thirdly, they erected eight columns in the form of tree trunks, the slenderest known to man, towering twelve times as high as they were thick. These innovations made Persian architecture more elegant and lighter than that of Assyria. Though the Persians had not made much progress in the arts, they were renowned for their honesty, sanity, and bravery. For two centuries, they reigned over Asia with a sovereignty that was the least cruel and unjust of its time.

Chapter 7

The Phoenicians

Phoenicia is a narrow strip of land, stretching one hundred and fifty miles long and twenty-four to thirty miles wide. It is enclosed between the sea of Syria and the high range of Lebanon. The terrain is a series of narrow valleys and ravines, surrounded by steep hills that slope towards the sea. During the early spring, small torrents formed by snow or rainstorms flow through the valleys, but in the summer, no water remains except in wells and cisterns. The mountains in this region were always covered with trees, and at the summit were the famous cedars of Lebanon. On the ridges, pines and cypresses grew, while lower down, palms grew even to the seashore. In the valleys, the olive, vine, fig, and pomegranate flourished. The Phoenician cities were located at intervals along the rocky coast, where promontories or islands formed natural harbors. Tyre and Arad were each built on a small island, and the people housed themselves in dwellings that were six to eight stories high. Fresh water was brought over by ships. The other cities, Gebel, Beirut, and Sidon, arose on the mainland. The soil was not enough to support the large population, so the Phoenicians were primarily seamen and traders. Unfortunately, not a single book of the Phoenicians has survived, not even a sacred book. The sites of their cities have been excavated, but the ruins have not been well-preserved. The Syrians violated the tombs to remove the jewels of the dead, demolished buildings to obtain stone for construction, and destroyed sculptures due to Muslim hatred of chiseled figures. As a result, very little is found beyond broken marble, cisterns, wine presses cut in the rock, and some sarcophagi hewn in the rock. This debris provides little information, and we know very little more about the Phoenicians than what Greek writers and Jewish prophets have taught us. The Phoenicians never built an empire. Each city had its own independent territory, assemblies, king, and government. For general state business, each city sent delegates to Tyre, which became the principal city of Phoenicia from the thirteenth century B.C. The Phoenicians were not a military people, and therefore, submitted themselves to all the conquerors, including the Egyptians, Assyrians, Babylonians, and Persians. They fulfilled all their obligations to them by paying tribute.

Tyre was a city of great renown, particularly in the thirteenth century. Its island was too small to contain its growing population, so a new city was constructed on the opposite coast. Tyrian merchants established colonies throughout the Mediterranean, receiving silver from the mines of Spain and goods from all corners of the ancient world. The prophet Isaiah referred to these traders as princes, while Ezekiel described the caravans that came to them from all directions. King Hiram of Tyre was the one whom Solomon requested workmen from to build his palace and temple in Jerusalem. Carthage, a colony of Tyre, surpassed even its mother city in power. In the ninth century, some Tyrians who were exiled by a revolution founded the city of Carthage on the African shore near Tunis. A woman named Elissar, whom we call Dido the fugitive, led them. According to legend, the locals were only willing to sell her enough land to cover a bull's hide, but she cut the hide into narrow strips that enclosed a vast territory, where she constructed a citadel. Situated at the center of the Mediterranean with two harbors, Carthage thrived, established colonies, made conquests, and eventually reigned over all the coasts of Africa, Spain, and Sardinia. It had commerce agencies and subjects who paid tribute everywhere. To protect its colonies from natives and keep its subjects in check, a strong army was necessary. However, a Carthaginian's life was too valuable to risk without necessity. Carthage preferred to pay mercenary soldiers, recruiting them from the barbarians of its empire and adventurers from all over. Its army was a strange mixture in which all languages were spoken, all religions were practiced, and every soldier wore different arms and costumes. There were Numidians clothed in lion skins that served as their couch, mounted bareback on small, fleet horses, and drawing their bows with the horse at full gallop. There were also Libyans with black skins, armed with pikes, Iberians from Spain in white garments adorned with red, armed with a long pointed sword, Gauls naked to the girdle, bearing enormous shields and a rounded sword that they held in both hands, and natives of the Balearic Islands, trained from infancy to sling stones or balls of lead. The generals were Carthaginians, but the government distrusted them, watched them closely, and had them crucified when they were defeated.

The Carthaginians were a people ruled by a senate comprised of the wealthiest merchants in the city, despite having two kings. Their focus was on commerce, making every state issue a matter of trade. Although they were despised by other nations for their cruelty, greed, and treachery, their powerful fleet, wealth, and efficient government allowed them to maintain their grip on the western Mediterranean for 300 years, from the sixth to the third century B.C., amidst a sea of barbarous and divided peoples. The Phoenicians and Carthaginians had a religion similar to that of the Chaldeans. Their male god, Baal, was a sun-god, as the sun and moon were considered the great forces of creation and destruction. Each city in Phoenicia had its divine pair, with Baal Sidon, the sun, and Astoreth, the moon, in Sidon; Baal Tammouz and Baaleth in Gebel, and Baal-Hamon and Tanith in Carthage. However, Baal's name changed depending on whether he was seen as a creator or destroyer. In Carthage, Baal was worshipped as Moloch, the destroyer. The gods were represented by idols, with their own temples, altars, and priests. As creators, they were honored with orgies and tumultuous feasts, while as destroyers, they were appeased with human sacrifices. Astoreth, the great goddess of Sidon, was represented by the crescent moon and the dove and had her cult in the sacred woods. Baal Moloch was depicted as a bronze colossus with extended and lowered arms. To appease him, children were placed in his hands and fell into a pit of fire. During the siege of Carthage by Agathocles, the city's leaders sacrificed as many as two hundred of their children to Moloch. This religion, with its sensuality and bloodshed, horrified other nations, yet they imitated it. The Jews sacrificed to Baal on the mountains, while the Greeks worshipped Astarte of Sidon as Aphrodite and Baal Melkhart of Tyre as Herakles.

Phoenician Commerce

In the ancient world, the Phoenicians were known as the masters of commerce. Despite their small territory, they made their living through trade, something that no other people in the East or West dared to do. The Egyptians, Chaldeans, Assyrians, Spaniards, Gauls, and Italians had no navy, but the Phoenicians did. They were the commission merchants of their time, traveling to every corner of the world to buy and sell goods. They used caravans to transport goods over land and ships to sail the seas. Their caravans went in three directions. The first was towards Arabia, where they brought back gold, agate, onyx, incense, myrrh, pearls, spices, ivory, ebony, ostrich plumes, and apes from India. The second was towards Assyria, where they found cotton and linen cloths, asphalt, precious stones, perfumes, and silk from China. The third was towards the Black Sea, where they received horses, slaves, and copper vases made by the mountaineers of the Caucasus. Their ships were made from the cedars of Lebanon and were propelled by both oars and sails. They were skilled sailors who knew how to navigate by the polar star and were not afraid to venture into the open ocean. They sailed to the shores of England and perhaps even Norway. In fact, Phoenicians in the service of a king of Egypt circumnavigated Africa in the seventh century B.C. and returned after three years by way of the Red Sea. Another expedition from Carthage sailed along the coast of Africa to the Gulf of Guinea, and the commander Hanno wrote an account of the voyage that still exists today.

Commodities were the lifeblood of the Phoenicians, who sold their wares to civilized peoples and scoured barbarous lands in search of goods not found in the Orient. Along the coast of Greece, they harvested shellfish to extract a red dye known as purple, which was used to color cloth worn by kings and great lords throughout ancient times. From Spain and Sardinia, the Phoenicians procured silver from the mines. Tin, necessary for making bronze, was not found in the Orient, so they sought it on the coasts of England, in the Isles of Tin or the Cassiterides. Slaves were also a valuable commodity, and the Phoenicians procured them through various means, including purchasing them and raiding coasts to capture women and children. The Phoenicians were secretive about their trade routes, not wanting to invite competition from other mariners. They concealed the road they traveled on their return from far-off lands, and no one in antiquity knew the location of the famous Isles of the Cassiterides. Carthage even went so far as to drown foreign merchants found in Sardinia or on the shore of Gibraltar, and a Carthaginian merchantman once ran aground to prevent a foreign ship from following it. In the countries where they traded, the Phoenicians established factories or branch houses, and fortified posts on natural harbors where they landed their merchandise. The natives brought their own commodities to exchange, much like modern-day European merchants trading with Africans. Phoenician markets could be found in Cyprus, Egypt, and all the then-barbarous countries of the Mediterranean, including Crete, Greece, Sicily, Africa, Malta, Sardinia, and on the coasts of Spain at Malaga and Cadiz, and possibly in Gaul at Monaco. Around these Phoenician buildings, the natives often set up their cabins, and the market would grow into a city. Even after the city became Greek, the inhabitants would continue to worship Phoenician gods, such as the dove-goddess, Melkhart, or the god with the bull-face that devours human victims.

The Phoenicians, in their pursuit of trade, were not concerned with anything beyond their own interests. However, their colonies ultimately contributed to the advancement of civilization. The Western barbarians were introduced to the refined cloths, jewels, and utensils of the Eastern peoples, and through imitation, they too learned to create such objects. For a significant period of time, the Greeks only possessed vases, jewels, and idols that were brought to them by the Phoenicians, and these items served as their models. The Phoenicians also brought industry and commodities from both Egypt and Assyria. Simultaneously, they exported their alphabet. The Phoenicians did not invent writing; the Egyptians had been writing for centuries before them, even using letters that represented individual sounds, similar to our alphabet. However, the Egyptian alphabet was still encumbered with ancient signs that represented either a syllable or an entire word. The Phoenicians required a simpler system for their books of commerce, and so they discarded all the syllabic signs and ideographs, preserving only twenty-two letters, each of which represented a sound or articulation of their language. Other peoples imitated this alphabet of twenty-two letters. Some, like the Jews, wrote from right to left, just as the Phoenicians themselves did, while others, like the Greeks, wrote from left to right. Although the form of the letters has slightly changed over time, the Phoenician alphabet serves as the foundation for all alphabets, including Hebrew, Lycian, Greek, Italian, Etruscan, and Iberian, and perhaps even the Norse runes. It is the Phoenicians who taught the world how to write.

Chapter 8

The Origin of The Hebrews

The Bible is an aggregation of sacred books that were united by the Jews. These books also became sacred to the Christians. The Bible is not only the history of the Jewish nation, but it is also the source of all our knowledge of the sacred people. The Hebrews were a tribe of Semites who left the plains of the Euphrates during the first Chaldean empire and migrated to the country of Jordan beyond Phoenicia. They were a race of nomadic shepherds who lived in tents and moved from place to place with their herds of cattle, sheep, and camels. The tribe of Hebrews was like a great family, with the chief having absolute authority over all. These tribal chiefs were called patriarchs, and the principal ones were Abraham and Jacob. Both were chosen by God to be the scions of a sacred people. Abraham made a covenant with God that he and his descendants would obey him, and God promised him a posterity more numerous than the stars of heaven. Jacob received from God the assurance that a great nation would issue from himself. Jacob took the name of Israel, meaning contender with God, after being moved by a vision. His tribe was called Beni-Israel or Israelites. According to the Bible, Jacob and his house settled on the eastern frontier of Egypt after being invited by Joseph, one of his sons who had become a minister of a Pharaoh, due to famine. The sons of Israel lived there for several centuries and multiplied until they became six hundred thousand men, not counting women and children.

And so it came to pass that the Pharaoh of Egypt began to oppress the Israelites, forcing them to toil in the construction of his great cities, making mortar and bricks for his ambitious projects. But in the midst of this despair, a man named Moses heard the call of God. As he tended to his herds on the mountain, an angel appeared to him in a burning bush, declaring, "I am the God of Abraham, Isaac, and Jacob. I have seen the affliction of my people in Egypt, I have heard their cries against their oppressors, and I have come to deliver them from the Egyptians and bring them to a land flowing with milk and honey, to the place of the Canaanites. Come now, and I will send you to Pharaoh to bring forth my people, the children of Israel, out of Egypt." And so Moses led the Israelites out of Egypt, through the desert, and to the foot of Mount Sinai, where they received the law of God. But their journey was not without its challenges. Many of the Israelites longed to turn back, yearning for the fish, cucumbers, melons, leeks, and onions they had left behind in Egypt. But Moses held them to obedience, and they eventually reached the land promised to them by God. This land, known as Canaan or Palestine, was a harsh and arid country, scorching in the summer sun, but also a land of mountains. The Bible describes it as a "good land, a land of brooks of water, of fountains and depths that spring out of valleys and hills, a land of wheat, and barley, and vines, and fig-trees, and pomegranates; a land of oil olive and honey, wherein thou shalt eat bread without scarceness, thou shalt not lack anything in it." The Israelites, numbering 601,700 men capable of bearing arms, divided among twelve tribes, set out to conquer this land, which was already occupied by several small peoples known as the Canaanites. Through battle and conquest, the Israelites eventually exterminated the Canaanites and claimed their territory as their own.

The Religion of Israel

In the ancient world, many peoples worshipped multiple gods. However, the Israelites believed in only one God, who is immaterial and created and governs the world. According to the book of Genesis, "In the beginning, God created the heavens and the earth." God also created plants, animals, and humans, whom he made in his own image. Therefore, all people are the handiwork of God. God chose the children of Israel to be his people. He made a covenant with Abraham, saying, "I will establish my covenant between me and thee and thy seed after me.

to be a God unto thee and to thy seed." God also appeared to Jacob, telling him, "I am God, the God of thy father; fear not to go down into Egypt, for I will make of thee there a great nation." When Moses asked God for his name, he replied, "Thou shalt say to the children of Israel, The Lord, the God of thy fathers, the God of Abraham, the God of Isaac, the God of Jacob hath sent me unto you. This is my name forever." Therefore, there is a covenant between the Israelites and God. Jehovah or the Eternal, loves and protects the Israelites, who are "a holy nation" and "his most precious jewel among all the nations." In return, the Israelites swear to worship him, serve him, and obey him in everything as a lawgiver, judge, and sovereign. Jehovah, the lawgiver of the Israelites, dictated his precepts to Moses on Mount Sinai amidst lightning and thundering. These precepts were inscribed on two tables, the Tables of the Law, in the following terms: "Hear, O Israel, I am Jehovah, thy God, who brought you out of the land of Egypt, from the land of bondage." Then follow the ten commandments, which can be found in the twentieth chapter of the book of Exodus.

Besides the ten commandments, the Israelites are required to obey many other divine ordinances. These are all delivered to them in the first five books of the Bible, the Pentateuch, and constitute the Law of Israel. The Law regulates the ceremonies of religion, establishes the feasts-including the Sabbath every seven days, the Passover in memory of the escape from Egypt, the week of harvest, the feast of Tabernacles during the vintage; it organizes marriage, the family, property, government, fixes the penalty of crimes, indicates even foods and remedies. It is a code at once religious, political, civil, and penal. God, the ruler of the Israelites, has the right to regulate all the details of their lives. The Israelites did not receive with docility the government of God. Moses on his deathbed could say to the Levites in delivering to them the book of the law, "'Take this book that it may be a witness against you, Israel, for I know thy rebellion and thy stiff neck", Deuteronomy chapter 31 verse 27. "During my life, you have been rebellious against the Lord, and how much more after my death." During these centuries, some of the Israelites, often the majority of the nation, had been idolaters. They became similar to the other Semites of Syria. Only the Israelites who remained faithful to God formed the Jewish people. It is the religion of Jehovah which has transformed an obscure tribe into the holy nation, a small nation, but one of the most significant in the history of the world. Once established in Palestine, the Hebrews remained divided for several centuries. "In those days," says the Bible, "there was no king in Israel; every man did that which was right in his own eyes." Often the Israelites forgot Jehovah and served the gods of neighboring tribes. Then "the anger of the Lord was kindled against the Israelites, and he delivered them into the hands of their enemies." When they had repented and had humbled themselves, "the Lord raised up judges who delivered them out of the hand of those that spoiled them." "But it came to pass that at the death of the judge they corrupted themselves anew. bowing themselves to other gods." These judges, Gideon, Jephthah, and Samson, were warriors who came in the name of Jehovah to free the people. Then they fell at once into idolatry again and their servitude was repeated.

The Monarchs

Finally, the Israelites grew tired and requested a king from Samuel, the chief priest. Samuel reluctantly appointed Saul as their leader. This king was meant to be a faithful servant of God's will, but he dared to disobey Him. The chief priest told him, "You have rejected the word of the Lord, and the Lord has rejected you from being king over Israel." David, a war chief, was appointed in his place. He defeated all of Israel's enemies, captured Mount Zion from them, and made it his capital. This became Jerusalem. Compared to Babylon or Thebes, Jerusalem was a modest capital. The Hebrews were not builders, and their religion prevented them from constructing temples. The homes of individuals were shaped like cubes of rock, which can still be seen today on the sides of Lebanon amidst vines and fig trees. However, Jerusalem was the holy city of the Hebrews. The king had his palace there, including Solomon's palace, which amazed the Hebrews with its ivory throne. Jehovah had His temple there, which was the first Hebrew temple. The symbol of the covenant between God and Israel was a large cedarwood chest with gold rings, which contained the tables of the Law. This was carried before the people on important feast days, and it was known as the Ark of the Covenant. To protect this ark and other necessary objects of worship, Moses is said to have built the Tabernacle. This was a wooden pavilion covered with skins and hangings, and it was a portable temple that the Hebrews carried with them until they could build a permanent temple in the promised land.

The Temple, a grand structure erected by Solomon, was comprised of three distinct areas. The Holy of Holies, located at the rear, housed the ark of the covenant and was accessible only to the high priest once a year. In the middle was the Holy Place, home to the altar of incense, the candlestick with seven arms, and the table of shew-bread. The priests entered this area to present offerings and burn incense. The front area was the Court, open to the people, where the great altar was used for sacrifices. The Temple of Jerusalem served as the nation's center, attracting people from all over Palestine to witness its ceremonies. The high priest, who oversaw the worship, often held more power than the king. Following the reign of Solomon, the kingdom of Israel was formed by ten tribes who worshipped the golden calves and Phoenician gods. Only two tribes remained loyal to Jehovah and the king in Jerusalem, forming the kingdom of Judah. The two kingdoms engaged in war with each other, ultimately leading to their downfall at the hands of Eastern conquerors. Israel was destroyed by Sargon, king of Assyria in 722, and Judah fell to Nabuchodonosor or Nebuchadrezzar, king of Chaldea in 586. Faithful Israelites viewed these disasters as a punishment from God for their disobedience. They believed that God would deliver them from their conquerors, as he had done before. The children of Israel had sinned against Jehovah, their God, by building high places in every city, imitating the nations around them, making idols of brass, bowing before the stars, and worshipping Baal. As a result, Jehovah rejected all of Israel and allowed them to be afflicted and plundered.

The Seers, also known as the prophets, emerged onto the scene: Elijah, Jeremiah, Isaiah, and Ezekiel. They hailed from the desert, where they fasted, prayed, and meditated. In the name of Jehovah, they came not as warriors of judgment, but as preachers. They called upon the Israelites to repent, cast aside their idols, and return to Jehovah. They prophesied the woes that would befall them if they did not reconcile with Him. They preached and prophesied simultaneously. These men, ablaze with divine spirit, found the official religion in Jerusalem to be lackluster and unfeeling. Why should they, like the idolaters, slaughter cattle and burn incense in God's honor? "Hear the word of Jehovah," says Isaiah: "To what purpose is the multitude of your sacrifices? I am full of the burnt offerings of rams and of the fat of fed beasts, and I delight not in the blood of bullocks, or of lambs, or of goats. Bring no more vain oblations, your incense is an abomination to me. When ye spread forth your hands, I will hide mine eyes from you. for your hands are full of blood. Wash you, make you clean. Cease to do evil, learn to do well; seek judgment, relieve the oppressed, judge the fatherless, plead for the widow. Though your sins be as scarlet, they shall be as white as snow." Instead of sacrifices, the prophets would focus on justice and good works. Israel deserved its afflictions, but there would be a limit to the chastisement. "O my people," says Isaiah in the name of Jehovah, "be not afraid of the Assyrian. He shall smite thee with a rod, after the manner of Egypt. For yet a very little while and the indignation shall cease, and the burden shall be taken away from off thy shoulder." The prophets taught the people to anticipate the coming of the Messiah, who would deliver them. They paved the way for the Messiah.

The Jewish people longed for their homeland, even as they were exiled to the plains of the Euphrates. They sang of their beloved Zion, mourning their displacement in a foreign land. But after seventy years of captivity, Cyrus allowed them to return to Palestine. They rebuilt Jerusalem, restored the temple, and renewed their covenant with Jehovah. For seven centuries, the Jews maintained their kingdom, paying tribute to various masters but always faithful to Jehovah. They lived by the law of Moses, celebrating feasts and sacrifices in Jerusalem. The high priest and council of elders preserved the law, while scribes copied and doctors expounded it. The Pharisees were known for their zeal in fulfilling its requirements. As the Jews spread beyond Judah for trade, they established synagogues to read and comment on the word of God. Though they could not raise additional temples, they were determined to preserve their religion. These synagogues became places of gathering and learning, scattered throughout the great cities of the world.

The destruction of the Temple was a pivotal moment in history, for it was at this moment that the Christ appeared. The Jews, fearing his message, crucified him and persecuted his disciples not only in Judaea but in every city where they found them in any number. In the year 70 A.D., Jerusalem, in revolt against the Romans, was taken by assault, and all the inhabitants were massacred or sold into slavery. The Romans burnt the temple and carried away the sacred utensils. From that time there was no longer a center of the Jewish religion. But the Jewish nation survived the ruin of its capital. The Jews, scattered throughout the world, learned to dispense with the temple. They preserved their sacred books in the Hebrew tongue. Hebrew is the primitive language of Israel; the Jews since the return from Babylon no longer spoke it, but adopted the languages of the neighboring peoples, the Syriac, the Chaldean, and especially the Greek. The Rabbis, however, instructed in the religion, still learned Hebrew, explained it, and commented on the Scripture. Thus the Jewish religion was preserved and, thanks to it, the Jewish people. It made converts even among the Gentiles; there were in the empire proselytes, that is, people who practiced the religion of Jehovah without being of the Jewish race. The Christian Church, powerful since the fourth century, began to persecute the Jews. In these times, the Jews were tolerated on account of their wealth and because they transacted most banking operations, but they were kept apart, and not permitted to hold any office. In the majority of cities, they were compelled to wear a special costume, to live in a special quarter, gloomy, filthy, unhealthy, and sometimes at Easter time to send one of their numbers to suffer insult. The people suspected them of poisoning fountains, killing children, or profaning the consecrated host; often, the people rose against them, massacred them, and pillaged their houses. Judges, under the least pretext, had them imprisoned, tortured, and burned. Sometimes the church tried to convert them by force; sometimes, the government exiled them en masse from the country and confiscated their goods. The Jews, at last, disappeared from France, Spain, England, and Italy. In Portugal, Germany, Poland, and the Mohammedan lands, they maintained themselves. From these countries, after the cessation of persecution, they returned to the rest of Europe.

Chapter 9

Greece and the Greeks

Greece is a small country, barely larger than Switzerland, but do not let its size fool you. It is a land of great diversity, with towering mountains and deep gulfs that have influenced the character of its inhabitants for centuries. The Pindus mountain range runs through the center of Greece, covering the land with its rocky terrain. As it nears the isthmus of Corinth, it becomes lower, but the Peloponnesus on the other side of the isthmus rises to an elevation of about 2,000 feet above sea level. Its lofty chains, abrupt and snowy, fall perpendicularly into the sea like a citadel crowned with a fortress. Even the islands scattered along the coast are nothing more than submerged mountains whose peaks rise above the surface of the sea. Tillable ground is scarce in this diverse land, with almost everywhere bare rock. The streams, like brooks, leave only a narrow strip of fertile soil between their half-dried channels and the sterile mountain rock. Some forests, cypresses, laurels, and palms can be found scattered here and there, along with vines on the rocky hillsides. But there are no rich harvests or green pastures to be found. This rugged landscape produces wiry mountaineers, active and sober. Greece is a land of shores, with a coastline as long as Spain's, despite its size being smaller than Portugal. The sea penetrates it with numerous gulfs, coves, and indentations, surrounded by projecting rocks or approaching islands that form natural ports. The sea is like a lake, with a calm and lustrous surface, often described as the color of violets, as Homer once said. This sea is perfect for small ships, with the north wind rising every morning to guide the barques of Athens to Asia, and the south wind bringing them back to port in the evening. The islands between Greece and Asia Minor are like stepping stones, with land always in sight on a clear day. Such a sea beckons people to cross it.

And cross it, the Greeks have. They have been sailors, traders, travelers, pirates, and adventurers, much like the Phoenicians before them. They have spread over the ancient world, carrying with them the merchandise and inventions of Egypt, Chaldea, and Asia.

The climate of Greece is mild, with Athens experiencing freezing temperatures only once every twenty years. During the summer months, the heat is tempered by the sea breeze. Even today, people can be found lounging in the streets from May to September. The air is crisp and clear, with the statue of Pallas visible from miles away. The distant mountains are not shrouded in haze, but stand out distinctly against the azure sky. Greece is a beautiful country that inspires one to live life to the fullest, for everything around is filled with joy. "Walking in the gardens at night, listening to the chirping of the grasshoppers, playing the lute under the moonlight, drinking from the mountain spring, carrying wine to drink while singing, and spending days dancing-these are the pleasures of the Greeks, a race that is poor, economical, and forever young." In this country, people do not suffer from extreme heat or cold. They live outdoors, happy, and without spending much money. They do not require large quantities of food, warm clothing, or comfortable homes. A Greek can survive on a handful of olives and a sardine. Their clothing consists of sandals, a tunic, and a large mantle. Often, they go barefoot and bareheaded. Their homes are meager and easily permeated by the air. A bed with some coverings, a chest, some beautiful vases, and a lamp are their only furnishings. The walls are bare and whitewashed. Their homes are only for sleeping. The Greeks who inhabited this charming little land were Caucasian people, related to the Hindus and Persians. They, like their ancestors, came from the mountains of Asia or the steppes beyond the Caspian Sea. The Greeks had forgotten the long journey made by their ancestors and believed that they, like the grasshoppers, were the children of the soil. However, their language and the names of their gods leave no doubt about their origin. Like all Caucasians, the primitive Greeks nourished themselves with milk and the flesh of their herds. They moved about under arms, always ready to fight, and grouped themselves into tribes governed by patriarchs.

The Legends

The Greeks, like all other ancient peoples, were ignorant of their origin. They did not know where their ancestors came from when they settled in Greece, or what they did there. To preserve the exact memory of things as they occur, there is a need for some means of fixing them. However, the Greeks did not know how to write until about the eighth century B.C. They had no way of calculating the number of years. Later, they began counting the years according to the great feast celebrated every four years at Olympia. A period of four years was called an Olympiad. But the first Olympiad was placed in 776 B.C., and the chronology of the Greeks does not rise beyond this date. And yet, in Greece, they used to tell a great number of legends about this primitive period. These were especially the exploits of ancient kings and heroes who were adored as demigods. These stories were so mingled with fable that it is impossible to know how much truth they may contain. They said at Athens that the first king, Cecrops, was half man and half serpent. At Thebes, they said that Cadmus, founder of the city, had come from Phoenicia to seek his sister Europa who had been stolen by a bull. He had killed a dragon and had sown his teeth, from which was sprung a race of warriors. The noble families of Thebes descended from these warriors. At Argos, it was said that the royal family was the issue of Pelops, to whom Zeus had given a shoulder of ivory to replace the one devoured by a goddess. Thus, each country had its legends, and the Greeks continued to the end to relate them and to offer worship to their ancient heroes namely Perseus, Bellerophon, Herakles, Theseus, Minos, Castor and Pollux, Meleager, and Oedipus. The majority of the Greeks, even among the better-educated, admitted, at least in part, the truth of these traditions. They accepted as historical facts the war between the two sons of Oedipus, king of Thebes, and the expedition of the Argonauts, sailing forth in quest of the Golden Fleece, which was guarded by two brazen-footed bulls vomiting flames.

The tale of the Trojan War is among the most celebrated legends of all time. It tells of the powerful city of Troy, which ruled over the coast of Asia in the twelfth century. Paris, a prince of Troy, traveled to Greece and took Helen, the wife of Menelaus, king of Sparta, as his own. Agamemnon, the king of Argos, formed a league with the kings of Greece, and together they sailed with a fleet of two hundred galleys to besiege Troy. The siege lasted ten years, as Zeus, the supreme god, had taken the side of the Trojans. All the Greek chiefs were involved in this epic adventure. Achilles, the bravest and most beautiful of them all, killed Hector, the main defender of Troy, and dragged his body around the city. Achilles wore divine armor given to him by his mother, a goddess of the sea, but he was ultimately killed by an arrow to his heel. The Greeks, unable to take the city by force, devised a trick. They pretended to leave and left behind a massive wooden horse, inside of which were the chiefs of the army. The Trojans brought the horse into the city, and during the night, the chiefs emerged and opened the gates to the Greeks. The city of Troy was burned, the men slaughtered, and the women taken as slaves. However, the chiefs of the Greeks faced a tempestuous return journey. Some perished at sea, while others were cast onto foreign shores. Odysseus, the most cunning of the chiefs, was buffeted from one land to another for ten years, losing all his ships and becoming the sole survivor of the disasters. Throughout antiquity, the Trojan War was believed to be true. The year 1184 B.C. was considered the end of the siege, and the location of the city was known. In 1874, Schliemann set out to excavate the site, which was buried under layers of debris from many cities. At a depth of around fifty feet, he discovered the remains of a great city reduced to ashes, and inside the ruins of the main building, he found a casket filled with gold gems, which he called the Treasury of Priam. There were no inscriptions, and the city whose entire wall was uncovered, was quite small. Many small, crude idols were also found depicting an owl-headed goddess representing the Greek goddess Pallas. However, no evidence has been found to prove that this city was indeed Troy.

The Homeric Poems are the stuff of legend, known throughout the world for their epic tales of the Trojan War. The Iliad tells of the Greeks' battles and the heroic deeds of Achilles before the walls of Troy, while the Odyssey recounts the incredible adventures of Odysseus also known as Ulysses after the city's fall. For centuries, these two poems were passed down through oral tradition, recited by wandering singers known as rhapsodists at feasts and gatherings. It wasn't until the sixth century that Pisistratus, a prince of Athens, had them collected and edited. From that time on, they became the most revered works of Greek literature. The Greeks believed that Homer, a blind old man from Ionia, was the author of these poems. Although seven towns claimed to be his birthplace, this tradition was widely accepted. However, in the eighteenth century, a German scholar named Wolf noticed inconsistencies in the poems and argued that they were not the work of a single poet, but rather a collection of fragments from different sources. This theory has been hotly debated ever since, with passionate arguments for and against the existence of Homer. Today, we may never know the truth, but one thing is certain: these poems are ancient, likely dating back to the ninth century. The Iliad was likely composed in Asia Minor and may be a combination of two separate poems, one about the Trojan battles and the other about Achilles' exploits. The Odyssey, on the other hand, appears to be the work of a single author, though it cannot be definitively linked to the same author as the Iliad.

The Greeks in the Time of Homer

We cannot journey far back into the annals of Greek history, but the Homeric poems stand as their oldest historical account. When these works were written, around the ninth century B.C., there was no universal name for all the inhabitants of Greece. Homer referred to them by their primary tribes. From his descriptions, it appears that they had made some progress since their departure from Asia. They knew how to cultivate the land, construct fortified cities, and organize themselves into small communities. They were obedient to their kings, had a council of elders, and an assembly of the people. They were proud of their institutions and looked down upon their less advanced neighbors, whom they called Barbarians. Odysseus, in an effort to demonstrate the Cyclops' rudeness, said, "They have no rules of justice nor places where they deliberate; each one governs himself, his wife, and children, and has no association with others." However, these Greeks were themselves half-barbarians, as they did not know how to write, coin money, or work with iron. They were hesitant to trust themselves to the sea and believed that Sicily was inhabited by monsters. The Dorians. The name "Dorians" was given to the sons of mountaineers who had migrated from the north and had either expelled or subjugated those who lived in the plains and along the Peloponnesian coast. The latter, confined to a small area, sent colonies into Asia. The most famous of these mountain groups came from a small canton called Doris and retained the name "Dorians." These invaders told stories of how certain kings of Sparta, descendants of Herakles, had been ousted by their subjects and had gone to the mountains to seek the Dorians. The mountain people, motivated by their love for Herakles, had followed his descendants and restored them to their throne. In doing so, they dispossessed the inhabitants and took their place. They were a martial, robust, and healthy people, accustomed to cold weather, meager food, and a sparse existence. Both men and women wore short tunics that did not extend to the knee. They spoke a crude and primitive dialect. The Dorians were a race of soldiers, always required to remain armed. They were the least cultured in Greece, as they were far from the sea and retained the customs of the barbaric age. However, they were the most Greek because, being isolated, they could not mix with outsiders or adopt their ways.

The Ionians were a people of Attica, the islands, and the coast of Asia. Their name's origin is unknown, but they were a race of sailors and traders, the most cultured in Greece, and they gained knowledge from contact with the most civilized peoples of the Orient. They were the least Greek because they associated with Asiatics and had partially adopted their dress. The Ionians were peaceful and industrious, living luxuriously, speaking a smooth dialect, and wearing long flowing garments like the Orientals. The Hellenes were composed of two opposing races, the Dorians and the Ionians, who were the most remarkable and powerful in Greece. Sparta was Dorian, and Athens was Ionian. However, the majority of Greeks were neither Dorians nor Ionians, but rather called Aeolians, which is a vague name that covers very different peoples. All Greeks, from early times to the present day, take the name "Hellenes." The origin of the term is unknown, but they said only that Dorus and Aeolus were sons of Hellen, and Ion was his grandson. The Hellenes were still in small groups, like at the time of Homer. Greece's land, cut by mountains and sea, breaks naturally into many small cantons, each isolated from its neighbor by an arm of the sea or a wall of rocks, making it easy to defend the land but difficult to communicate with other parts. Each canton constituted a separate state called a city, and there were more than a hundred of these, including colonies, which numbered over a thousand. To us, a Greek state seems like a miniature. The whole of Attica was only slightly larger than the state of Delaware, and Corinth or Megara was much smaller. Usually, the state was only a city with a strip of shore and a harbor, or some villages scattered in the plain around a citadel. From one state, one can see the citadel, mountains, or harbor of the next state. Many of them counted their citizens only by thousands, and the largest included hardly 200,000 or 300,000.

The Hellenes, though not united as one nation, shared a common language, religion, and way of life. They looked down upon other peoples whom they deemed barbarians. Despite their constant fighting, the Hellenes established colonies in neighboring lands. From the islands of the Archipelago to the coasts of France and Spain, Greek cities sent out colonists to found new settlements. These colonies were established in various ways, by conquest or agreement with the natives, and were founded by mariners, merchants, exiles, or adventurers. Despite their diverse origins, the colonies shared common characteristics. They were established at once, according to fixed rules, and with a religious ceremony. The colonists arrived together under a leader, and the new city was founded in one day. The founder traced a sacred enclosure, constructed a sacred hearth, and lit the holy fire.

The Founding of Colonies

The tales of old regarding the establishment of some of these colonies allow us to observe how they differed from modern colonies. The story of the founding of Marseilles goes like this: Euxenus, a citizen of Phocaea, arrived in Gaul aboard a merchant ship and was invited by a Gallic leader to attend his daughter's wedding. As per the custom of the Gauls, the young girl carried a cup during the feast that she would present to the man she chose as her husband. She stopped in front of the Greek and offered him the cup. This impromptu act seemed to be divinely inspired. The Gallic leader gave his daughter to Euxenus and allowed him and his companions to establish a city on the Gulf of Marseilles. Later, the Phocaeans, seeing their city under siege by the Persian army, loaded their families, belongings, statues, and temple treasures onto their ships and set sail, abandoning their city. As they departed, they threw a mass of red-hot iron into the sea and swore never to return to Phocaea until the iron rose to the surface. Many broke this oath and returned, but the rest continued their voyage and, after many trials, arrived in Marseilles. In Miletus, the Ionians who founded the city did not bring wives with them. They conquered a city inhabited by natives of Asia, killed all the men, and forcibly married the women and girls of their victims' families. It was said that the women, outraged by this treatment, swore never to eat with their captors or call them "husband." This custom persisted among the women of Miletus for centuries. The colony at Cyrene in Africa was founded by the direct order of the oracle Apollo. The inhabitants of Thera, who received this command, were hesitant to go to an unfamiliar land. They only relented after seven years of famine on their island, believing that Apollo had brought misfortune upon them as punishment. Nonetheless, the citizens sent out to establish the colony attempted to abandon the endeavor. Their fellow citizens attacked them and compelled them to return. After spending two years on an island with no success, they finally settled in Cyrene, which quickly became a thriving city.

The Significance of the Colonies

Wherever the colonists settled, they established a new state that did not obey their mother town in any way. Consequently, the entire Mediterranean was surrounded by independent Greek cities. Many of these cities became wealthier and more powerful than their mother towns, possessing larger and more fertile territories and, as a result, greater populations. Sybaris, for example, had 300,000 men capable of bearing arms, while Croton could field an infantry force of 120,000 men. Even Sparta and Athens were surpassed in terms of army size by cities such as Syracuse in Sicily and Miletus in Asia. South Italy was known as Great Greece, and in comparison, the home country was only a small Greece. As a result, the Greeks were much more numerous in neighboring countries than in Greece proper, and many of the most celebrated names in Greek history came from these colonies. Homer, Alcaeus, Sappho, Thales, Pythagoras, Heraclitus, Democritus, Empedocles, Aristotle, Archimedes, Theocritus, and many others are among the people of the colonies who have achieved great renown.

Chapter 10

Greek Religion

The Gods: Polytheism

The Greeks, much like the ancient Caucasians, believed in a multitude of gods. They did not possess the sentiment of infinity or eternity, nor did they conceive of God as a being for whom the heavens were merely a tent and the earth a footstool. To the Greeks, every force of nature, the air, the sun, the sea, was divine. Since they did not consider all these phenomena as originating from a single cause, they assigned each to a specific god. This is why they believed in multiple gods, making them polytheists. Anthropomorphism. Each god represented a force in nature and had a distinct name. The Greeks, with their lively imagination, envisioned a living being of beautiful form and human characteristics under this name. A god or goddess was depicted as a beautiful man or woman. When Odysseus or Telemachus encountered a person who was particularly great and beautiful, they would inquire if they were a god. Homer, describing the army depicted on Achilles' shield, wrote, "Ares and Athena led the army, both clad in gold, beautiful and great, as becomes the gods, for men were smaller." Greek gods were men, possessing clothing, palaces, and bodies similar to ours. Though they could not die, they could be wounded. Homer recounts how Ares, the god of war, was wounded by a warrior and fled, howling with pain. This method of depicting gods as humans is called Anthropomorphism. Mythology. The gods, being human-like, had parents, children, and property. Their mothers were goddesses, their brothers were gods, and their offspring were either other gods or half-divine humans. This genealogy of the gods is known as the Theogony. The gods also had a history, and their birth, youth, and exploits were recounted. Apollo, for example, was born on the island of Delos, where his mother, Latona had fled. He killed a monster that was ravaging the country at the foot of Parnassus. Each region of Greece had its own tales of the gods, which are referred to as myths. The collection of these myths is known as Mythology, or the history of the gods.

The gods of ancient Greece were not merely figures of myth and legend, but were seen as manifestations of the natural world. They were both human and divine, embodying the forces of nature that surrounded the Greeks in their daily lives. The Naiad, for example, was not only a young woman, but also a bubbling fountain. The river Xanthus was not just a body of water, but a god that could throw itself upon Achilles in a fit of fury. Even the weather was personified, with the Greeks saying "Zeus rains" or "Zeus thunders." Each city had its own set of gods, reflecting the unique landscape and environment of the region. These local gods were known as Poliades, or gods of the city, and were worshipped in small sanctuaries and grottos throughout the countryside. Every torrent, wood, and mountain had its own deity, though these minor gods were often only known to the people of the surrounding area. Above these countless local gods were a select group of great divinities that were worshipped throughout Greece. These gods represented the major forces of nature, such as the sky, sun, earth, and sea. They were known by the same names across the country and had temples or sanctuaries in every city. Despite their importance, there were only a few of these great gods; in fact, even fewer than twenty. Their true names were Zeus, Hera, Athena, Apollo, Artemis, Hermes, Hephaistos, Hestia, Ares, Aphrodite, Poseidon, Amphitrite, Proteus, Kronos, Rhea, Demeter, Persephone, Hades, and Dionysos. It was these great gods that were worshipped in the grand temples of Greece and invoked in the prayers of the people. Though they were seen as divine beings, they were also intimately connected to the natural world, reflecting the Greeks' deep reverence for the forces that shaped their lives.

Attributes of the Gods

In ancient times, the great gods of Greece were revered and worshipped by their followers. Each god had their own unique form, costume, and instruments-known as their attributes-which were used to represent them in sculptures and in the imaginations of their faithful. These gods also had distinct characters that were well known to their worshippers, and each had a role to play in the world, often aided by secondary divinities who obeyed their commands. Athena, the clear-eyed virgin, was often depicted standing, armed with a lance, a helmet on her head, and gleaming armor on her breast. She was the goddess of clear air, wisdom, and invention, exuding an air of dignity and majesty. Hephaistos, the god of fire, was often represented as a lame and ugly blacksmith, wielding a hammer. It was he who forged the thunderbolt, a powerful weapon used by the gods. Artemis, the shy maiden, was often depicted armed with a bow and quiver, coursing through the forests with a troop of nymphs. She was the goddess of the woods, the chase, and of death. Hermes, often represented with winged sandals, was the god of the fertile showers. But he had other offices as well, serving as the god of streets and squares, commerce, theft, and eloquence. He was also the guide of souls of the dead, the messenger of the gods, and the deity presiding over the breeding of cattle. To the Greeks, a god often had several functions, which may have seemed dissimilar to outsiders but were related in some way to the Greeks. Olympus and Zeus. Each of the gods was like a king in their own domain, but the Greeks believed that all the forces of nature operated in harmony, and that the gods were in accord with the administration of the world. They believed that the gods, like men, had laws and government among them and that Zeus, the king of the gods, presided over all. The Greeks believed that the gods were responsible for the order and harmony of the universe, and that their power was to be respected and revered.

In the northern reaches of Greece, there stood a mountain whose peak was shrouded in snow and had never been scaled by any man. This was Olympus, a place where it was believed the gods convened. Under the open sky, they gathered to discuss the affairs of the world. Zeus, the most powerful of them all, presided over these meetings. He was the god of the heavens and the light, the one who commanded the clouds and hurled the thunderbolt. A venerable figure with a flowing beard, he sat upon a throne of gold, and all the other gods bowed before him. Should any of them dare to defy him, Zeus would threaten them. As Homer recounted, he once said, "Bind a chain of gold to heaven and let all the gods and goddesses put their weight upon it. Even if you all pull together, you cannot bring me, the sovereign ruler, down to earth. But if I wished to pull the chain to myself, I could bring the earth and the sea with it. Then I would attach it to the summit of Olympus, and the entire universe would hang suspended. That is how much greater I am than gods and men." The morality of Greek mythology was a curious thing. Many of their gods were depicted as violent, bloodthirsty, deceitful, and debauched. They were known for their scandalous affairs and dishonest deeds. Hermes was infamous for his thievery, Aphrodite for her flirtatiousness, and Ares for his savagery. They were all so vain that they would persecute those who failed to offer them sacrifices. Niobe, for example, had boasted of her large family, and as punishment, Apollo had killed all of her children with arrows. The gods were so jealous that they could not bear to see a man truly happy. For the Greeks, prosperity was the greatest danger, for it never failed to draw the wrath of the gods. This anger was personified as a goddess named Nemesis, and there were many tales told about her. One such story involved Polycrates of Samos, who had become very powerful. Fearing the jealousy of the gods, he threw a gold ring into the sea so that his good fortune would not be entirely without misfortune. Sometime later, a fisherman caught an enormous fish, and inside its belly was the very same ring. This was seen as a sure sign of impending doom. Polycrates was besieged in his city, captured, and crucified. The gods had punished him for his good fortune.

In ancient Greece, the gods were not always the best role models for mortals. The philosophers of the time, such as Xenophanes, criticized the poets who spread stories of the gods' immoral behavior. According to a disciple of Pythagoras, even the great Homer and Hesiod were punished in the afterlife for their portrayals of the gods. Xenophanes believed that the gods were often depicted as having the same flaws as humans, and that there was only one god who was truly divine and did not resemble mortals in any way. This idea was not without merit, as the Greeks tended to create their gods in their own image. As the people of Greece became more civilized, they began to see the flaws in their gods and were no longer comfortable with their immoral behavior. However, the ancient traditions and stories of the gods were already set in stone, and later generations were hesitant to change them. Despite the questionable behavior of the gods, the heroes of Greece were revered and respected. These were men who had become famous for their deeds and were believed to have become powerful spirits after their deaths. They were not gods, but they possessed a higher power than any mortal and were able to help or harm those who sought their aid. Every city, tribe, and family had their own hero who was worshipped and who protected them. In Greece, the gods may have been flawed, but the heroes were revered for their strength and power.

Different Kinds of Heroes

Of these heroes, many are legendary figures like Achilles, Odysseus, and Agamemnon. Some, without a doubt never existed, such as Herakles and Oedipus. Others, like Hellen, Dorus, and Aeolus, are only names. But their worshippers regarded them as men of the olden time, and in fact, most of the heroes lived at one time. Many are historical personages, such as generals like Leonidas and Lysander, philosophers like Democritus and Aristotle, and legislators like Lycurgus and Solon. The people of Croton even adored one of their fellow citizens, Philip by name, because he had been in his time the most beautiful man in Greece. The leader who had guided a band of colonists and founded a city became for the inhabitants the Founder. A temple was raised for him, and every year sacrifices were offered to him. The Athenian Miltiades was thus worshipped in the city of Thrace. The Spartiate Brasidas, killed in the defense of Amphipolis, had divine honors paid to him in that city, for the inhabitants had come to regard him as their Founder. Presence of the Heroes. The hero continued to reside in the place where his body was interred, either in his tomb or in the neighborhood. A story told by Herodotus depicts this belief in a lively way. The city of Sicyon adored the hero Adrastus, and in a public place was a chapel dedicated to his honor. Cleisthenes, the tyrant of Sicyon, took a fancy to rid himself of this hero. He went to the oracle at Delphi to ask if it would aid him in expelling Adrastus. The oracle replied to his question that Adrastus was king of the Sicyonians and Cleisthenes was a brigand. The tyrant, not daring to evict the hero, adopted a ruse. He sent to Thebes to seek the bones of Melanippus, another hero, and installed them with great pomp in the sanctuary of the city. "He did this," says Herodotus, "because Melanippus during his life had been the greatest enemy of Adrastus and had killed his brother and his son-in-law." Then he transferred to Melanippus the festivals and the sacrifices formerly paid to the honor of Adrastus. He was persuaded, and all the Greeks with him, that the hero would be irritated and would flee.

Intervention of the Heroes

The heroes possess divine power, akin to that of the gods, and can, according to their whims, send good or evil. Stesichorus, the poet, spoke ill of the famous Helen, who, as legend has it, was carried away to Troy. Suddenly, he became blind. However, when he retracted his statement, the heroine restored his sight. The protecting heroes of a city shielded it from plagues and famine, and even fought against its enemies. During the battle of Marathon, the Athenian soldiers saw Theseus, the mythical founder of Athens, clad in shining armor, standing in their midst. At the battle of Salamis, the heroes Ajax and Telamon, former kings of Salamis, appeared on the highest point of the island, extending their hands to the Greek fleet. "It is not we," said Themistocles, "that have vanquished the Persians; it is the gods and heroes." In Sophocles' tragedy, "Oedipus at Colonus," Oedipus, at the point of death, receives a visit from the king of Athens and the king of Thebes, both of whom, as gods, request him to have his body interred in their territory and become a protecting hero. Oedipus eventually consents to be buried in the soil of the Athenians and says to the king, "Dead, I shall not be a useless inhabitant of this country. I shall be a rampart for you, stronger than millions of warriors." A hero alone was as effective as an entire army; his spirit was mightier than all living men.

The Principles of Worship of the Gods

The gods and heroes, powerful as they were, bestowed upon men all good or evil fortune according to their will. It was perilous to have them against you, but wise to have them on your side. They were seen as similar to men, becoming irritated if they were neglected, but contented if they were revered. Worship was based on this principle. It consisted of doing things agreeable to the gods to obtain their favor. Plato expressed the thought of the common man as follows: "To know how to say and do those things that are pleasing to the gods, either in prayers or offerings, this is piety which brings prosperity to individuals and states. The reverse is impiety which ruins everything." Xenophon stated, "It is natural that the gods should favor those who not only consult them in need, but honor them in the day of prosperity." Religion was first and foremost a contract. The Greeks sought to delight the gods and in return required their services. "For a long time," said a priest of Apollo to his god, "I have burned fat bullocks for you; now grant my petitions and discharge your arrows against my enemies." The Great Festivals. Since the gods had the emotions of men, they were to be pleased in the same way as men. Wine, cakes, fruits, and food were brought to them. Palaces were built for them. Festivals were given in their honor, for they were "joyous gods" who loved pleasure and beautiful spectacles. A festival was not simply an occasion of rejoicing, but a religious ceremony. On those days free from daily toil, men were required to rejoice in public before the gods. The Greeks undoubtedly delighted in these festivities, but it was for the god and not for himself that he celebrated them. "The Ionians," said an ancient hymn to Apollo, "delight thee with trial of strength, the hymn, and the dance." The Sacred Games. From these diversions offered to the gods originated the solemn games. Each city had them to honor its gods; ordinarily, only its citizens were admitted to them. However, in four districts of Greece, games were celebrated

THE ECHO OF ANCIENT CIVILIZATIONS

in which all Greeks could be present and participate. These are called the Four Great Games.

The foremost of these four festivals was the one held at Olympia. It occurred every four years to honor Zeus and lasted for five or six days. People from all over Greece filled the amphitheater. They began by sacrificing animals and praying to Zeus and the other gods. Then came the competitions: The footrace around the stadium. The Pentathlon, which included five exercises. Competitors had to jump, run from one end of the stadium to the other, throw a metal discus, hurl a javelin, and wrestle. Boxing, where fighters had their arms bound with hide thongs. Chariot races, held in the hippodrome. The chariots were light and drawn by four horses. The judges of the games wore purple robes and laurel crowns. After each competition, a herald announced the name of the winner and their city to the entire assembly. The victor received only an olive wreath, but their fellow citizens welcomed them back as heroes. Sometimes, they even knocked down part of the city wall to allow them entry. The victor arrived in a chariot drawn by four horses, wearing purple robes and accompanied by the people. "These victories, which today we leave to the athletes of public shows, were then considered the greatest of all. The most renowned poets celebrated them. Pindar, the most famous lyric poet of ancient times, wrote extensively about chariot races. Legend has it that a man named Diagoras saw his two sons crowned on the same day and was carried in triumph by them in front of the audience. The people thought this honor was too great for a mortal and shouted, 'Die, Diagoras, for you cannot become a god.' Overcome with emotion, Diagoras died in his sons' arms. In his eyes and the eyes of the Greeks, his sons possessing the strongest fists and the most nimble limbs in Greece was the pinnacle of earthly happiness." The Greeks admired physical prowess for a reason: in their wars, where they fought hand-to-hand, the most vigorous athletes were the best soldiers.

Omens

The Greeks believed that their gods required service in exchange for the homage, festivals, and offerings they received. The gods protected their worshippers, granted them health, wealth, and victory, and shielded them from harm by sending signs that men interpreted as Omens. Herodotus said, "When a city is about to suffer some great misfortune, this is usually anticipated by signs. The people of Chios had omens of their defeat: of a band of one hundred youths sent to Delphi but two returned; the others had died of the plague. At about the same time, the roof of a school in the city fell on the children who were learning to read, but one escaped of the one hundred and twenty. Such were the anticipating signs sent them by the deity." The Greeks believed that supernatural signs could appear in dreams, the flight of birds, the entrails of animals sacrificed, earthquakes, eclipses, and even a simple sneeze. During the Sicilian expedition, Nicias, the Athenian general, was about to embark his army for the retreat when an eclipse of the moon occurred. He thought that the gods had sent this prodigy to warn the Athenians not to continue their enterprise. So Nicias waited for twenty-seven days, offering sacrifices to appease the gods. In the meantime, the enemy closed the port, destroyed the fleet, and exterminated his army. When the Athenians learned of this news, they reproached Nicias for not knowing that the eclipse of the moon was a favorable sign for an army in retreat. During the retreat of the Ten Thousand, Xenophon, the general, was addressing his soldiers when a soldier sneezed. At once, all adored the god who had sent this omen. Xenophon exclaimed, "Since at the very instant when we are deliberating concerning our safety, Zeus the savior has sent us an omen, let us with one consent offer sacrifices to him."

The Oracles

Frequently, the deity responds to the faithful who seek guidance, not through silent gestures, but through the words of an inspired individual. The faithful enter the god's sanctuary in search of answers and advice. These are the Oracles. Oracles existed in many places throughout Greece and Asia. The most renowned were located at Dodona in Epirus and at Delphi, situated at the base of Mount Parnassus. At Dodona, it was Zeus who spoke through the rustling of sacred oaks. At Delphi, it was Apollo who was consulted. Beneath his temple, in a cavern, a stream of cool air emerged from a crevice in the ground. The Greeks believed that this air was sent by the god, as it caused those who inhaled it to become frenzied. A tripod was placed over the opening and a woman, the Pythi, who had bathed in the sacred spring, sat on the tripod and received inspiration. Immediately, seized with a nervous frenzy, she uttered cries and fragmented sentences. Priests surrounding her captured these expressions, put them into verse, and presented them to the one seeking the god's guidance. The Pythia's oracles were frequently obscure and ambiguous. When Croesus asked if he should wage war against the Persians, the response was, "Croesus will destroy a great empire." Indeed, a great empire was destroyed, but it was Croesus's own. The Spartans had immense faith in the Pythia and never began a campaign without consulting her. Other Greeks followed suit, and Delphi became a kind of national oracle.

Amphictyonies

In ancient Greece, the sanctuary of Delphi was a precious site that required protection. To ensure its safety, twelve of the most significant peoples of Greece formed an association known as an Amphictyony. Each year, delegates from these groups gathered at Delphi to celebrate the festival of Apollo and ensure that the temple was not under threat. This temple was a treasure trove of immense wealth, making it a tempting target for pillagers. In the sixth century, the people of Cirrha, a neighboring city of Delphi, stole these treasures. The Amphictyons declared war against them for sacrilege. The city of Cirrha was taken and destroyed, and its inhabitants were sold into slavery. The territory was left fallow. In the fourth century, the Amphictyons waged war against the Phocians, who had seized the treasury of Delphi, and the people of Amphissa, who had cultivated a field dedicated to Apollo. However, it is essential to note that the assembly of the Amphictyons did not resemble a Greek senate. It was solely concerned with the temple of Apollo and not at all with political affairs. The Amphictyony did not even prevent its members from fighting one another. While the oracle and the Amphictyony of Delphi were more potent than other oracles and amphictyonies, they never united the Greeks into a single nation.

Chapter 11

Sparta

Laconia, a land of great beauty and harshness, was settled by the Dorian mountaineers when they invaded the Peloponnesus. The main body of them settled in Sparta, which is located in Laconia, a narrow valley with a considerable stream called the Eurotas flowing between two massive mountain ranges with snowy summits. The country is described by a poet as "a land rich in tillable soil, but hard to cultivate, deep set among perpendicular mountains, rough in aspect, inaccessible to invasion." The Dorians of Sparta lived in this enclosed country in the midst of the ancient inhabitants who had become their subjects or serfs. There were three classes in Laconia: Helots, Perioeci, and Spartiates. The Helots, who dwelt in scattered cottages in the plain and cultivated the soil, were not free to leave the land they worked on. They were like the serfs of the Middle Ages, peasants attached to the soil from father to son. They labored for a Spartiate proprietor who took the greater part of their harvest. The Spartiates instructed them, feared them, and ill-treated them. They compelled them to wear rude garments, beat them unreasonably to remind them of their servile condition, and sometimes made them intoxicated to disgust their children with the sight of drunkenness. A Spartiate poet compared the Helots to "loaded asses stumbling under their burdens and the blows inflicted." The Perioeci inhabited a hundred villages in the mountains or on the coast. They were sailors, engaged in commerce, and manufactured the objects necessary for life. They were free and administered the business of their village, but they paid tribute to the magistrates of Sparta and obeyed them. The Helots and Perioeci despised the Spartiates, their masters. "Whenever one speaks to them of the Spartiates," says Xenophon, "there isn't one of them who can conceal the pleasure he would feel in eating them alive." Once an earthquake nearly destroyed Sparta, and the Helots rushed from all sides of the plain to massacre those of the Spartiates who had escaped the catastrophe. At the same time, the Perioeci rose and refused obedience. The Spartiates' bearing toward the Perioeci was certain to exasperate them. At the end of a war in which many of the Helots had fought in their army, they bade them choose those who had specially distinguished themselves for bravery, with the promise of freeing them. It was a ruse to discover the most energetic and those most capable of revolting. Two thousand were chosen; they were conducted about the temples with heads crowned as evidence of their manumission; then the Spartiates put them out of the way, but how it was done no one ever knew.

In ancient Sparta, the oppressed classes outnumbered their masters tenfold. The Helots alone numbered over 200,000, while the Perioeci numbered 120,000. In contrast, there were never more than 9,000 Spartiate heads of families. In life or death situations, a Spartiate needed to be worth ten Helots. As battles were fought hand-to-hand, the Spartans required agile and robust men. Sparta was like a camp without walls, with its people always ready for battle. Education in Sparta began at birth. Infants were brought before a council, and if they were found to be deformed, they were exposed on a mountain to die. The children who were allowed to live were taken from their parents at the age of seven and trained together as a group. They went barefoot in both summer and winter and had only one mantle. They slept on a heap of reeds and bathed in the cold waters of the Eurotas. They ate little and quickly to teach them not to overindulge. They were grouped by the hundreds, each under a chief, and often had to fight with blows of feet and fists. At the feast of Artemis, they were beaten before the goddess's statue until blood flowed. Some died under this ordeal, but their honor required them not to weep. They were taught to fight and suffer. Often, they were given nothing to eat and had to forage for food. If they were captured on these expeditions, they were roughly beaten. One Spartiate boy who had stolen a little fox and hidden it under his mantle let the animal gnaw out his vitals rather than betray himself. They were taught to escape from perplexing situations when in the field. They walked with lowered glances, silent, hands under their mantles, without turning their heads and "making no more noise than statues." They were not allowed to speak at the table and had to obey all men they encountered. This was to accustom them to discipline.

The Maidens

In ancient Greece, most fathers kept their daughters locked away in the house, spinning flax. But the Spartans were different. They believed that strong women would produce strong children. And so, their daughters were trained just like their sons. In the gymnasia, they ran, leaped, and threw the discus and javelin. One poet even wrote of Spartiate girls, "Like colts with flowing manes, they make the dust fly about them." These girls were known as the healthiest and bravest women in all of Greece. The Regiment. The men of Sparta lived a regimented life, just like soldiers. With so many enemies, they could not afford to be weak. At the age of seventeen, a Spartiate became a soldier, and he remained one until he turned sixty. Everything about his life was regulated, from his clothing to his meals to his exercise routine. Since he was only meant to be a warrior, he trained for war every day. He ran, leaped, and practiced with his weapons, making sure that every part of his body was strong. He was not allowed to engage in trade, work in any industry, or even farm the land. He was a soldier, and nothing else. He could not even live with his family as he pleased. Instead, he ate with his fellow soldiers in squads, and he could not leave the country without permission. It was like living in enemy territory. Laconic Speech. The Spartans were known for their rough and simple way of life. They spoke in short phrases, which we now call "laconic." The Greeks told many stories about their Spartan neighbors and their curt expressions. For instance, when a garrison was in danger of being surprised, the government sent this message: "Attention!" When the king of Persia ordered a Spartan army to lay down their arms, the general replied, "Come and take them." And when Lysander captured Athens, he wrote simply, "Athens is fallen."

Music and Dance

The arts of Sparta were those that pertained to an army. The Dorian conquerors brought with them a peculiar sort of music-the Dorian style, serious, strong, even harsh. It was military music; the Spartiates went into battle to the sound of the flute so that the step might be regular. Their dance was a military movement. In the "Pyrrhic" the dancers were armed and imitated all the movements of a battle; they made the gestures of striking, of parrying, retreating, and throwing the javelin. Heroism of the Women. The women stimulated the men to combat; their exhibitions of courage were celebrated in Greece, so much so that collections of stories of them were made. A Spartan mother, seeing her son fleeing from battle, killed him with her hand, saying; "The Eurotas does not flow for deer." Another, learning that her five sons had perished, said, "This is not what I wish to know; does victory belong to Sparta?" "Yes." "Then let us render thanks to the gods." THE INSTITUTIONS OF SPARTA. The Kings and the Council. The Spartiates had at first, like the other Greeks, an assembly of the people. All these institutions were preserved, but only in form. The kings, descendants of the god Herakles, were loaded with honors; they were given the first place at the feasts and were served with a double portion; when they died all the inhabitants made lamentation for them. But no power was left to them and they were closely watched. The Senate was composed of twenty-eight old men taken from the rich and ancient families, appointed for life; but it did not govern. The Ephors. The real masters of Sparta were the Ephors, five magistrates who were renewed every year. They decided peace and war, and had judicial functions. When the king commanded the army, they accompanied him, directed the operations, and sometimes made him return. Usually, they consulted the senators and took action in harmony with them. Then they assembled the Spartiates in one place, announced to them what had been decided, and asked their approbation. The people without discussing the matter approved the action by acclamation. No one knew whether he had the right to refuse assent; accustomed to obey, the Spartiate never refused. It was, therefore, an aristocracy of governing families. Sparta was not a country of equality. Some men were called Equals, but only because they were equal among themselves. The others were termed Inferiors and had no part in the government.

The Army was the backbone of Spartan society. Their way of life was centered around military training and warfare. This resulted in a lack of focus on other areas such as art, architecture, philosophy, and oration. However, their expertise in the military arts made them the instructors of other Greeks. They introduced two significant innovations: a better method of combat and a better method of athletic exercise. Before the Spartans, Greek armies marched into battle in disarray. The leaders rode on horseback or in light chairs, while the soldiers followed on foot, each armed in their own way. This led to chaos and an inability to act together or resist. Battles became a series of duels and massacres. The Spartans, on the other hand, all had the same arms: a breastplate covering the chest, a casque protecting the head, greaves over the legs, and a buckler held before the body. For offense, they carried a short sword and a long lance. This uniformity allowed them to be called hoplites. The Spartan hoplites were organized into regiments, battalions, companies, and squads, with an officer commanding each group. This allowed for the same movement to be executed throughout the whole army, making it an astonishing novelty to the Greeks. When facing the enemy, the soldiers arranged themselves in line, forming a compact mass called a Phalanx, usually eight ranks deep, with each man close to his neighbor. The king sacrificed a goat to the gods, and if the entrails were propitious, he raised a chant that the whole army took up in unison. Then they advanced, with rapid and measured steps, to the sound of the flute, with lance couched and buckler before the body. They met the enemy in dense array, overwhelmed them with their mass and momentum, put them to rout, and only checked themselves to avoid breaking the phalanx. As long as they remained together, each was protected by their neighbor, forming an impenetrable mass on which the enemy could secure no hold. These tactics were simple but effective enough to overcome a disorderly troop. Isolated men could not resist such a body. The other Greeks understood this, and as far as they were able, imitated the Spartans, arming themselves as hoplites and fighting in phalanx formation.

Gymnastics played a crucial role in ancient Greek society. To effectively engage in battle, soldiers needed to be agile and strong. Thus, the Spartans established athletic exercises, which were subsequently adopted by other Greeks. Gymnastics became a national art, highly esteemed, and a key feature of major festivals. Even in far-flung regions, Greek cities were recognized by their gymnasiums. These were large squares surrounded by porticoes and located near springs, with baths and halls for exercise. Citizens would gather here to socialize and walk. All young men were required to enter the gymnasium and train for at least two years. They learned to leap, run, throw the disc and javelin, and wrestle by seizing their opponent around the waist. To toughen their muscles and skin, they would plunge into cold water, avoid using oil on their bodies, and scrape their skin with a strigil. Many individuals continued these exercises throughout their lives, becoming known as Athletes. Some became renowned for their skills, such as Milo of Croton in Italy, who was said to have carried a bull on his shoulders and stopped a chariot in its tracks by seizing it from behind. These athletes sometimes served as soldiers or generals in combat, as gymnastics was seen as a school of war. The Spartans were the most skilled wrestlers and soldiers, and they taught the other Greeks how to exercise and fight. They were always recognized as the best and most respected by the rest of Greece. When the Greeks had to unite against the Persians, they chose the Spartans as their leaders without hesitation. As an Athenian orator once said, this was a just decision.

Chapter 12

Athens

Attica, a land of ancient heritage, has been home to the Athenians for generations. According to their legends, their forefathers sprang from the very soil itself. The conquerors who swept through the southern lands bypassed Attica, as it held little allure for them. Attica is a triangular mass of rocks that juts out into the sea. These rocks are famous for their marble blocks and the honey produced by their bees. However, they are barren and unproductive. Between the rocks and the sea lie three small, poorly irrigated plains that cannot sustain a large population, especially during the dry summer months. Athens, the largest of these plains, is located a league from the sea, and it is built at the foot of a massive, isolated rock. The old city, known as the Acropolis, sits atop this rock. Initially, the people of Attica did not form a single state. Instead, they founded separate villages, each with its own king and government. Later, these villages united under the king of Athens, establishing a single city. However, this did not mean that everyone lived in one town. The people continued to live in their villages and cultivate their lands, but they all worshipped the same goddess, Athena, and obeyed the same king. Eventually, the kings were replaced by nine archons who changed every year. Little is known about this period since no written records have survived. However, it is said that for centuries, the Athenians lived in discord. The nobles, known as the Eupatrids, oppressed the peasants on their estates, and creditors held their debtors as slaves. To restore order, the Athenians commissioned Solon, a wise man, to draft a code of laws for them in 594.

In ancient Athens, Solon, a wise and just leader, enacted three major reforms that forever altered the course of Athenian history. Firstly, he reduced the value of the currency, which allowed debtors to easily free themselves from their debts. Secondly, he granted the peasants ownership of the land they worked, resulting in a greater number of small landowners in Attica than in any other part of Greece. Lastly, he divided all citizens into four classes based on their income, requiring each to pay taxes and provide military service according to their wealth, with the poor being exempt from such duties. Following Solon's rule, the Athenians came under the leadership of Pisistratus, a powerful and cunning citizen. However, in 510 B.C., dissension once again arose in Athens. Enter Cleisthenes, a leader of one of the parties, who used the opportunity to enact a sweeping revolution. Athens was home to many foreigners, particularly seamen, and traders living in Piraeus near the harbor. Cleisthenes granted these individuals citizenship and equal rights to the native inhabitants, creating two distinct populations in Athens: the people of Attica and those of Piraeus. This physical difference persisted for three centuries, with the people of Attica resembling other Greeks and those of Piraeus resembling Asians. This expansion of the Athenian people resulted in a new, dynamic population, one of the most active in all of Greece.

In the fifth century, Athens was a society with three distinct classes: slaves, foreigners, and citizens. The slaves were the majority of the population, and even the poorest Athenian had at least one slave. The wealthy owned hundreds of them. Most slaves worked in the homes of their masters, grinding grain, baking bread, weaving cloth, cooking, and cleaning. Others worked in shops as blacksmiths, dyers, or in mines. The master provided food for the slaves but sold anything they produced for profit, giving them only enough to survive. Domestic servants, miners, and most artisans were slaves. They lived in society but had no part in it. They were considered property, often referred to as "a body." Slaves had no rights and were subject to the will of their masters, who could make them work, imprison them, deprive them of food, or beat them. If a citizen went to court, his opponent could demand that the former's slaves be tortured for information. Athenian orators praised this practice as a way to obtain truthful testimony. "Torture," said Isaeus, "is the best way to prove the truth. When you want to resolve a dispute, you don't ask free men. Instead, you torture slaves to find out what really happened."

Foreigners were known as Metics in Athens. This term referred to individuals of foreign origin who had established themselves in the city. Unlike our modern citizenship laws, being born in the country was not enough to become an Athenian citizen. One had to be the son of a citizen. Even if some aliens had lived in Attica for generations, their families might not have become Athenian. The Metics could not engage in government, marry a citizen, or acquire land. However, they were personally free and had the right to commerce by sea, banking, and trade, provided they had a patron to represent them in court. Athens had over ten thousand families of Metics, with the majority of them being bankers or merchants. To become a citizen of Athens, both parents had to be citizens. When Athenians reached maturity, around eighteen years of age, they appeared before the popular assembly, received their arms, and took an oath. The oath was as follows: "I swear never to dishonor these sacred arms, not to quit my post, to obey the magistrates and the laws, to honor the religion of my country." They became both citizen and soldier and owed military service until they turned sixty. This gave them the right to sit in the assembly and fulfill the functions of the state. Occasionally, Athens would accept a man who was not the son of a citizen into their citizenship, but this was rare and a sign of great favor. The assembly had to vote the stranger into its membership, and then, nine days after, six thousand citizens had to vote for him on a secret ballot. The Athenian people were like a closed circle, and no new members were admitted except those pleasing to the old members. They admitted few besides their sons. The Athenians referred to their government as a democracy, a government by the people. However, this people was not the mass of inhabitants, but the body of citizens, a true aristocracy of 15,000 to 20,000 men who governed the whole nation as masters. This body had absolute power and was the true sovereign of Athens. They assembled at least three times a month to deliberate and vote.

The assembly was held in the open air on the Pnyx, with citizens sitting on stone benches arranged in an amphitheater. The magistrates sat before them on a platform and opened the session with a religious ceremony and a prayer. A herald then proclaimed the business to occupy the assembly and asked, "Who wishes to speak?" Every citizen had the right to this privilege, and the orators mounted the tribune according to age. When all had spoken, the president put the question, and the assembly voted by a show of hands before dissolving.

The Courts were where the people, being sovereign, passed judgment. Any citizen of thirty years of age could participate in the judicial assembly, known as the Heliaea. The heliasts sat in great halls in sections of five hundred, making the tribunal composed of one thousand to fifteen hundred judges. Unlike us, the Athenians had no prosecuting officer. Instead, a citizen took it upon himself to make the accusation. The accused and the accuser appeared before the court, each delivering a plea that was not to exceed the time marked off by a water-clock. Then, the judges voted by depositing a black or white stone. If the accuser did not obtain a certain number of votes, he himself was condemned. The sovereign people needed a council to prepare the business for discussion and magistrates to execute their decisions. The council was composed of five hundred citizens drawn by lot for one year. The magistrates were very numerous, including ten generals to command the army, thirty officials for financial administration, and sixty police officials to superintend the streets, the markets, weights, and measures, among other things. The power in Athens did not pertain to the rich and the noble, as in Sparta. In the assembly, everything was decided by a majority of votes, and all the votes were equal. All the jurors, all the members of the council, and all the magistrates except the generals were chosen by lot. The citizens were equal not only in theory but also in practice. Socrates said to a well-informed Athenian who did not dare to speak before the people, "Of what are you afraid? Is it of the fullers, the shoemakers, the masons, the artisans, or the merchants? For the assembly is composed of all these people." Many of these people had to ply their trade to make a living and could not serve the state gratuitously, so a salary was instituted. Every citizen who sat in the assembly or in the courts received three obols for every day of session, which is about eight cents of our money. This sum was just sufficient to maintain life at that time. From this day, the poor administered the government.

The Demagogues

In ancient Athens, the most influential men were those who spoke the best. Since all important affairs were decided by discussion and discourse, the people listened to the orators, followed their counsel, and even appointed them as generals or charged them with embassies. These men were called Demagogues, or leaders of the people. However, the party of the rich scoffed at them. In a comedy by Aristophanes, the people were represented by an old man who had lost his wits. The rich accused the people of being foolishly credulous, letting flatterers and intriguers pull them around by the nose, and being enraptured when they were harangued. The chorus addressed a charlatan, saying that he was rude, vicious, had a strong voice, an impudent eloquence, and violent gestures, and believed that he had all that was necessary to govern Athens. Private Life. The Athenians created so many political functions that a part of the citizens were engaged in fulfilling them. The citizen of Athens was absorbed in public affairs, like a functionary or soldier of our days. Warring and governing were the whole of his life. He spent his days in the assembly, the courts, the army, the gymnasium, or the market. Almost always, he had a wife and children, for his religion commanded this, but he did not live at home. The Children. When a child was born, the father had the right to reject it. In this case, the child was laid outside the house where it died from neglect unless a passer-by took it and brought it up as a slave. Athens followed this custom, as did all the Greeks. Girls were especially exposed to death. According to a writer of comedy, a son was always raised even if the parents were in the last stage of misery, but a daughter was exposed even though the parents were rich.

In ancient times, if a father welcomed his child, that child would become a part of the family. Initially, the child would stay with the mother in the women's quarters. The girls would remain there until they married, while the boys would leave when they turned seven years old. At that point, the father would entrust the boy to a preceptor, whose job was to teach him how to behave and obey. The preceptor was often a slave, but the father would give him the right to discipline his son. This was the norm in those days. Later on, the boy would attend school where he would learn how to read, write, do math, recite poetry, and sing in the chorus or to the sound of the flute. Finally, he would learn gymnastics. This was the extent of his education, which aimed to make him physically strong and mentally calm, or what the Greeks called "good and beautiful." As for the young girl, she would stay secluded with her mother and would not receive any education in the liberal arts. It was considered enough for her to learn how to obey. Xenophon, a wealthy and well-educated Athenian, once spoke about his wife to Socrates, saying, "She was barely twenty years old when I married her, and until then she had been under strict surveillance. They didn't want her to learn anything. Wasn't it enough that she could spin flax to make clothes and assign tasks to the slaves?" When her husband suggested that she become his assistant, she was surprised and asked, "How can I help you? What am I capable of? My mother always taught me to be prudent." Prudence and obedience were the virtues expected of Greek women.

At the age of fifteen, the girl was married off by her parents. The husband was chosen by them, usually a man from a neighboring family or a long-time friend of the father, but always a citizen of Athens. Rarely did the young girl know him, nor was she ever consulted in the matter. Herodotus, speaking of a Greek man named Callias, noted that he gave his daughters a rich dowry, allowed them to choose husbands from all the people, and then married them to the men of their choice. In the Athenian household, the women had a secluded apartment called the gynaeceum. Only the husband and relatives were allowed to visit, and the mistress of the household spent her day there with her slaves. She directed them, managed the housekeeping, and distributed flax for them to spin. She wove garments and rarely left the house except for religious festivals. She never appeared in the company of men, and Athenian women who frequented society could not maintain a good reputation. The wife, secluded and ignorant, was not an enjoyable companion. The husband had taken her not as a lifelong companion, but to keep his house in order, be the mother of his children, and fulfill Greek custom and religion, which required him to marry. Plato believed that one did not marry because they wanted to, but because the law compelled them to do so. The comic poet Menander once said, "Marriage, to tell the truth, is an evil, but a necessary evil." As a result, women in Athens, as in most other states of Greece, held little place in society.

Chapter 13

The Greeks and the Persian Wars

Beginning of the Persian Wars

As the Greeks were organizing their cities, the Persian king was uniting all the nations of the East into a single empire. Eventually, Greeks and Orientals would find themselves face to face, and it was in Asia Minor where they first met. On the coast of Asia Minor, there were rich and populous Greek colonies. Cyrus, the king of Persia, desired to subject them to his rule. These cities sent for help to the Spartans, who were reputed as the bravest of the Greeks. This action was reported to Cyrus, who replied, "I have never feared this sort of people that has in the midst of the city a place where the people assemble to deceive one another with false oaths." He was thinking of the marketplace. The Greeks of Asia were subdued and made subject to the Great King. Thirty years later, King Darius found himself in the presence of the Greeks of Europe. But this time, it was the Greeks who attacked the Great King. The Athenians sent twenty galleys to aid the revolting Ionians. Their soldiers entered Lydia, took Sardis by surprise, and burned it. Darius revenged himself by destroying the Greek cities of Asia, but he did not forget the Greeks of Europe. He had decreed, they say, that at every meal an officer should repeat to him, "Master, remember the Athenians." He sent envoys to the Greek cities to demand earth and water, a symbol in use among the Persians to indicate submission to the Great King. Most of the Greeks were afraid and yielded, but the Spartans cast the envoys into a pit, bidding them to take thence earth and water to carry to the king. This was the beginning of the Median Wars.

The contrast between the two worlds that clashed is well marked by Herodotus in the form of a conversation between King Xerxes and Demaratus, a Spartan exile. "I assure you," said Demaratus, "that the Spartans will offer you battle even if all the rest of the Greeks fight on your side, and if their army should not amount to more than one thousand men." "What!" said Xerxes, "one thousand men attack so immense an army as mine! I fear your words are only boasting; for although they be five thousand, we are more than one thousand to one. If they had a master like us, fear would inspire them with courage; they would march under the lash against a larger army; but being free and independent, they will have no more courage than that with which nature has endowed them." "The Spartans," replied Demaratus, "are not inferior to anybody in a hand-to-hand contest, and united in a phalanx they are the bravest of all men. Yet, though free, they have an absolute master, the Law, which they dread more than all your subjects do you; they obey it, and this law requires them to stand fast to their post and conquer or die." This is the difference between the two parties to the conflict: on the one side, a multitude of subjects united by force under a capricious master; on the other, little martial republics whose citizens govern themselves according to laws that they respect. There were two Persian wars. The first was simply an expedition against Athens; six hundred galleys sent by Darius disembarked a Persian army on the little plain of Marathon, seven hours distant from Athens. Religious sentiment prevented the Spartans from taking the field before the full moon, and it was still only the first quarter; the Athenians had to fight alone. Ten thousand citizens armed as hoplites camped before the Persians. The Athenians had ten generals, having the command on successive days; of these Miltiades, when his turn came, drew up the army for battle. The Athenians charged the enemy in serried ranks, but the Persians seeing them advancing without cavalry and archers, thought them fools. It was the first time that the Greeks had dared to face the Persians in battle array. The Athenians began by turning both flanks and then engaged the center, driving the Persians in disorder to the sea and forcing them to re-embark on their ships.

In the year 490 B.C., the Athenians achieved a great victory at Marathon, which brought them fame throughout Greece. Ten years later, the Second Persian War began with an invasion led by Xerxes. The Persian army was massive, consisting of 1,700,000 men from various regions of the empire. They were equipped with different weapons and armor, including iron cuirasses, bows and arrows, clubs, and daggers. The Persian fleet, consisting of 1,200 galleys, sailed along the shores of Thrace, passing through the canal at Mount Athos, which Xerxes had built for this purpose. The Greeks were terrified and, for the most part, submitted to the Great King and joined their armies to the Persian force. The Athenians, however, sought guidance from the oracle of Delphi, which gave them a cryptic response. The god said that Athens would be destroyed from base to summit, but also granted them a wall of wood that would not be taken, in which they and their children would find safety. The priests advised the

Athenians to leave Attica and establish themselves elsewhere, but Themistocles interpreted the "wall of wood" as referring to their ships. He urged them to retreat to the fleet and fight the Persians on the sea. Thus began the famous naval battle of Salamis, which saw the Greeks emerge victorious over the Persians. The victory at Salamis marked a turning point in the war and secured the freedom of Greece. The Athenians had once again proven their bravery and military prowess, and their name would be remembered for generations to come.

In ancient times, Athens and Sparta decided to resist the Persians and sought to unite the Greeks against them. However, few cities dared to join the league, and those that did placed themselves under the command of the Spartans. Despite the odds, the Greeks were able to settle the war in just four battles. At Thermopylae, King Leonidas of Sparta attempted to block the entrance to a defile, but was ultimately outflanked and overwhelmed. At Salamis, the Persian fleet was defeated by the Greek navy in a narrow space where the ships were crowded together. The rest of the Persian army left in Greece was annihilated by the Greek hoplites at Plataea, with only 40,000 of the original 300,000 men escaping. On the same day, the Greeks landed at Mycale on the coast of Asia and routed the Persians. With these victories, the Greeks conquered the Great King. Despite the odds, the Greeks were able to emerge victorious due to several factors. The war was not a national one between Greeks and barbarians, as many Greeks fought on the Persian side. In reality, it was a fight between the Great King and his subjects against Sparta, Athens, and their allies. The conquest of such a great horde by two small peoples was seen as a prodigy at the time, with the Greeks believing that the gods had fought for them. However, upon closer examination, it becomes clear that the Persian army was innumerable and that Xerxes believed that victory was simply a matter of numbers. The multitude of soldiers ultimately proved to be an embarrassment to itself, as they struggled to secure food and choked themselves on the day of combat. The ships were also arranged in too close of an order, causing them to collide with one another and shatter their oars. Additionally, many of the soldiers were not true soldiers, but rather men who had been forced into the war and were ill-equipped and lacked discipline. In contrast, the Spartans and their allies were well-equipped and marched in a solid line, making them nearly unstoppable. They broke the enemy with their long pikes, and the battle quickly became a massacre. Overall, the Greeks were able to emerge victorious due to their superior strategy and equipment, as well as the disorganization and lack of discipline among the Persian soldiers.

The Persian Wars had far-reaching consequences for Greece. Although Sparta had commanded the troops, it was Athens who truly delivered Greece by setting an example of resistance and constituting the fleet of Salamis. As a result, Athens reaped the benefits of victory. All the Ionian cities of the Archipelago and the coast of Asia revolted and formed a league against the Persians. The Spartans, being mountain men, were unable to conduct a maritime war and thus withdrew. The Athenians immediately became the leaders of the league. In 476 B.C., Aristides, commanding the fleet, assembled the delegates of the confederate cities. They decided to continue the war against the Great King and agreed to provide ships and warriors and to pay each year a contribution of 460 talents which is equivalent to 350,000 dollars. The treasure was deposited at Delos in the temple of Apollo, the god of the Ionians. Athens was charged with the leadership of the military force and with collecting the tax. To make the agreement irrevocable, Aristides had a mass of hot iron cast into the sea, and all swore to maintain the oaths until the day that the iron should mount to the surface. However, a day came when the war ceased, and the Greeks, always the victors, concluded a peace, or at least a truce, with the Great King. He surrendered his claim to the Asiatic Greeks about 449 B.C. The question then arose: what was to become of the treaty of Aristides? Were the confederate cities still obligated to pay their contribution now that there was no more fighting? Some refused it even before the war was over. Athens, however, asserted that the cities had made their engagements in perpetuity and forced them to pay up.

The war was over, and the Delos treasury had no further use. The Athenians transferred the money to Athens and used it to build their monuments. They claimed that the allies paid for their deliverance from the Persians and had no claim against Athens as long as she defended them from the Great King. The allies were now the tributaries of Athens and her subjects. Athens increased the tax on them, required their citizens to bring their cases before the Athenian courts, and even sent colonists to seize a part of their lands. Athens, the mistress of the league, was sovereign over more than 300 cities spread over the islands and coasts of the Archipelago, and the tribute paid to her amounted to 600 talents a year. The Greek states found themselves divided between two leagues after the foundation of the Athenian empire in the Archipelago. The maritime cities were subject to Athens, while the cities of the interior remained under the domination of Sparta. After much friction, war arose between Sparta and her continental allies on one side and Athens and her maritime subjects on the other. This was the Peloponnesian War, which continued for 27 years from 431 to 404. When it ceased, it was revived under other names until 360. These wars were complicated affairs, fought simultaneously on land and sea in Greece, Asia, Thrace, and Sicily, ordinarily at several points at once. The Spartans had a better army and ravaged Attica, while the Athenians had a superior fleet and made descents on the coasts of the Peloponnesus. Then Athens sent its army to Sicily, where it perished to the last man in 413. Lysander, a Spartan general, secured a fleet from the Persians and destroyed the Athenian fleet in Asia in 405. The Athenian allies who fought only under compulsion abandoned her. Lysander took Athens, demolished its walls, and burnt its ships. Sparta was for a time mistress on both land and sea. "In those days," says Xenophon, "all cities obeyed when a Spartan issued his orders." But soon the allies of Sparta, wearied of her domination, formed a league against her. The Spartans, driven at first from Asia, still maintained their power in Greece for some years by virtue of their alliance with the king of the Persians in 387. But the Thebans, having developed a strong army under the command of Epaminondas, fought them at Leuctra in 371 and at Mantinea in 362. The allies of Sparta detached themselves from her, but the Thebans could not secure from the rest of the Greeks the recognition of their supremacy. From this time, no Greek city was sovereign over the others.

The wars between the Greek cities were savage and brutal. A few examples illustrate their ferocity. At the start of the war, Sparta's allies threw all the merchants from hostile cities into the sea. In retaliation, the Athenians put to death the ambassadors of Sparta without allowing them to speak. When the town of Plataea was taken by capitulation, the Spartans promised that no one would be punished without a trial. However, Spartan judges demanded that every prisoner reveal if they had aided the Peloponnesians during the war. If the prisoner replied negatively, they were condemned to death, and the women were sold as slaves. When the city of Mytilene revolted from Athens, they were retaken, and the Athenians deliberated and decreed that all the people of Mytilene should be put to death. Although they revised the decree the next day, over a thousand Mytileneans were executed. After the Syracusan disaster, the Athenian army was taken captive, and the conquerors slaughtered all the generals and many of the soldiers. The remainder were consigned to the quarries, which served as a prison. They were left there crowded together for seventy days, exposed without protection to the burning sun of summer and then to the chilly nights of autumn. Many died from sickness, cold, and hunger, and their corpses remained on the ground, infecting the air. Finally, the Syracusans drew out the survivors and sold them into slavery. Typically, when an army invaded a hostile state, they leveled houses, felled trees, burned crops, and killed laborers. After the battle, they made short shrift of the wounded and killed prisoners in cold blood. In a captured city, everything belonged to the captor, and men, women, and children were sold as slaves. Such was the right of war at this time. Thucydides summed up the case as follows: "Business is regulated between men by the laws of justice when there is an obligation on both sides, but the stronger does whatever is in his power, and the weaker yields. The gods rule by a necessity of their nature because they are strongest; men do likewise." These wars did not unite the Greeks into one body. No city, not even Sparta, was able to force the others to obey her. They only exhausted themselves by fighting one another. The king of Persia profited from their strife. Not only did the Greek cities not unite against him, but they all allied themselves with him against the other Greeks. In the Peace of Antalcidas in 387, the Great King declared that all the Greek cities of Asia belonged to him, and Sparta recognized this claim. Athens and Thebes did the same some years later. An Athenian orator said, "It is the king of Persia who governs Greece; he needs only to establish governors in our cities. Is it not he who directs everything among us? Do we not summon the Great King as if we were his slaves?" The Greeks, through their strife, had lost the advantage that the Median war had gained for them.

Chapter 14

The Arts in Greece

In the middle of the fifth century, Athens found itself as the most powerful city in Greece. Pericles, descended from one of the noble families, was then the director of the affairs of the state. He was a man of few words and never sought to flatter the vanity of the people. But the Athenians respected him and acted only in accordance with his counsels; they had faith in his knowledge of all the details of administration and the resources of the state, and so they permitted him to govern. For forty years, Pericles was the soul of the politics of Athens. As Thucydides, his contemporary, said, "The democracy existed in name; in reality, it was the government of the first citizen." In Athens, as in the majority of Greek cities, the houses of individuals were small, low, and packed closely together, forming narrow streets, tortuous, and ill-paved. The Athenians reserved their display for their public monuments. After they levied heavy war taxes on their allies, they had large sums of money to expend, and these were employed in erecting beautiful edifices. In the marketplace, they built a portico or Poikile adorned with paintings, in the city a theatre, a temple in honor of Theseus, and the Odeon for the contests in music. But the most beautiful monuments rose on the rock of the Acropolis as on a gigantic pedestal. There were two temples of which the principal, the Parthenon, was dedicated to Athena, the protecting goddess of the city. A colossal statue of bronze represented Athena, and a staircase of ornamental character led up to the Propylaea. Athens was from this time the most beautiful of the Greek cities. Athens became at the same time the city of artists. Poets, orators, architects, painters, sculptors, some Athenians by birth, others come from all corners of the Greek world, met here and produced their masterpieces. There were, without doubt, many Greek artists elsewhere than at Athens. There had been before the fifth century, and there was a long time afterward; but never were so many assembled at one time in the same city. Most of the Greeks had fine sensibilities in matters of art; but the Athenians more than all others had a refined taste, a cultivated spirit, and a love of the beautiful. If the Greeks have gained renown in the history of civilization, it is that they have been a people of artists. Neither their little states nor their small armies have played a great role in the world. This is why the fifth century is the most beautiful moment in the history of Greece; this is why Athens has remained renowned above all the rest of the Greek cities.

Epistles

Athens, the city of eloquence, holds sway over all. The speeches delivered in the assembly determine matters of war, peace, taxes, and all other state affairs of importance. The speeches given before the courts either condemn or acquit citizens and subjects. The orators hold the power; the people follow their counsel and often entrust them with important public functions. Cleon is appointed general, and Demosthenes directs the war against Philip. The orators wield great influence, employing their talents in eloquence to accuse their political enemies. Often, they possess wealth, for they are paid for supporting one party or the other. Aeschines is retained by the king of Macedonia, and Demosthenes accepts fees from the king of Persia. Some of the orators, instead of delivering their own speeches, wrote them for others. When an Athenian citizen had a case in court, he did not desire, as we do, an advocate to plead his case for him. The law required that each person speaks in person. Therefore, he sought an orator and had him compose a speech, which he learned by heart and recited before the tribunal. Other orators traveled through the cities of Greece speaking on subjects that pleased their fancy. Sometimes, they gave lectures, as we would say. The oldest orators spoke simply, limiting themselves to an account of the facts without oratorical flourishes. On the platform, they were almost rigid, without loud speaking or gesticulation. Pericles delivered his orations with a calm air, so quietly that no fold of his mantle was disturbed. When he appeared at the tribune, his head, according to custom, crowned with leaves, he might have been taken, said the people, "for a god of Olympus." But the orators who followed wished to move the public. They assumed an animated style, pacing the tribune in a declamatory and agitated manner. The people became accustomed to this form of eloquence. The first time that Demosthenes came to the tribune, the assembly shouted with laughter. The orator could not enunciate, and he carried himself poorly. He disciplined himself in declamation and gesture and became the favorite of the people. Later, when he was asked what was the first quality of the orator, he replied, "Action, and the second, action, and the third, action." Action, that is delivery, was more important to the Greeks than the sense of the discourse.

In ancient times, there were a group of learned men in Asia called the Sages. They were wise and knowledgeable, delving into the fields of physics, astronomy, and natural history. They were also scholars, reflecting on the world around them. The Seven Sages of Greece were among the most celebrated of these wise men during the seventh century. However, around the time of Pericles, a new group of men emerged in Athens called the Sophists. They claimed to teach wisdom and charged fees for their lessons. They often criticized the religion, customs, and institutions of Greek cities, arguing that they were not based on reason. They believed that humans could not know anything with certainty and that nothing was true or false. They were skeptics who believed that nothing existed, and even if it did, humans could not know it. Some of these Sophists were also skilled orators. Socrates, an old man from Athens, opposed the Sophists. He was not wealthy or eloquent like the Sophists, but he went around the city talking to people and asking them questions that led them to discover what he had in mind. He especially sought out young men and gave them guidance and instruction. Socrates did not claim to be a scholar, saying that his only knowledge was that he knew nothing. He called himself a philosopher, meaning a lover of wisdom. He was not interested in the sciences or the nature of the world but focused solely on humanity. His motto was "Know thyself," and he preached about virtue. However, the Athenians mistook Socrates for a Sophist because he spoke about morals and religion. In 399, he was brought before the court on charges of not worshipping the city's gods, introducing new gods, and corrupting the youth. He did not try to defend himself and was sentenced to death at the age of seventy.

Xenophon, one of the followers of the great philosopher Socrates, took it upon himself to transcribe their conversations and even wrote an apology on his behalf. Another of his pupils, Plato, wrote a series of dialogues in which Socrates was the main character. Since then, Socrates has been hailed as the "father of philosophy." Plato himself went on to establish a school, and Aristotle, one of his students, compiled all the scientific knowledge of his time in his books. Other philosophers who came after them aligned themselves with either Plato or Aristotle, with Plato's followers calling themselves Academicians and Aristotle's disciples naming themselves Peripatetics. The Greeks had a tradition of dancing in their religious ceremonies, with young men performing a series of noble and expressive poses around the altar dedicated to the god. This dance, accompanied by chants in honor of the god, was known as the Chorus. Each city had its festival chorus, with the children of the most prominent families participating after a long period of preparation. The god deserved nothing less than a group worthy of him. In the flatlands surrounding Athens, young men celebrated the god of the vintage, Dionysos, with religious dances each year. One of these dances was solemn and depicted the actions of the god, with the leader of the chorus portraying Dionysos, and the chorus itself playing the role of his companions, the satyrs. Over time, they began to portray the lives of other gods and ancient heroes. It was then that Thespis, a Greek innovator, came up with the idea of setting up a stage on which an actor could perform while the chorus rested. This new form of entertainment was perfected and moved to the city, where it was performed under a black poplar tree in the marketplace. And thus, Tragedy was born.

In ancient Greece, the art of theatre was born. Two types of plays were performed: tragedy and comedy. Tragedies were serious, featuring heroes and their struggles, while comedies were lighthearted and made fun of everyday life. The masked dancers who performed the comic dances chanted praises to Dionysos mixed with jeers towards the audience and humorous observations about current events. This is how comedy was born. Even when performed in the theatre, both types of plays were still played before the altar of the god. The choir continued to dance and chant around the altar, even after the actors became the most important part of the spectacle. In comedies, sarcastic remarks about the government were made during the Parabasis. To ensure that all Athenians could attend these spectacles, a theatre was built on the side of the Acropolis that could hold 30,000 people. The theatre was open to the sky and made up of tiers of rock arranged in a half-circle around the orchestra, where the chorus performed and the stage where the play was given. Plays were only produced during the festivals of the god, but they continued for several days in a row. Each day began at sunrise and ended at torchlight with the production of a trilogy of tragedies followed by a satirical drama. Each trilogy was the work of one author, and the public determined the victor in a competition between poets. The most famous competitors were Aeschylus, Sophocles, and Euripides. There were also contests in comedy, but only the works of one comic poet, Aristophanes, remain.

Greek Temples

In Greece, the most magnificent structures were erected to honor the gods. When we think of Greek architecture, it is their temples that come to mind. A Greek temple is not like a Christian church, which is designed to receive worshippers who come to pray. Instead, it is the palace where the god resides, represented by an idol. Men feel compelled to make this palace splendid. The majority of worshippers do not enter the temple's interior; they remain outside, surrounding the altar in the open air. At the center of the temple is the "chamber" of the god, a mysterious sanctuary without windows, dimly lit from above. On the floor stands the idol, made of wood, marble, or ivory, adorned with gold garments and jewels. The statue is often colossal. In the temple of Olympia, Zeus is depicted sitting, and his head almost touches the summit of the temple. "If the god should rise," they said, "his head would shatter the roof." This sanctuary, a kind of reliquary for the idol, is hidden from view on every side. To enter, one must pass through a porch formed by a row of columns. Behind the "chamber" is the "rear chamber," where the valuable property of the god is kept-his riches and often the gold and silver of the city. Therefore, the temple serves as a storehouse, treasury, and museum. Rows of columns surround the building on four sides, like a second wall protecting the god and his treasures. There are three orders of columns that differ in base and capital, each bearing the name of the people who invented it or used it most frequently. They are, in order of age, the Doric, the Ionic, and the Corinthian. The temple is named after the style of the columns that support it.

Above the columns, encircling the structure, are sculpted surfaces of marble, known as the metopes, which alternate with plain blocks of marble, known as the triglyphs. Together, the metopes and triglyphs make up the frieze. The temple is crowned with a triangular pediment adorned with statues. Greek temples were polychromatic, meaning they were painted in multiple colors, including yellow, blue, and red. For a long time, modern scholars refused to believe this, thinking that the Greeks had too refined a taste to add color to their buildings. However, traces of paint have been found on several temples, leaving no doubt about the matter. It has since been concluded that these bright colors were used to enhance the lines of the building. The characteristics of Greek architecture are unique. At first glance, a Greek temple appears to be a simple, unadorned structure, just a long box of stone perched on a rock, with a square facade topped by a triangle. However, upon closer inspection, it is discovered that not a single line is truly straight. The columns bulge in the middle, the vertical lines are slightly inclined, and the horizontal lines bulge a little at the center. These subtle details are so fine that precise measurements are required to detect them. Greek architects discovered that to create a harmonious whole, they needed to avoid geometrical lines that would appear stiff and instead take into account the illusions of perspective. As a Greek writer once said, "The aim of the architect is to invent processes for deluding the sight." Greek artists worked conscientiously, as they were creating structures for the gods. As a result, their monuments were elaborated in every detail, even those that were not visible to the eye. They were constructed so solidly that they would still be standing today had they not been destroyed by violence. The Parthenon, for example, was still standing in the seventeenth century before an explosion of gunpowder destroyed it.

The Greeks crafted their architecture with a blend of solidity and elegance, simplicity and science. While most of their temples have vanished, a few remain in ruins, with roofs collapsed and only rows of columns standing. Yet, even in this state, they captivate those who lay their eyes upon them. Sculpture was a mere accessory ornament for the Egyptians and Assyrians, but for the Greeks, it was the principal art. Their most celebrated artists, Phidias, Praxiteles, and Lysippus, were all sculptors. They created bas-reliefs to embellish the walls of a temple, its facade, or pediment. One such work is the renowned frieze of the Panathenaic procession, which was carved around the Parthenon. It depicts young Athenian women on the day of the great festival of the goddess. Most of the sculptures were statues that represented gods and served as idols, while others depicted victorious athletes in the great games and served as their reward. The earliest Greek statues were stiff and unrefined, akin to Assyrian sculptures, and often colored. Gradually, they became graceful and elegant. The most exceptional works were those of Phidias in the fifth century and Praxiteles in the fourth. The statues of the following centuries were more graceful but less noble and less powerful.

In ancient Greece, there existed thousands of statues, each city having its own. For five centuries, sculptors worked tirelessly, producing an abundance of art. Unfortunately, only about fifteen complete statues have survived to this day. None of the celebrated masterpieces of Greek art remain. The most famous Greek statues we have are either copies or works from the period of decadence. However, we still have enough fragments of statues and bas-reliefs to provide a general understanding of Greek sculpture. Greek sculptors aimed to represent the most beautiful bodies in a calm and noble attitude. They had numerous opportunities to view beautiful bodies of men in beautiful poses, such as at the gymnasium, in the army, and in sacred dances and choruses. They studied these bodies and learned to reproduce them with unparalleled precision. Greek statues typically feature a small head, a face without emotion, and a dull expression. The Greeks did not strive for facial expressions, as we do. Instead, they focused on the beauty of the line and did not sacrifice the limbs for the head. In Greek statues, the entire body is beautiful. Pottery was also a significant art form in Greece. The Greeks called it Ceramics, and it was not held in the same esteem as other arts. However, it has the advantage of being better known than the others. While temples and statues have fallen into ruin, the achievements of Greek potters are preserved in tombs, where they are still found today. Over 20,000 specimens of painted vases and statuettes of baked earth have been collected in museums across Europe. There were also illustrious painters in Greece, such as Zeuxis, Parrhasius, and Apelles. Unfortunately, we know little about them beyond some anecdotes and descriptions of their paintings. To get an impression of Greek painting, we are limited to the frescoes found in the houses of Pompeii, an Italian city from the first century of our era. However, this is not enough to truly understand the art of Greek painting.

Chapter 15

The Greeks in Asia Before Alexander

The Persian Empire was in decline, despite the Greeks ceasing their attacks and even taking orders from the Great King. The satraps, or governors, no longer obeyed the government and became little kings in their provinces, waging war as they pleased. The Great King had little power to remove them, resorting to assassination. The Persians were no longer feared by other Asian peoples. Greek captain Xenophon, who had been in their pay, described them as decadent, reclining on tapestries wearing gloves and furs. Even their servants were transformed into knights for the sake of pay. Although their armies were large, they were of no service, as their enemies moved more freely through the empire than their friends. They lacked courage and military strength, conceding their inferiority and only daring to fight with Greek auxiliaries on their side. This weakness was evident in 400 when Cyrus, brother of the Great King Artaxerxes, marched against him to secure his throne. Cyrus hired ten thousand Greek mercenaries, and they crossed Asia to Babylon without resistance. In battle, the Greeks chased the barbarians who fled before they could even shoot arrows. They let the war chariots through their ranks without receiving any harm except for one who was wounded with an arrow. Cyrus was killed, and his army disbanded without fighting. The Persians did not dare to attack the Greeks, but they killed their leaders and soldiers who came to conclude a truce. Xenophon recorded their expedition.

The mercenaries, without friends to guide them, elected new leaders and set fire to their tents and chariots before beginning their retreat. They trekked through the rugged mountains of Armenia, facing famine, snow, and the arrows of hostile natives who sought to stop them. Despite these obstacles, they reached the Black Sea and returned to Greece after traversing the entire Persian empire. Upon their return in 399, their numbers still totaled 8,000. Three years later, Agesilaus, the king of Sparta, invaded the wealthy regions of Asia Minor, including Lydia and Phrygia, with a small army. He battled the satraps and planned to invade Asia, but the Spartans ordered him to return home to fight the armies of Thebes and Athens. Agesilaus was the first Greek to dream of conquering Persia, but he was distressed to see his fellow Greeks fighting amongst themselves. When they informed him of their victory at Corinth, where only eight Spartans had died compared to 10,000 of the enemy, he did not rejoice. Instead, he sighed and lamented, "Alas, unhappy Greece, to have lost enough men to have subjugated all the barbarians!" On another occasion, he refused to destroy a Greek city, stating, "If we exterminate all the Greeks who fail in their duty, where shall we find the men to vanquish the barbarians?" This sentiment was uncommon at the time. Xenophon, his biographer, exclaimed, "Who else regarded it as a misfortune to conquer when he was making war on peoples of his own race?" After a century of war, Sparta and Athens were exhausted and had given up their fight against the Persian king. The Macedonians, a rough and uncultured people similar to the ancient Dorians, took up the cause and brought it to an end. They were shepherds and soldiers who lived in two large valleys that opened to the sea far north of Greece. The Greeks held little respect for them, considering them half-barbarians. However, since the kings of Macedon claimed to be descendants of Herakles, they were allowed to participate in the Olympian games' horse races, which gave them some standing as Greeks.

In the heartland of Greece, far from the sea, the kings held little sway over the wars of their fellow Greeks. But in the year 359 B.C., a young, bold, and ambitious man named Philip rose to the throne of Macedon. He had three goals in mind: to build a strong army, to conquer all the ports along the coast of Macedon, and to unite all the Greeks under his command against the Persians. It took him twenty-four long years, but he succeeded in all three of his aims. The Greeks mostly left him alone, and some even helped him. In every city, he bribed people to speak in his favor. "No fortress is impregnable," he would say, "if only one can introduce within it a mule laden with gold." And by these means, he conquered one city after another in northern Greece. The most famous opponent of Philip was an orator named Demosthenes. He was the son of an armorer and was orphaned at the age of seven. His guardians had stolen some of his money, so when he came of age, he sued them and won. He studied the speeches of Isaeus and the history of Thucydides, which he memorized. But when he spoke in public, people laughed at him because his voice was weak and he couldn't speak for very long. For years, he worked hard to improve his voice. It is said that he locked himself away for months with half of his head shaved so he wouldn't be tempted to go outside. He practiced speaking with pebbles in his mouth and on the seashore so he could be heard over the noise of the crowd. When he returned to the public forum, he was a master of his voice. He always prepared his speeches carefully, and he became the most polished and powerful orator in all of Greece.

The rulers of Athens, led by Phocion, desired to maintain peace. Athens lacked the resources to resist the Macedonian king, so Phocion advised waiting until they were ready to make war. However, Demosthenes misunderstood Philip and believed him to be a barbarian. He aligned himself with the party that wanted to make war and used his oratory skills to convince the Athenians to abandon their policy of peace. For fifteen years, Demosthenes delivered speeches urging war, with many of them solely focused on attacking Philip. These speeches were called Philippics, and there were three of them. The speeches given to enlist Athenian aid for Olynthus when it was besieged by Philip were called Olynthiacs. The first Philippic was delivered in 352. Demosthenes urged the Athenians to equip fifty galleys and be prepared to man them themselves. He rejected the idea of an army of 10,000 or 20,000 foreign soldiers, preferring only citizen soldiers. In the third Philippic, delivered in 341, Demosthenes reminded the Athenians of the progress Philip had made due to their inaction. He criticized the Greeks for not preventing Philip, a hated barbarian, from destroying Greek cities and even celebrating the Pythian games. He urged the Greeks to work together to stop Philip's increasing power, warning that the disaster would eventually affect everyone. Finally, when Philip took Elatea to the borders of Boeotia, the Athenians, following Demosthenes' advice, decided to go to war and sent envoys to Thebes. Demosthenes led the embassy and convinced the Thebans to ally with Athens and undertake the war. The Athenian and Theban army, hastily assembled, was defeated by Philip's veteran soldiers at the Battle of Chaeronea in Boeotia. Demosthenes, then forty-eight years old, fought as a private soldier.

Macedonian Supremacy

After his triumph at Chaeronea, Philip stationed a military force in Thebes and proposed peace to Athens. He then traveled to the Peloponnesus, where he was welcomed as a liberator by the people who had been oppressed by Sparta. From that moment on, he faced no opposition. In 337, he arrived in Corinth and gathered representatives from all the Greek states, except for Sparta. In Corinth, Philip announced his plan to lead a Greek army in an invasion of Persia. The representatives approved the proposal and established a general confederation of all the Greek states. Each city would govern itself and live in peace with its neighbors. A general council was created to prevent wars, civil strife, proscriptions, and confiscations. The confederation formed an alliance with the king of Macedon and appointed him as the commander of all Greek troops and navies. Every Greek was forbidden from making war on Philip, on pain of banishment. Alexander. In 336, Philip of Macedon was assassinated, leaving his twenty-year-old son, Alexander, to succeed him. Like all Greeks of good lineage, Alexander was accustomed to athletic exercises, a fierce fighter, and an excellent horseman. He alone had been able to tame Bucephalus, his war horse. However, he was also knowledgeable in politics, eloquence, and natural history, having studied under Aristotle, the greatest scholar of Greece, from the age of thirteen to seventeen. He avidly read the Iliad, considering it a guide to military strategy, and aspired to emulate its heroes. He was truly born to conquer, as he loved to fight and was eager to distinguish himself. His father once told him, "Macedon is too small to contain you." The Phalanx. Philip left behind a powerful tool of conquest: the Macedonian army, the best that Greece had ever seen. It consisted of a phalanx of infantry and a corps of cavalry.

The mighty phalanx of Macedonians was comprised of 16,000 soldiers, arranged in a formation of 1,000 men at the front and 16 men deep. Each warrior wielded a sarissa, a spear of about twenty feet in length. On the battlefield, the Macedonians did not march towards the enemy in a single direction. Instead, they held their position and presented their pikes to the enemy on all sides. Those in the back held their spears above the heads of the soldiers in the front ranks. The phalanx looked like a monstrous beast bristling with iron, ready to face any enemy. While the phalanx guarded the field of battle, Alexander led his cavalry to charge the enemy. The Macedonian cavalry was a distinguished group of young nobles. Alexander departed in the spring of 334 with 30,000 infantry, mostly Macedonians, and 4,500 knights. He carried only seventy talents, which was less than eighty thousand dollars, and supplies for forty days. He had to fight not only the poorly armed peoples that Xerxes had brought together but also an army of 50,000 Greeks who had enlisted in the service of the Great King under the leadership of a competent general, Memnon of Rhodes. These Greeks could have withstood Alexander's invasion, but Memnon died, and his army dispersed. Alexander, freed from his only dangerous opponent, conquered the Persian empire in just two years. Three victories secured the empire for Alexander. In Asia Minor, he defeated the Persian troops stationed behind the Granicus River in May of 333. In the ravines of Cilicia, at Issus, he routed King Darius and his army of 600,000 men in November of the same year. At Arbela, near the Tigris, he scattered and massacred an even larger army in 331. This was a repeat of the Median wars. The Persian army was ill-equipped and knew nothing of maneuvering. It was weighed down by its mass of soldiers, servants, and baggage. Only the elite troops gave battle, while the rest were scattered and massacred. Between battles, the conquest was a triumphant procession. No one resisted, except for the city of Tyre, a commercial rival of the Greeks. The peoples of the empire did not care whether they were subject to Darius or Alexander.

Each victory gave Alexander control of the entire country. The Granicus opened up Asia Minor, Issus secured Syria and Egypt, and Arbela gave him the rest of the empire.

Master of the Persian Empire, Alexander saw himself as the successor to the Great King. He donned Persian attire, observed the customs of the Persian court, and compelled his Greek generals to bow before him as was customary in Persia. He even took a wife from the land and married eighty of his officers to daughters of Persian nobles. His goal was to expand his empire to the farthest reaches of the ancient kings, and he marched all the way to India, fighting against the fierce natives. Upon returning to Babylon with his army in 324 B.C., he died at the young age of thirty-three from a brief fever. It is difficult to discern Alexander's true intentions. Did he conquer for the sheer thrill of it, or did he have a grand design? Did he aim to unite all the peoples of his empire, or was he merely following Persia's example? Or perhaps he emulated the Great King simply for his own vanity? We cannot know for sure. Nonetheless, his actions yielded significant results. He founded seventy cities, including several in Egypt, Tartary, and India. He distributed the treasures that had been hoarded in the Great King's chests to his subjects. He encouraged Greek scholars to study the flora, fauna, and geography of Asia. Most importantly, he readied the people of the Orient to adopt the language and customs of the Greeks. It is for this reason that Alexander is known as "the Great."

The Hellenes in the Orient

The Empire of Alexander dissolved after his death, and his generals fought for twenty years over who would succeed him. They each had a portion of the Macedonian army or some Greek mercenaries on their side, and they fought over who would possess Asia. Eventually, only three generals remained, and each had carved out a great kingdom for themselves: Ptolemy had Egypt, Seleucus had Syria, and Lysimachus had Macedonia. Other smaller kingdoms were also separated or detached themselves later. In these new kingdoms, the king was

Greek, and he preserved his language, religion, and customs while his subjects were Asiatics. He sought to maintain a Greek court around him and recruited his army with Greek mercenaries. His administrative officers were Greeks, and he invited Greek poets, scholars, and artists to his court. Before the time of the Persian kings, there were already many Greeks in the empire as colonists, merchants, and soldiers. The Greek kings attracted even more of them, and they came in such numbers that eventually, the natives adopted the costume, religion, manners, and language of the Greeks. The Orient ceased to be Asiatic and became Hellenic. By the first century B.C., the Romans found only peoples like the Greeks who spoke Greek.

Alexandria, a city founded on the order of Alexander the Great, became the capital of the Greek kings of Egypt, descendants of Ptolemy. These rulers accepted the title of Pharaoh, wore the diadem, and were worshipped as children of the Sun, just like the ancient kings. However, they surrounded themselves with Greeks and built their capital on the edge of the sea in a Greek city. Alexandria was more regular than other Greek cities, built on a simple plan with streets intersecting at right angles. A great highway, 100 feet broad and three and a half miles in length, traversed the whole length of the city. The city was bordered by great monuments such as the Stadium, where public games were presented, the Gymnasium, the Museum, and the Arsineum. The harbor was enclosed with a dike nearly a mile long, which united the mainland to the island of Pharos. At the very extremity of this island, a tower of marble was erected, on the summit of which was maintained a fire always burning to guide the mariners who wished to enter the port. Alexandria superseded the Phoenician cities and became the great port of the entire world. The Museum was an immense edifice of marble connected with the royal palace. The kings of Egypt purposed to make it a great scientific institution. The Museum contained a great library, and the chief librarian was commissioned to buy all the books that he could find. Every book that entered Egypt was brought to the library, copyists transcribed the manuscript, and a copy was rendered to the owner to indemnify him. Thus, they collected 400,000 volumes, an unheard-of number before the invention of printing. Until then, the manuscripts of celebrated books were scarce, always in danger of being lost; now it was known where to find them. In the Museum were also a botanical and zoological garden, an astronomical observatory, a dissecting room established notwithstanding the prejudices of the Egyptians, and even a chemical laboratory.

The Museum, a sanctuary for scholars, mathematicians, astronomers, physicians, and grammarians, provided them with lodgings at the state's expense. The king often dined with them to show his esteem. They held conferences and gave lectures, attracting auditors from all corners of the Greek world. Alexandria was the destination for instruction, with nearly 14,000 students in the city. The Museum was a library, academy, and school, much like a university, which was unheard of before its time. Alexandria became the meeting place for Orientals, including Greeks, Egyptians, Jews, and Syrians, who brought their religion, philosophy, and science, all mingling together. For centuries, Alexandria remained the scientific and philosophical capital of the world. In Asia Minor, the kingdom of Pergamum was small and weak, but its capital city, like Alexandria, was a hub for artists and literature. Pergamum's sculptors were renowned in the third century B.C. King Attalus assembled all the ancient authors' manuscripts in the city's great library. Pergamum also invented the art of preparing skins to replace papyrus for writing, giving rise to parchment, which preserved the manuscripts of antiquity.

Chapter 16

The Last, Decadent Years of Greece

In nearly all Greek cities, wealthy families controlled the land, trade, and ships that brought in money. The majority of citizens, however, had no land or money. So, what could a poor citizen do to make a living? Work as a farmer, artisan, or sailor? Unfortunately, the wealthy families already had their own farms, workshops, and ships, all run by slaves who were cheaper than free workers because they were poorly fed and not paid. If poor citizens wanted to work on their own, money was scarce and borrowing was not an option because interest rates were at 10 percent. Plus, custom prevented citizens from becoming artisans. The philosophers believed that trade harmed the body, weakened the soul, and left no time for public affairs. Aristotle even said that a well-run city should not allow artisans to become citizens. The citizens of Greece were a noble class whose only honorable duties, like the nobles of ancient France, were to govern and go to war. Working with their hands was considered degrading. As a result of the competition with slaves and their elevated status, most citizens were reduced to extreme poverty. The poor were in charge of the cities but had no way to earn a living. They decided to take from the rich, who then formed associations to resist them. Every Greek city was divided into two groups: the rich, called the minority, and the poor, called the majority or the people. The rich and the poor hated each other and fought each other. When the poor gained power, they exiled the rich and took their belongings. They even did two extreme things: they abolished debts and redistributed land. When the rich regained power, they exiled the poor. In many cities, the rich swore to always be an enemy of the people and to harm them as much as possible. There was no way to reconcile the two groups. The rich would not give up their property, and the poor did not want to starve. According to Aristotle, all revolutions start because of the distribution of wealth. Polybius said, "Every civil war is initiated to subvert wealth." They fought brutally, as neighbors often do. "In Miletus, the poor were initially in charge and forced the rich to leave the city. Later, regretting that they had not killed them all, they took the children of the exiles, gathered them in barns, and had them trampled by cattle. The rich returned to the city and became its masters. They took the children of the poor, covered them in pitch, and burned them alive."

Democracy and Oligarchy were the two favored forms of government among the rich and poor parties, respectively. When each party held the city, they put their preferred system into action. The Oligarchy, controlled by a select few, was the choice of the wealthy, while the Democracy, which gave power to an assembly of the people, was the preference of the poor. Both parties formed alliances with similar groups in other cities, resulting in the division of Greek cities into two leagues: the Oligarchy, or the league of the rich, and the Democracy, or the league of the poor. This arrangement began during the Peloponnesian War, with Athens supporting the Democratic party and Sparta favoring the Oligarchic. Cities where the poor held power allied themselves with Athens, while those where the rich governed joined Sparta. For instance, when the poor gained power in Samos, they killed 200 of the rich, exiled 400, and seized their property. Samos then adopted a democratic government and became an ally of Athens. However, when the Spartan army besieged Samos, they brought with them the exiled rich who wanted to return to the city by force. Samos was captured, set up an oligarchy, and joined the league of Sparta. Eventually, the poor realized that the democratic form of government was insufficient to maintain their power. In most cities, they agreed to have a leader, known as a Tyrant. The Tyrant ruled as a master with no regard for the law and could condemn people to death or confiscate their property at will. Mercenaries defended the Tyrant against his enemies. An anecdote illustrates the policy of the Tyrants: Periander, the Tyrant of Corinth, once asked Thrasybulus, the Tyrant of Miletus, for advice on how to govern safely. Thrasybulus took the envoy into a field of wheat and walked with him, striking off with his staff all heads that were higher than the others. He sent the envoy away without further advice. The messenger thought Thrasybulus was a fool, but Periander understood that Thrasybulus was advising him to kill the principal citizens.

Everywhere, the tyrant killed the wealthy and seized their possessions. Often, the wealth was distributed among the poor, which is why the people supported the tyrant. In Greece, there were tyrants as early as the sixth century. Some, like Pisistratus, Polycrates, and Pittacus, were respected for their wisdom. At that time, anyone who exercised absolute power outside the limits of the constitution was called a tyrant, and it was not considered an insult. However, when the tyrants waged constant war against the rich, they became violent and were hated. The story of Damocles illustrates their situation. Damocles told Dionysius, the tyrant of Syracuse, "You are the happiest of men." Dionysius replied, "I will show you the delight of being a tyrant." He treated Damocles to a sumptuous feast and ordered his servants to treat the guest with the same honors as himself. During the feast, Damocles looked up and saw a sword hanging from the ceiling by a single hair, directly above his head. The comparison was striking; the tyrant's life hung by a thread. The rich, his enemies, waited for an opportunity to cut it, and assassinating a tyrant was considered praiseworthy. This danger made Dionysius paranoid and cruel. He trusted no one, believed he was only secure after killing all his enemies, and condemned citizens to death on the slightest suspicion. Thus, the name tyrant became synonymous with injustice. The civil wars between the rich and poor continued for nearly three centuries, from 430 through 150 B.C., exhausting Greece. Many citizens were massacred, and even more, were exiled. These exiles wandered in poverty, knowing no trade but that of a soldier. They became mercenaries in the armies of Sparta, Athens, the Great King, the Persian satraps, and anyone who would hire them. There were 50,000 Greeks in Darius's service against Alexander, but few returned home.

And so it came to pass that the great cities of Greece were left empty, their people scattered and gone. Families grew smaller, with many men choosing not to marry or have children, and others having only one or two. As Polybius once said, "Is this not the root of the problem? When war or sickness takes one of two children, the home is left deserted and the city weakened." Eventually, there were not enough citizens left in the towns to resist a conqueror. This was the time of the Roman conquest when the Greeks began to see the danger that lay ahead. During the second war of Rome with Carthage, an assembly was held at Naupactus in 207 B.C. A wise Greek orator warned, "Turn your eyes to the West. The Romans and Carthaginians are fighting for something more than just the possession of Italy. A cloud is forming on that coast, and it grows larger every day, threatening Greece." At that time, the Greek cities were divided into two leagues that were hostile to each other. The Aetolians and Achaeans were two small peoples who directed the leagues, commanding the armies and deciding on peace and war, just as Athens and Sparta had done in the past. Each league supported one of the two political parties in the Greek states - the democratic party was supported by the Aetolian League, while the Achaean League supported the oligarchical party. However, neither of the two leagues was strong enough to unite all the Greek states. This is when the Romans appeared on the scene. Philip, the king of Macedon, and later Antiochus, the king of Syria, made war on the Romans. However, both were defeated by Rome. Rome destroyed their armies and made them surrender their fleets. Perseus, the new king of Macedon, was also conquered, made prisoner, and his kingdom was overthrown. The Greeks made no effort to unite for the common defense. Rich and poor persisted in their strife, and each hated the other more than the foreigner. The democratic party allied itself with Macedon, while the oligarchical party called in the Romans. Even among the Achaeans, Callicrates, a partisan of the Romans, prepared a list of a thousand citizens whom he accused of having been favorable to Perseus. These suspects were sent to Rome, where they were held for twenty years without trial. At Rhodes, all those who had acted or spoken against Rome were condemned to death.

The Final Battle

It was not long before the Romans were no longer seen as friends. In 197, after defeating the king of Macedon, Consul Flamininus traveled to the Isthmus of Corinth. There, he proclaimed to the gathered Greeks, "All Greek peoples are free." The crowd was overjoyed and approached Flamininus to thank him. They wanted to see their liberator, touch his hand, and crown him with garlands. The pressure was so great that Flamininus almost suffocated. The Romans soon began to assert their control and wished to command. The wealthy accepted their sovereignty, and Rome helped them by crushing the poor. This went on for forty years. Finally, in 147, while Rome was fighting Carthage, the democratic party gained power in Greece and declared war on the Romans. Some Greeks were terrified and betrayed their compatriots and themselves to the Roman soldiers. Others fled to safety or even took their own lives. The opposition leaders seized the property of the wealthy, canceled debts, and armed the slaves. It was a desperate struggle. Even after being defeated, the Achaeans regrouped and marched into battle with their families. General Dioeus locked himself in his house with his entire family and set it on fire. Corinth had been the center of resistance, but the Romans entered and massacred the men. They sold the women and children into slavery and pillaged and burned the city, destroying priceless works of art. Paintings by great artists were thrown to the ground, and Roman soldiers played dice on them.

The Greeks and Their Influence on Rome. When the Romans conquered the Greeks, they were a people without culture, lacking in literature, science, philosophy, and art. The Greeks, on the other hand, were rich in all these things, and the Romans sought to imitate them. Just as the Assyrians had imitated the Chaldeans and the Persians had imitated the Assyrians, the Romans imitated the Greeks. The Romans did not, however, adopt Greek customs, language, or religion. Instead, Greek scholars and artists flocked to Rome, establishing schools of literature and eloquence. Later, it became fashionable for the young men of wealthy Roman families to study in Athens and Alexandria. In this way, the arts and sciences of the Greeks gradually made their way into Rome. As Horace, the Roman poet, put it, "Vanquished Greece overcame her savage conqueror; she brought the arts to uncultured Latium." Although the Romans had their own national architecture, they borrowed the column from the Greeks and often imitated their buildings. Many Roman temples, for example, resemble Greek temples. A wealthy Roman's house typically consisted of two parts: the ancient Roman house and a Greek house added to it. The Greeks were renowned for their sculptures, which could be found in temples, public squares, gymnasia, and private homes. When the Romans conquered Greece, they believed themselves to be the rightful owners of everything that belonged to the vanquished people. Their generals, therefore, removed a great number of statues, transporting them to the temples and porticos of Rome. In the triumph of Aemilius Paullus, the victor over the king of Macedon Perseus, a notable spectacle was two hundred and fifty wagons full of statues and paintings.

Soon the Romans grew accustomed to adorning their theaters, council halls, and private villas with statues. Every great noble wished to have some and commissioned Greek artists to create them. Thus, a Roman school of sculpture was developed, which continued to imitate ancient Greek models. And so it was that Greek sculpture, though a little blunted and disfigured, was spread over all the world subject to the Romans. Literature-wise, the oldest Latin writer was a Greek, Livius Andronicus, a freedman, a schoolmaster, and later an actor. The first works in Latin were translations from Greek. Livius Andronicus translated the Odyssey and several tragedies. The Roman people took pleasure in Greek pieces and would have no others. Even the Roman authors who wrote for the theater did nothing but translate or arrange Greek tragedies and comedies. Thus, the celebrated works of Plautus and Terence are imitations of the comedies of Menander and of Diphilus, now lost to us. The Romans also imitated the Greek historians. For a long time, it was the fashion to write history, even Roman history, in Greek. The only great Roman poets declared themselves pupils of the Greeks. Lucretius wrote only to expound the philosophy of Epicurus; Catullus imitated the poets of Alexander; Vergil, Theocritus, and Homer; Horace translated the odes of the Greek lyrics. Epicureans and Stoics were two sects of Greek philosophers. The Romans had a practical and literal spirit, very indifferent to pure science and metaphysics. They took interest in Greek philosophy only so far as they believed it had a bearing on morals. For the Epicureans, pleasure is the supreme good, not sensual pleasure, but the calm and reasonable pleasure of the temperate man. Happiness consists of the quiet enjoyment of a peaceful life, surrounded by friends and without concern for imaginary goods. For the Stoics, the supreme good is virtue, which consists of conducting oneself according to reason, with a view to the good of the whole universe. Riches, honor, health, beauty, all the goods of earth are nothing for the wise man; even if one tortures him, he remains happy in the possession of the true good.

The Romans were a people divided, taking up the banner of one philosophy or another, often without truly understanding either. Those who claimed to be Epicureans spent their days indulging in food and drink, likening themselves to swine. Meanwhile, those who called themselves Stoics, such as Cato and Brutus, affected a rough language and solemn demeanor and focused on the hardships of life. Despite this, these doctrines gradually spread and helped to break down certain prejudices among the Romans. Epicureans and Stoics found common ground in two areas: they rejected the old religion and taught that all men, regardless of status or origin, are equal. Roman students of these philosophies abandoned certain old superstitions and learned to treat their slaves and other peoples with less cruelty and arrogance. When the Romans conquered Greece, they brought with them the arts, letters, and morals of the Greeks, just as the Greeks had spread their language, customs, and religion throughout the Orient during their conquest of the Persian empire.

Chapter 17

Rome and the Ancient People of Italy

The Etruscans were a people shrouded in mystery, both in ancient times and to this day. They were unlike their neighbors and likely originated from far-off lands such as Germany, Asia, or Egypt. However, no one can say for certain. We don't even know what language they spoke. While their alphabet is similar to that of the Greeks, the Etruscan inscriptions only contain proper names, which are too brief to offer any insight into their language. The Etruscans established a confederation of twelve cities in Tuscany, each with its own fortress, king, and government. They also had colonies on both coasts, with twelve in Campania near Naples and another twelve in the Po Valley. Etruria, the land of the Etruscans, was a warm and humid country where the air hung heavily over the inhabitants. The region where they had most of their cities was the famous Maremma, an incredibly fertile area covered in beautiful forests. However, the water had no outlet, forming marshes that poisoned the air. As the Italian proverb goes, "In the Maremma, one gets rich in a year, but dies in six months." Today, all that remains of the Etruscans are their city walls and tombs.

When one opens an Etruscan tomb, they are greeted with a porch supported by columns, leading to chambers with couches and bodies laid upon them. The space is adorned with ornaments of gold, ivory, and amber, as well as purple cloths, utensils, and large painted vases. The walls are decorated with paintings of combats, games, banquets, and fantastical scenes. Industry and Commerce. The Etruscans were skilled in utilizing their fertile soil, but their true forte was as mariners and traders. Like the Phoenicians, they embarked on long journeys to acquire ivory from India, amber from the Baltic, tin, Phoenician purple, Egyptian jewels adorned with hieroglyphics, and even ostrich eggs. All of these objects have been discovered in their tombs. Their navies sailed as far south as Sicily. The Greeks held a deep-seated hatred for them, referring to them as "savage Tyrrhenians" or "Etruscan pirates." At the time, every mariner was a pirate on occasion, and the Etruscans were particularly keen on excluding the Greeks so that they could monopolize the trade of Italy's west coast. The famous Etruscan vases, which have been extracted by the thousands from tombs to enrich our museums, were imitations of Greek vases but produced by the Etruscans. They depict scenes from Greek mythology, particularly the combats surrounding Troy, with human figures in red on a black background. Religion. The Etruscans were a somber people. Their gods were stern and often malevolent. The two most revered gods were "the veiled deities," about whom we know nothing. Below them were the gods who hurled lightning, forming a council of twelve gods. Gods of ill omen resided beneath the earth, in the abode of the dead, and are depicted on Etruscan vases. Mantus, the king of the lower world, a winged genius, sits with a crown on his head and a torch in his hand. Other demons, armed with swords or clubs and holding serpents, receive the souls of the dead. The principal figure, known as Charun or the Charon of the Greeks, is an old man of hideous form who wields a heavy mallet to strike his victims. The souls of the dead or the Manes, emerge from the lower world three days a year, wandering the earth, terrifying the living, and causing them harm. Human sacrifices are offered to appease their thirst for blood. The famous gladiatorial combats, which the Romans adopted, originated from bloody sacrifices in honor of the dead.

The Augurs

In ancient times, the Etruscans believed that a mischievous spirit named Tages emerged from a furrow and revealed the secrets of divination to the people. The Etruscan priests, who called themselves haruspices or augurs, had strict guidelines for predicting the future. They examined the entrails of sacrificial animals, observed thunderbolts, and most importantly, studied the flight of birds, hence their name "augurs." To begin, the augur faced north and held a crooked staff in hand, drawing a line that divided the sky into two sections. The right side was deemed favorable, while the left was unfavorable. A second line intersected the first at a right angle, and other lines parallel to these created a square in the sky, known as the Temple. The augur observed the birds that flew within this square, with some, like the eagle, representing good fortune, and others, like the owl, foretelling doom. The Etruscans predicted the future of their people, but they were unique in that they did not believe their civilization would last forever. According to their beliefs, Etruria would endure for ten centuries. These centuries were not precisely one hundred years each, but certain signs marked the end of each period. In the year 44, the year of Caesar's death, a comet appeared, and an Etruscan haruspex proclaimed to the Romans that this comet signaled the end of the ninth century and the beginning of the tenth, the final century of the Etruscan people. The Romans, a semi-barbaric people, often copied their more sophisticated neighbors, the Etruscans. They adopted many aspects of Etruscan religion, including the dress of the priests and magistrates, religious rituals, and the art of divination from birds, known as auspices. When the Romans founded a city, they followed Etruscan customs. The founder plowed a square enclosure with a bronze-tipped plow drawn by a white bull and heifer. Men followed behind, carefully casting the clods of earth from the furrow's side. The entire ditch left by the plow was considered sacred and could not be crossed. To enter the enclosure, the founder had to break the ditch at specific points, lifting the plow and carrying it for a moment. The resulting gap remained profane and became the gate by which one entered. Rome itself was founded using these rites, known as Roma Quadrata, and legend held that the founder had killed his brother for crossing the sacred furrow. Later, the limits of Roman colonies, camps, and even estates were traced according to religious rules and geometric lines.

In the rugged mountains of the Apennines, east and south of the Roman plain, there were many tribes. These people did not have the same name and did not form a single nation. They were Umbrians, Sabines, Volscians, Aequians, Hernicans, Marsians, and Samnites. However, they all spoke almost the same language, worshipped the same gods, and had similar customs. Like the Persians, Hindus, and Greeks, they were of the Caucasian race. Secluded in their mountains, remote from strangers, they remained like the Caucasians of the ancient period. They lived in groups with their herds scattered in the plains, and they had no villages or cities. Fortresses erected on the mountains defended them in times of war. They were brave and martial people, of simple and substantial manners. They later became the strength of the Roman armies. A proverb ran: "Who could vanquish the Marsians without the Marsians?" The Sacred Spring. According to legend, in the midst of pressing danger, the Sabines believed their gods to be angry and decided to appease their displeasure by sacrificing everything that was born during a certain spring to the god of war and death. This sacrifice was called a "Sacred Spring." All the children born in this year belonged to the god. When they reached manhood, they left the country and journeyed abroad. These exiles formed several groups, each taking for guidance one of the sacred animals of Italy, a woodpecker, a wolf, or a bull, and followed it as a messenger of the god. Where the animal halted, the band settled itself. It was said that many peoples of Italy originated in these colonies of emigrants and still preserved the name of the animal that had led their ancestors. Such were the Hirpines or people of the wolf, the Picentines or people of the woodpecker, and the Samnites, whose capital was named Bovianum or city of the ox. The Samnites. The Samnites were the most powerful of all. They were settled in the Abruzzi, a paradise for brigands. They descended into the fertile plains of Naples and Apulia and put Etruscan and Greek towns to ransom.

The Samnites, a fierce people who fought against the Romans for two centuries, were never able to overcome their lack of central administration and discipline. However, they continued to wage war against the Romans. In their final battle, an old man brought a sacred book written on linen to the chiefs of the army. The soldiers formed a wall of linen around an altar and stood with unsheathed swords. The bravest warriors entered the precinct one by one and swore to kill any fugitives and not to flee before the enemy. These warriors, numbering 16,000, donned linen garments and became known as the "linen legion." They engaged in battle and were slaughtered to the last man, but their bravery was legendary. The Greeks had many colonies in southern Italy, including Sybaris, Croton, and Tarentum. However, they avoided the Roman coast due to fear of the Etruscans. Only the city of Cumae had any significant relations with the Romans until the third century. The Latins, a small people who inhabited the hills and ravines south of the Tiber, were similar to other Italians in language, religion, and manners, but were slightly more advanced in civilization. They built strong cities and cultivated the soil. Each little independent group of people had its own city and government, forming miniature states known as cities. Thirty Latin cities formed a religious association similar to the Greek amphictyonies, and they celebrated a common festival every year at Alba, where they sacrificed a bull in honor of their common god, the Latin Jupiter.

On the frontier of Latium, near the borders of Etruria, in a marshy plain dotted with hills that followed the Tiber, stood the city of Rome, the hub of the Roman people dispersed throughout the plain. The land was plagued by malaria and desolation, but the location was advantageous. The Tiber acted as a barrier against the enemy from Etruria, and the hills served as fortresses. The sea was only six leagues away, far enough to avoid the threat of pirates, yet close enough to allow for the transportation of goods. The port of Ostia at the mouth of the Tiber was a suburb of Rome, similar to how Piraeus was to Athens. The area was therefore appealing to a people of warriors and traders. Of the first centuries of Rome, we only know some legends, and the Romans knew no more than we. According to their tales, Rome was a small square town confined to the Palatine Hill. The founder, whom they named Romulus, had traced the circuit with a plow in accordance with Etruscan customs. Every year, on the twenty-first April, the Romans celebrated the anniversary of these ceremonies: a procession circled the original enclosure, and a priest hammered a nail into a temple to commemorate it. It was estimated that the founding occurred in the year 754 B.C. On the other hills facing the Palatine, other small cities emerged. A group of Sabine mountaineers settled on the Capitoline, while a band of Etruscan adventurers established themselves on Mount Caelius. Perhaps there were still other peoples. All of these small settlements eventually joined Rome on the Palatine. A new wall was constructed to encompass the seven hills. The Capitol then became for Rome what the Acropolis was for Athens: the temples of the three protecting deities of the city-Jupiter, Juno, and Minerva rose here; as well as the citadel that housed the treasure and archives of the people. When laying the foundations, it was said that a recently severed human head was discovered. This head was an omen that Rome would become the head of the world.

Chapter 18

Roman Religion

The deities of Rome, much like those of Greece, were believed to be responsible for all occurrences in the world. However, instead of a single god directing the universe, the Romans had a god for each phenomenon they observed. There was a deity for seed germination, another for field boundaries, and yet another for fruit protection. Each had a name, gender, and specific functions. The major gods included Jupiter, the god of heaven; Janus, the two-faced god who opens; Mars, the god of war; Mercury, the god of trade; Vulcan, the god of fire; Neptune, the god of the sea; Ceres, the goddess of grains, the Earth, the Moon, Juno, and Minerva. Below these were minor deities. Some personified qualities such as Youth, Concord, Health, and Peace. Others presided over certain life events, such as a god to teach a child to speak, a goddess to teach a child to drink, and another to knit their bones. Two accompanied the child to school, and two took them home. In short, there were countless minor special deities. Other gods protected cities, sections of mountains, forests, rivers, fountains, and trees. An old woman in a Latin romance once exclaimed, "Our country is so full of gods that it is much easier to find a god than a man." Unlike the Greeks, the Romans did not give their gods a specific form. For a long time, there were no idols in Rome. They worshipped Jupiter as a rock and Mars as a sword. Later, they imitated the wooden statues of the Etruscans and the marble ones of the Greeks. Perhaps they did not initially think of the gods as having human forms. Unlike the Greeks, the Romans did not imagine marriage and kinship among their gods. They had no legends about these relationships, nor did they know of any Olympus where the gods gathered. The Latin language had a significant word for designating the gods: Manifestations. They were the manifestations of a mysterious divine power. This is why they were formless, without family relationships or legends. Everything known about the gods was that each controlled a natural force and could benefit or harm humans. The Romans were not fond of pale and frigid abstractions. They even seemed to fear them. When they invoked the gods, they covered their faces, perhaps so as not to see them. However, they believed that the gods were powerful and would serve them if they knew how to please them. "The man whom the gods favor," says Plautus, "they cause to gain wealth."

The Roman people view religion as a transaction of good deeds. The worshipper offers gifts and respect, and in return, the gods grant some benefit. If a man gives a gift to a god and receives nothing in return, he feels cheated. When Germanicus fell ill, the people made sacrifices for his recovery. However, when they learned of his death, they became angry and overturned altars and statues of the gods because they did not do what was expected of them. Even today, Italian peasants curse the saints who do not grant their wishes. Worship involves doing things that please the gods. They receive offerings of fruits, milk, wine, or animal sacrifices. Sometimes, statues of the gods are brought from their temples, placed on couches, and served with a feast. Magnificent temples were built for them, and entertainment was arranged. However, it is not enough to make a costly offering to the gods. The Roman gods are particular about the form of worship. They require that all acts of worship, sacrifices, games, and dedications follow the ancient rules or the rites. When offering a victim to Jupiter, one must choose a white animal, sprinkle salted meal on its head, and strike it with an axe. One must stand tall with hands raised to heaven, the home of Jupiter, and recite a sacred formula. If any part of the ceremony fails, the sacrifice is useless, and the god will not be pleased. A magistrate celebrating games in honor of the protecting deities of Rome must follow the rites strictly. If he alters a word in his formula, if a flute player rests, or if an actor stops short, the games do not conform to the rites and must be restarted. Therefore, a wise person seeks the help of two priests, one to recite the formula and the other to follow the ritual accurately.

Every year, the Arval Brothers, a group of priests, gather in a temple near Rome to perform a sacred dance and recite a prayer. The prayer is written in an old language that no one understands anymore, so each priest is given a written formulary at the beginning of the ceremony. Despite not comprehending the prayer, the priests continue to chant it without alteration. This is because the Romans place great importance on following the letter of the law when it comes to their gods. For them, the exactness of the prescribed ritual is their religion, and they consider themselves to be "the most religious of men." They believe that they may be inferior or equal to other people in all other aspects, but they excel in their worship of the gods. When a Roman prays, it is not to connect with a god on a spiritual level, but to ask for a favor. The first step is to identify which god can provide the requested service. According to Varro, "knowing what god can aid us in a special case is as important as knowing where the carpenter and baker live." Once the appropriate god is identified, the supplicant dons the proper attire and brings an offering, as the gods appreciate neatness and do not like empty-handed visitors. The worshipper then stands erect with their head veiled and invokes the god. However, they do not know the exact name of the god, as "no one knows the true names of the gods." Instead, they say something like "Jupiter, greatest and best, or whatever is the name that thou preferrest." The supplicant then makes their request, using clear language to avoid any misunderstandings. If a libation is offered, the worshipper says, "Receive the homage of this wine that I am pouring," to avoid any confusion about the type of wine being presented. The prayers are lengthy, verbose, and full of repetitions.

In ancient Rome, just as in Greece, the belief in omens was strong. The gods were thought to have knowledge of the future, and they would send signs that allowed men to interpret them. Before any action was taken, the Romans would consult the gods. For instance, a general about to go to battle would examine the entrails of victims, while magistrates would observe the flight of birds, known as "taking the auspices", before holding an assembly. If the signs were favorable, the gods were believed to approve of the enterprise; if not, they were against it. Sometimes, the gods would send a sign that had not been requested. Every unexpected phenomenon was seen as a presage of an event. For example, a comet appeared before the death of Caesar, and it was thought to have been a warning. When the assembly of the people deliberated, and there was thunder, it was believed that Jupiter did not want any decision to be made that day, and the assembly had to dissolve. Even the most insignificant fact could be interpreted as a sign, such as a flash of lightning, a word overheard, a rat crossing the road, or a diviner met on the way. To avoid being influenced by any portent, Marcellus had himself carried in a closed litter when he had determined on an enterprise. These were not the superstitions of the populace; the republic supported six augurs whose task was to predict the future. It carefully preserved a collection of prophecies, known as the Sibylline Books, and had sacred chickens guarded by priests. No public act, whether an assembly, election, or deliberation, could be done without taking the auspices, which involved observing the flight of birds. In the year 195, it was reported that lightning had struck a temple of Jupiter and hit a hair on the head of the statue of Hercules, and a governor wrote that a chicken with three feet had been hatched. The senate assembled to discuss these portents. In Rome, as in Greece, the priest was not responsible for the care of souls but existed only to serve the god. He would guard the temple, manage its property, and perform ceremonies in the god's honor. For example, the guild of the Salii, or leapers, watched over a shield that had supposedly fallen from heaven and was worshipped as an idol. Every year, they would perform a dance in arms, which was their sole function.

The augurs, those who read the signs of the gods, predicted the future. The pontiffs oversaw the ceremonies of worship, regulated the calendar, and determined the festivals to be celebrated throughout the year. Unlike in Egypt, the priests, augurs, and pontiffs in Rome did not form a separate caste. They were chosen from among the great families and continued to hold positions of power in the state, including judging, presiding over assemblies, and commanding armies. The Romans believed, like the Greeks and the Hindus, that the soul survived the body. If the body was buried properly, the soul would go to the lower world and become a god. If not, the soul would return to the earth and torment the living until proper burial was performed. Pliny the Younger tells of a ghost that haunted a house until bones were buried properly, and the shade of Emperor Caligula wandered until his body was reburied in the correct manner. It was important for both the living and the dead that proper funeral rites were observed. The family of the deceased would burn the body on a funeral pyre and place the ashes in an urn, which was then deposited in a tomb dedicated to the Manes, the souls that had become gods. The family would visit the tomb on fixed days of the year to bring food and offer nourishment to the soul. These funeral ceremonies were perpetuated for an indefinite period, with the family maintaining the tomb and holding funeral feasts. In return, the souls of their ancestors, now gods, loved and protected their posterity. Each family had its own guardian deities, known as Lares.

In the ancient Roman world, the hearth was a sacred object that every family cherished. The flame was considered a deity, and the hearth was an altar. The Romans believed that the flame should be kept burning day and night, and offerings of oil, fat, wine, and incense were made to it. The fire would then grow brighter and taller as if nourished by the offerings. Before every meal, the Romans would thank the god of the hearth, offer a portion of their food, and pour out a little wine as a libation. Even those who were skeptical, like Horace, would still offer libations and prayers before the hearth. Every Roman family had a sanctuary in their home where they kept the Lares, the souls of their ancestors, and the altar of the hearth. Rome also had its own sacred hearth, known as Vesta. The Vestals, four virgins from noble families, were tasked with keeping the hearth burning. Only pure beings could be trusted with this duty, as it was essential that the flame never be extinguished. If a Vestal broke her vow, she would be buried alive in a cave for committing sacrilege and endangering the entire Roman people. For the Romans, the family was a religious institution. All members of a family worshiped the same ancestors and gathered around the same hearth. They shared the same gods, and their religion was their own unique possession. The sanctuary where the Lares were kept was hidden within the home, and no stranger was allowed to approach it. This made the Roman family a little church, with its own religion and worship that only its members could access. The ancient family was vastly different from the modern family, as it was based on the principles of religion.

In ancient Rome, marriage was a sacred institution. The first rule of this religion was that one should be born of a regular marriage to have the right of adoring the ancestors of the family. The father of the bride would give her away outside the house, and a procession would conduct her to the groom's house, chanting an ancient sacred refrain, "Hymen, O Hymen!" The bride and groom would then divide a cake of meal between them before the altar of the husband, in the presence of the gods of the family. This period was called confarreatio, meaning communion through the cake. Later, another form of marriage was invented, where a relative of the bride, in the presence of witnesses, would sell her to the husband, who would declare that he buys her for his wife. This was called marriage by sale or coemptio. For the Romans, marriage was a religious duty ordained by religion to ensure that the family did not become extinct. When a Roman married, he declared that he takes his wife to perpetuate the family through their children. A noble Roman who sincerely loved his wife repudiated her because she brought him no children. The Roman woman was never free. As a young girl, she belonged to her father, who would choose her husband for her. Once married, she would come under the power of her husband, and the jurisconsults would say that she was under his "manus", meaning she was in the same position as his daughter. The woman always had a master who had the right of life and death over her. And yet, she was never treated like a slave. She was equal in dignity to her husband and was called the mother of the family, just as her husband was called the father of the family. She was the mistress of the house, and he was the master. She would give orders to the slaves, charging them with all the heavy tasks such as grinding the grain, making bread, and cooking. She would sit in the seat of honor, spin and weave, apportion work to the slaves, watch the children, and direct the house. She was not excluded from associating with the men, like the Greek woman. She would eat at the table with her husband, receive visitors, go into town to dinner, and appear at public ceremonies, the theatre, and even the courts. However, she was ordinarily uncultured, and the Romans did not care to instruct their daughters. The quality they most admired in a woman was gravity, and on her tomb, they would write by way of eulogy, "She kept the house and spun linen."

The young in Rome are treated as possessions of their fathers. If the father so chooses, he may abandon the child in the street. However, if he decides to keep the child, it is raised within the household. Girls are taught to spin and weave under the guidance of their mothers and remain in the family home until they are married. Boys, on the other hand, accompany their fathers to the fields and are trained in the art of warfare. Artistic pursuits are not valued by the Romans, and children are taught only the basics of reading, writing, and arithmetic. They are raised to be disciplined, reserved, and obedient. The head of the household is known as the paterfamilias, or the father of the family. He is the owner of the estate, the priest of the ancestral cult, and the ruler of the household. He holds complete authority over his household, with the power to reject his wife, disown his children, and even sell them into slavery. All possessions and earnings of his wife and children belong to him, as they are not allowed to own property.

In ancient Rome, the father of the family held immense power over his household. He had the ultimate authority, including the right to decide the fate of his family members. If any of them committed a crime, it was not the magistrate who punished them, but the father who judged them. In 186 B.C., the Roman Senate passed a decree that imposed the death penalty for all those who participated in the cult of Bacchus. While the men were executed, the guilty women were left in the hands of their fathers. The Senate had to seek the fathers' permission to condemn their wives or daughters to death. The elder Cato famously declared that the husband was the judge of his wife. He had complete control over her, and if she committed any wrongdoing, he could punish her as he saw fit. If she drank wine or was unfaithful, he could even condemn or kill her. When Catiline plotted against the Senate, a senator discovered that his own son was involved in the conspiracy. The father had his son arrested, tried, and sentenced to death. The father's power lasted until his death, and his son was never free from it, even if he became a consul. When the father passed away, his sons inherited his power and became fathers of their own families. As for the wife, she could never attain freedom and remained under the power of her husband's heir, even subject to her own son.

Chapter 19

The Reign of the Kings

Legend has it that Rome was ruled by kings for two and a half centuries. They not only knew the names and dates of death of each king but also the life story of each one. According to tradition, there were seven kings. Romulus, the first king, hailed from the Latin city of Alba, founded a settlement on the Palatine, and killed his brother for committing the sacrilege of leaping over the sacred furrow surrounding the settlement. He then formed an alliance with Tatius, a Sabine king. Later legends added that he established a quarter surrounded by a palisade at the foot of the hill city, where he welcomed all the adventurers who wished to join him. Numa Pompilius, the second king, was a Sabine. He organized the Roman religion and sought counsel from a goddess, the nymph Egeria, who lived in a nearby forest. The third king, Tullus Hostilius, was a warrior. He waged war against Alba, the capital of the Latin confederation, and successfully conquered and destroyed it. Ancus Marcius, the fourth king, was Numa's grandson. He constructed a wooden bridge over the Tiber and founded the port of Ostia, which facilitated commerce up the river to Rome. The last three kings were Etruscans. Tarquin the Elder expanded Rome's territory and introduced religious ceremonies from Etruria. Servius Tullius organized the Roman army, admitting all citizens regardless of birth, and dividing them into centuries or companies based on wealth. The final king, Tarquinius Superbus, oppressed the great families of Rome. Some of the nobles conspired against him and successfully expelled him. From that point on, there were no more kings. The Roman state, or as they called it, the commonwealth or res publica, was governed by two magistrates, the consuls, who were elected each year. It is difficult to determine the accuracy of this tradition, as it was formed long after the Romans began recording their history and contains many legends that cannot be fully accepted.

In ancient times, the names of kings were thought to represent a particular race or class. The early history of Rome has been reconstructed in various ways, but the more effort put into it, the less agreement among scholars. Around the fifth century B.C., Rome had two distinct classes of people: the patricians and the plebeians. The patricians were the descendants of the old families who had lived in the vicinity of the city for generations. They had the exclusive right to participate in religious ceremonies, hold office, and appear in the assembly of the people. They considered themselves the true people of Rome because their ancestors had founded the Roman state and bequeathed it to them. On the other hand, the plebeians were the descendants of foreigners and conquered peoples of nearby cities. Although they obeyed the government of Rome, they had no part in it. They did not practice the Roman religion nor participate in its ceremonies, and they were not allowed to intermarry with patrician families. They were known as the plebs, or the multitude, and were not considered part of the Roman people. The people and the plebs were like two distinct peoples, one of masters and the other of subjects. However, the plebeians were similar to the patricians. They served in the army at their own expense and risked their lives in the service of the Roman people. They lived on their own domains and were often wealthy and of ancient lineage. The only difference was that they were descended from a great family of some conquered Latin city, while the patricians were the scions of an old family in the conquering city. In ancient times, the prayers often included the formula "For the welfare of the people and the plebs of Rome." Despite the strife between the patricians and plebeians, they were both integral parts of the Roman state.

In the early days of Rome, the plebeians, feeling mistreated and undervalued, took up arms and withdrew to a nearby mountain, intent on breaking away from the Roman people. The patricians, alarmed by this move, sent Menenius Agrippa to negotiate with the plebeians. He told them the fable of the members and the stomach, which convinced the plebs to return to Rome. However, they made a treaty with the people, which granted their chiefs, known as tribunes of the plebs, the right to protect the plebeians from the magistrates of the people and to veto any measure against them. By uttering the word "veto," the tribunes could halt any action, as religion forbade attacks on a tribune under penalty of being devoted to the infernal gods. The struggle between the two orders continued for two centuries, from 494 B.C. to about 300 B.C. The plebeians, who were more numerous and wealthier, eventually emerged victorious. They secured the adoption of laws that were common to both orders and allowed marriage between patricians and plebeians. However, the most challenging task was to obtain the high magistracies, as the gods had to approve the choice of a magistrate before they could be named. The auspices, or the flight of birds, were consulted to determine the gods' approval, but the old Roman religion allowed the auspices to be taken only on the name of a patrician. The plebeian families, who were determined to be the equals of the patrician families in dignity, gradually forced the patricians to open all offices to them, starting with the consulship and ending with the great pontifical office. The first plebeian consul was named in 366 B.C., and the first plebeian pontifex maximus in 302 B.C. Eventually, the patricians and plebeians merged, forming one people.

The Roman People

The Right of Citizenship. In Rome, as in Greece, the people are not all the inhabitants, but only the body of citizens. Only those who have the right of citizenship are considered citizens, not every man who lives in the territory. The citizen has many privileges: 1. He is the only member of the body politic and has the right to vote in the assemblies of the Roman people, serve in the army, attend religious ceremonies in Rome, and be elected a Roman magistrate. These are known as public rights. 2. The citizen is the only one protected by Roman law. He has the right to marry legally, become the head of a family, have power over his wife and children, make a will, and buy or sell property. These are known as private rights. Those who are not citizens are excluded from the army and assembly. They cannot marry, have absolute power over their families, own property legally, or demand justice at a Roman tribunal. Thus, citizens are considered the aristocracy among the other inhabitants of the city. However, citizens are not equal among themselves as there are class differences or ranks. The Nobles. In the first rank are the nobles. A citizen is noble if one of his ancestors has held a magistracy. The magisterial office in Rome is an honor that ennobles the occupant and his posterity.

When a citizen ascends to the positions of aedile, praetor, or consul, he is granted a toga with a purple border, a curule chair, and the privilege of having a statue made in his likeness. These statues, initially crafted from wax and later silver, are placed in the atrium, the sacred space of the home, near the hearth and the family's gods. There, they stand in niches like idols, revered by future generations. When a member of the family passes away, the statues are brought out and carried in the funeral procession, and a relative delivers the eulogy. It is these statues that elevate a family that preserves them. The more statues a family has, the more distinguished it is. The Romans referred to those who were "noble by one image" and those who were "noble by many images." The noble families of Rome which numbered less than 300, were scarce, as the magistracies that granted nobility were typically bestowed upon those who were already noble. Beneath the nobility were the knights, who were wealthy but not noble. Their wealth, as recorded in the treasury's registers, had to amount to at least 400,000 sesterces. They were merchants, bankers, and contractors who did not govern but amassed riches. At the theater, they had reserved seating behind the nobles. If a knight were elected to a magistracy, the nobles dubbed him a "new man," and his son gained nobility. Those who were neither nobles nor knights constituted the bulk of the population, the plebs. The majority of them were farmers who cultivated small plots in Latium or the Sabine region. They were the descendants of the Latins or Italians who were subjugated by the Romans. Cato the Elder, in his book on Agriculture, provides insight into their customs: "Our ancestors, when they wished to praise a man, said 'a good workman,' 'a good farmer'; this compliment seemed the greatest of all."

In the days of Rome, the backbone of the army was made up of hardworking, thrifty laborers. These folks were the ones who did the heavy lifting, and they were also the ones who had a say in who got elected to office. The nobles who wanted to be magistrates knew they had to win over these peasants, and they did so by seeking them out on the parade ground and shaking their hands. If a candidate found a laborer's hand to be rough, he might make a joke about the man walking on his hands. But if he did, he could kiss his chances of winning goodbye. At the bottom of the heap were the freedmen. These were folks who had once been slaves, or whose parents had been slaves. Even though they were technically free, they still carried the stigma of their past, and they were not allowed to serve in the army. When it came time to vote, they had to wait until everyone else had had their say. The government of Rome was called a republic, which meant that it was supposed to be a thing of the people. The citizens were the ones who elected the magistrates, decided whether to go to war or make peace and made the laws. The law was whatever the people said it was. Even after more than half a million people became citizens, they still had to go to Rome in person to exercise their rights. The people met in one place, the Comitia. When the people gathered to vote, they were led by a magistrate. Sometimes they were called together by the sound of a trumpet, and they would gather on the parade ground, dividing themselves into groups. This was the Comitia by centuries. Other times, they would meet in the marketplace, dividing themselves into thirty-five tribes. Each tribe would then go into a separate area to cast their votes. This was the Comitia by tribes. The magistrate would tell the people what they were voting on, and when they were done, they would go their separate ways. The people were in charge, but they were used to following their leaders.

The Magistrates held great power in Rome. Every year, the people elect officials to govern them, and these officials are given absolute power. They are called magistrates, or "masters." Lictors march before them, carrying a bundle of rods and an axe, symbols of their power to punish and execute. The magistrate presides over the popular assembly and the senate, sits in court, and commands the army. He is the master of everything. He can call the assembly and dissolve it at will, render judgments alone, and do as he pleases with the soldiers, even putting them to death without consulting his officers. During a war against the Latins, Manlius, a Roman general, forbade his soldiers from leaving camp. His son, provoked by an enemy, left camp and killed him. Manlius had his son arrested and executed immediately. This shows the extent of the magistrate's power, which is said to be equal to that of a king. However, this power is brief and divided. The magistrate is elected for only one year, and he has a colleague with the same power. In Rome, two consuls govern the people and command the armies, as well as several praetors who serve as subordinate governors or commanders and pronounce judgments. There are also other magistrates, such as two censors, four aediles who supervise the public ways and markets, ten tribunes of the plebs, and quaestors who care for the state treasure. The highest of all magistrates are the censors. They take the census every five years, which is the enumeration of the Roman people. All citizens must appear before them and declare their name, the number of their children and slaves, and the amount of their fortune under oath. This information is recorded in the registers. The censors also draw up the list of senators, knights, and citizens, assigning each person their proper rank in the city. They are responsible for the lustrum, a great ceremony of purification that occurs every five years.

On this day, all the citizens of Rome are gathered on the Campus Martius, standing in formation like soldiers in battle. Three times, a bull, a ram, and a swine are led around the assembly as expiatory victims. These animals are then killed, and their blood is sprinkled on the people. This ritual purifies the city and reconciles it with the gods. The censors hold the power of registration and rank citizens as they see fit. They can demote a senator by striking him from the senate list, a knight by not registering him among the knights, and a citizen by not placing his name on the registers of the tribes. This power allows them to punish those they deem at fault and reach those whom the law does not condemn. They have even been known to demote citizens for poor farming practices and for owning an expensive carriage. They have demoted senators for possessing ten pounds of silver and for divorcing their wives. This overbearing power is known as the supervision of morals and makes the censors the masters of the city. The Senate is made up of approximately 300 individuals appointed by the censor. However, the censor does not choose randomly. They only select wealthy citizens who are respected and come from high-ranking families, most of whom are former magistrates. Typically, the censor appoints those who are already members of the Senate, which means that one usually remains a senator for life. The Senate is a gathering of Rome's most prominent men, which gives it its authority. When business is presented, one of the magistrates calls the senators to a temple, presents the matter, and then asks, "What do you think concerning this matter?" The senators respond one by one, following the order of their rank.

In the ancient city of Rome, the Senate is the ultimate authority. Their decisions, known as senatus consultum, are not laws but are treated as such by the people. The Senate is made up of nobles who have more experience than the common folk, and their decisions are rarely challenged by magistrates who fear their peers. The Senate regulates all public business, from declaring war to fixing the budget. The people ratify these decisions, and the magistrates execute them. In 200 B.C., the Senate decided on war with the king of Macedon, but the people were afraid and refused to approve it. The Senate then ordered a magistrate to give a more persuasive speech, and the people voted for war. In Rome, the people reigned, but the Senate governed, much like the king in England. To become a magistrate or senator in Rome is not a profession, but an honor. Only nobles, knights, and the rich can enter these positions, and they must first serve in the army for ten campaigns. Then they may become a quaestor, managing the state treasury, followed by the position of aedile, responsible for policing the city and providing the corn supply. After that, they may become a praetor, giving judgment in the courts, and finally, a consul, commanding an army and presiding over the assemblies. The highest position one can aspire to is the censorship, which is only attainable around the age of fifty. In Rome, the path to power is long and arduous, but those who succeed are honored and respected by all.

The same man, therefore, has been a financier, administrator, judge, general, and governor before attaining the original function of censor, which involves the political distribution of the Roman people. This sequence of offices is known as the "order of honors." Each of these roles lasts only one year, and to ascend to the next one, a new election is necessary. In the year preceding the election, one must continuously show oneself in the streets, "circulate" as the Romans say hence the word "ambition", and solicit the votes of the people. During this entire time, it is customary to wear a white toga, which gives the very sense of the word "candidate" or white garment.

Chapter 20

Roman Conquest and the Roman Army

In order to serve in the Roman army, one must first be a Roman citizen. It is necessary to have enough wealth to equip oneself at one's own expense, as the state does not provide any arms to its soldiers. Until 402 B.C., it did not even pay them. Therefore, only citizens who are provided with at least a small fortune are enrolled. The poor, known as the proletariat, are exempt from service, or rather, they have no right to serve. Every citizen who is rich enough to be admitted to the army owes the state twenty campaigns. Until these are completed, the man remains at the disposition of the consul, from the age of seventeen to forty-six. In Rome, as in the Greek cities, every man is at once a citizen and soldier. The Romans are a people of small proprietors disciplined in war. The Levy. When there was a need for soldiers, the consul ordered all citizens qualified for service to assemble at the Capitol. There, the officers elected by the people chose as many men as necessary to form the army. This was the enrollment, which the Romans called the Choice. Then came the military oath. The officers first took the oath, and then the rank and file. They swore to obey their general, to follow him wherever he led them, and to remain under the standards until he released them from their oath. One man pronounced the formula, and each in turn advanced and said, "I also." From this time, the army was bound to the general by the bonds of religion. Legions and Allies. The Roman army was initially called the Legion, or levy. When the population increased, several legions were formed. The legion was a body of 4,200 to 5,000 men, all Roman citizens. The smallest army had at least one legion, and every army commanded by a consul had at least two. However, the legions constituted hardly half of the Roman army. All the subject peoples in Italy were required to send troops, and these soldiers, who were called allies, were placed under the orders of Roman officers.

In the Roman army, the allies outnumbered the citizens of the legions. Typically, with four legions consisting of 16,800 men, there were also 20,000 archers and 40,000 horses from the allies. During the Second Punic War in 218 B.C., 26,000 citizens and 45,000 allies were called to serve. Therefore, the Roman people utilized both their citizens and subjects in warfare. Military exercises were conducted on the parade ground, the Campus Martius, on the opposite side of the Tiber, as Rome had no gymnasium. There, young men marched, ran, leaped under the weight of their arms, fenced with their swords, hurled javelins, wielded mattocks, and then swam across the Tiber, covered in dust and perspiration. Even the older men and generals joined in with the young men, as the Romans never ceased to exercise. During campaigns, the men were not allowed to be unoccupied. They were required to take exercise at least once a day, and when there was no enemy to fight or intrenchment to erect, they were employed in building roads, bridges, and aqueducts. The Roman soldier carried a heavy burden, consisting of his arms, utensils, rations for seventeen days, and a stake, totaling sixty Roman pounds. The army moved more rapidly as it was not encumbered with baggage. Each time a Roman army halted for camp, a surveyor traced a square enclosure, and the soldiers dug a deep ditch along its lines. The excavated earth was thrown inside, forming a bank that was fortified with stakes. The camp was thus defended by a ditch and a palisade. In this improvised fortress, the soldiers erected their tents, and the Praetorium, the general's tent, was set in the middle. Sentinels mounted guard throughout the night, preventing the army from being surprised.

The Arrangement of Forces

When facing the enemy, the soldiers did not form a solid mass like the Greeks. Instead, the legion was divided into small groups of 120 men, known as maniples, because they carried bundles of hay as standards. These maniples were arranged in a quincunx formation in three lines, with each separated from the neighboring maniple to maneuver separately. The soldiers of the first line maniples threw their javelins, drew their swords, and began the battle. If they were repulsed, they withdrew to the rear through the vacant spaces. The second line of maniples then marched to the combat. If it was repulsed, it fell back on the third line. The third line was composed of the best men of the legion and was equipped with lances. They received the others into their ranks and threw themselves on the enemy. The army was no longer a single mass incapable of maneuvering; the general could form his lines according to the nature of the ground. At Cynoscephalae, where the Roman legion and the Macedonian phalanx met for the first time, the ground was bristling with hills. On this rugged ground, the 16,000 Macedonian hoplites could not remain in order, their ranks were opened, and the Roman platoons threw themselves into the gaps and demolished the phalanx. Discipline. The Roman army obeyed strict discipline. The general had the right of life and death over all his men. The soldier who left his post or deserted in battle was condemned to death. The lictors bound him to a post, beat him with rods, and cut off his head. Alternatively, the soldiers may have killed him with blows of their staves. When an entire body of troops mutinied, the general separated the guilty into groups of ten and drew by lot one from every group to be executed. This was called decimation. The others were placed on a diet of barley bread and made to camp outside the lines, always in danger of surprise from the enemy. The Romans never admitted that their soldiers were conquered or taken prisoners. After the battle of Cannae, the 3,000 soldiers who escaped the carnage were sent by the senate to serve in Sicily without pay and honors until the enemy should be expelled from Italy. The 8,000 left in the camp were taken by Hannibal who offered to return them for a small ransom, but the senate refused to purchase them.

In the lands that were not yet fully under Roman control, the Romans established small garrisons of soldiers who founded towns that served as fortresses. These towns were called Colonies, and the lands around them were divided into small domains and given to the soldiers. Despite being Roman citizens, the colonists remained obedient to Rome. Unlike Greek colonies which often declared independence and even waged war against their mother cities, Roman colonies remained loyal. They were essentially Roman garrisons stationed in the midst of enemy territory. Most of these military posts were in Italy, but some were located in other places, such as Narbonne and Lyons, which were once Roman colonies. To maintain control over these territories and to transport their armies over long distances, the Romans constructed military roads. These roads were built in straight lines and made of limestone, stone, and sand. They covered the entire empire. Even today, in a country like France, one can find traces of these ancient Roman roads. The Roman people were constantly at war, and for five hundred years of the republic, the temple of Janus, the god of war, remained open. Only once was it closed, and that was for just a few years. Rome had the strongest army of the time, and it eventually conquered all other peoples and overcame the ancient world. Rome began by subjugating its neighboring peoples, such as the Latins, followed by the smaller peoples of the south, including the Volscians, the Aequians, and the Hernicans. Later, it conquered the Etruscans and the Samnites, and finally, the Greek cities. This was the most difficult and prolonged of Rome's conquests, beginning in the time of the kings and lasting for four centuries until 266.

In the early days of Rome, they found themselves fighting against their own people, those who were just as strong and courageous as they were. Those who refused to submit were wiped out, leaving behind only the desolate swamps of the Volscians, now known as the Pontine Marshes. Even three hundred years after the war, the forty-five camps of Decius and the eighty-six of Fabius were still visible in the land of the Samnites. Though the camps themselves had long since disappeared, the solitude of the area was a testament to the battles that had taken place there. When Rome ventured into Sicily, they found themselves at odds with Carthage, leading to the Punic Wars. There were three of these wars, the first lasting from 264 to 241. Rome emerged victorious, having taken control of Sicily. Legend has it that Rome had no warships at the time, but this is untrue, as the Roman navy had long been established. The second war, from 218 to 201, was led by Hannibal. The third and final war was a brutal one, resulting in the destruction of Carthage and the subjugation of Africa by Rome.

These were the wars that shook Rome to its core. Carthage boasted a superior navy, but its soldiers were mercenaries, fighting not for their homeland but for coin. They were lawless and brutal, especially under the command of a general like Hannibal. Hannibal, the scion of the powerful Barcas family, led the Carthaginian forces in the second war and nearly succeeded in capturing Rome. His father, Hamilcar, had fought in the first Punic war and later attempted to conquer Spain. Hannibal was just a child when he accompanied his father on these campaigns. Before departing, Hamilcar made young Hannibal swear to forever hate Rome after a sacrifice to the gods. Hannibal grew up among the soldiers and became the best horseman and archer in the army. War was his sole purpose in life, and he required only a horse and weapons. He was so beloved that when the army's commander, Hasdrubal, died, the soldiers elected Hannibal as their new leader without waiting for orders from the Carthaginian senate. At just 21 years old, he commanded an army that answered only to him. He began the war by laying siege to Saguntum, a Greek colony allied with Rome, and ultimately destroyed it, ignoring the senate's orders. Hannibal's greatness lay in his audacity. He didn't wait for the Romans to attack; instead, he marched into Italy to take the fight to them. Lacking a navy, he chose to march through the Pyrenees, cross the Rhone and the Alps, and secure the support of the Gallic peoples. He led an army of 60,000 African and Spanish mercenaries, along with 37 war elephants. When a Gallic tribe tried to block his path at the Rhone, Hannibal sent a detachment to attack them from behind, while the bulk of his army crossed the river on boats and the elephants on rafts.

He journeyed up the valley of the Isere and reached the Alps in late October, crossing them despite the snow and attacks from the mountain folk. Many men and horses tumbled down the cliffs, but after nine days, he reached the summits. The descent was treacherous, with the pass covered in ice, forcing him to carve a path out of the rock. By the time he reached the plain, his army was halved. Hannibal faced three Roman armies, defeating them all at the Ticinus and Trebia rivers and near Lake Trasimene in Etruria. As he advanced, his army grew, with warriors from Cisalpine Gaul joining him against the Romans. He positioned himself beyond Rome in Apulia, where the Roman army attacked him. Though his army was half the size of theirs, he had African cavalrymen on swift horses. He formed his lines in the plain of Cannae, with the sun in the Romans' faces and the wind driving dust at them. The Roman army was surrounded and nearly destroyed in 216. Though many expected Hannibal to march on Rome, he deemed himself too weak to do so. The Carthaginian senate sent no reinforcements. Hannibal tried to take Naples and have Rome attacked by the king of Macedon but only managed to gain a few towns, which Rome besieged and destroyed. Hannibal remained in southern Italy for nine years. Eventually, his brother Hasdrubal set out with the army of Spain to assist him, making his way almost to central Italy. The two Carthaginian armies marched to unite their forces, each opposed by a Roman army under the command of a consul. Nero, facing Hannibal, boldly crossed central Italy to unite with his colleague, who was entrenched against Hasdrubal. One morning, Hasdrubal heard the Roman trumpets sounding twice, signaling two consuls in the camp. He believed his brother was defeated and retreated. The Romans pursued him, and he and his entire army were massacred. Nero then rejoined the army he had left before Hannibal and threw Hasdrubal's head into the Carthaginian camp in 207. Hannibal, left with only his own troops, remained in Calabria for five more years.

The Roman army descended upon Africa, forcing Hannibal to leave Italy. He massacred the Italian soldiers who refused to accompany him and set sail for Carthage in the year 203. The battle of Zama in 202 marked the end of the war. Hannibal had hoped to draw the Romans into his lines and surround them, but Scipio, the Roman general, kept his troops in order. On a second attack, Scipio put the enemy's army to rout. Carthage was forced to negotiate for peace, relinquishing everything outside of Africa and ceding Spain to the Romans. They agreed to surrender their navy and elephants, pay over ten million dollars, and not make war without Rome's permission. Hannibal reorganized Carthage for a new war, which concerned the Romans. They demanded that the Carthaginians put him to death. Hannibal fled to Antiochus, king of Syria, and proposed inciting a revolt in Italy against Rome. However, Antiochus distrusted Hannibal and invaded Greece, where his army was captured. Hannibal then withdrew to the king of Bithynia. The Romans sent Flamininus to capture him, but Hannibal, seeing his house surrounded, took the poison he always had by him in 183. The Greek kings, successors of Alexander, divided the Orient among themselves. The most powerful of these kings took up war against Rome, but they were defeated. Philip, the king of Macedon, was defeated in 197, his son Perseus in 168, and Antiochus, the king of Syria, in 190. From this time on, the Romans had a free field and conquered all the lands that were useful to them one by one: Macedon in 148, the kingdom of Pergamum in 129, the rest of Asia from 74 to 64 after the defeat of Mithridates, and Egypt in 30. With the exception of the Macedonians, the Orient opposed the Romans with mercenaries or undisciplined barbarians who fled at the first attack. In the great victory over Antiochus at Magnesia, only 350 Romans were killed. At Chaeronea, Sulla was victorious with the loss of only twelve men. The other kings, now terrified, obeyed the Senate without resistance.

Antiochus the Great, king of Syria, had conquered a portion of Egypt. However, Popilius, acting under the command of the Senate, ordered him to abandon his conquest. Antiochus hesitated, but Popilius, taking a rod in his hand, drew a circle around the king and said, "Before you move from this circle, give an answer to the Senate." Antiochus submitted and surrendered Egypt. The king of Numidia asked the Senate to regard his kingdom as the property of the Roman people. Prusias, the king of Bithynia, prostrated himself before the Senate in the garb of a freedman with a shaved head. Mithridates, the king of Pontus, was the only one who resisted, but after thirty years of war, he was driven from his states and compelled to take his life by poison. The Romans found it more challenging to conquer the barbarous and warlike peoples of the West. It took a century to conquer Spain. The shepherd Viriathus made guerilla warfare on them in the mountains of Portugal from 149 to 139 B.C., overwhelmed five armies, and even compelled a consul to treat for peace. The Senate got rid of him by assassination. Against the single town of Numantia, they had to send Scipio, the best general of Rome. The little and obscure peoples of Corsica, Sardinia, and the mountains of Genoa or the Ligurians, were always reviving the war with Rome. But the most indomitable of all were the Gauls. Occupying the whole of the valley of the Po, they threw themselves on Italy to the south. One of their bands had taken Rome in 390. Their big white bodies, long red mustaches, blue eyes, and savage yells terrified the Roman soldiers. As soon as their approach was learned, consternation seized Rome, and the Senate proclaimed the levy of the whole army or what they called the "Gallic tumult". These wars were the bloodiest but the shortest. The first, which lasted from 225 to 222 B.C., gave the Romans all Cisalpine Gaul or northern Italy; the second the Rhone lands namely Languedoc, Provence, Dauphine; the third, from 58 to 51 B.C., all the rest of Gaul.

Roman Warfare

When a general emerged victorious in battle, the Senate granted him the privilege of celebrating a triumph, a grand religious procession to the temple of Jupiter. The magistrates and senators led the way, followed by chariots filled with spoils of war, captives bound by their feet, and finally, the victorious general on a golden chariot pulled by four horses and adorned with laurel. His soldiers trailed behind, chanting the solemn refrain "Io, Triomphe." The procession paraded through the city in festive attire and ascended to the Capitol, where the victor presented his laurel to Jupiter and thanked him for granting victory. After the ceremony, the captives were imprisoned, executed, or left to die in dungeons. The triumph of Aemilius Paullus, conqueror of Macedon, lasted three days. The first day featured a procession of 250 chariots bearing pictures and statues, the second day showcased weapons trophies and 25 casks of silver, and the third day displayed gold vases and 120 sacrificial bulls. King Perseus walked at the rear, dressed in black and surrounded by his chained followers and three young children who begged for pity. In ancient times, the victor claimed everything that belonged to the defeated, including weapons, camp supplies, treasure, movable property, livestock, men, women, and children. In Rome, the booty did not belong to the soldiers but to the people. The prisoners were enslaved, and the property was sold, with the profits going to the public treasury. Thus, every war was a profitable enterprise. The kings of Asia had amassed enormous wealth, which Roman generals transported to Rome. The conqueror of Carthage deposited over 100,000 pounds of silver in the treasury, while the victor over Antiochus contributed 140,000 pounds of silver and 1,000 pounds of gold, not including the minted metals. The conqueror of Persia remitted 120,000,000 sesterces.

The Allies of Rome were many, for in the ancient world, there were countless kings, small peoples, and cities that despised one another. They never banded together to resist, and so Rome absorbed them one by one. Those who were not attacked remained neutral and apathetic, and often even joined forces with the Romans. In most of Rome's wars, she did not fight alone but had the aid of allies. Against Carthage, she had the king of Numidia; against the king of Macedon, the Aetolians; and against the king of Syria, the Rhodians. In the east, many kings proudly took on the title of "Ally of the Roman People." In countries divided into small states, some peoples called upon the Romans to help them against their neighbors, welcoming the Roman army, providing it with provisions, and guiding it to the borders of the enemy's land. Thus, in Gaul, it was Marseilles that brought the Romans into the valley of the Rhone, and it was the people of Autun, the Aedui, who allowed them to establish themselves in the heart of the land. The Romans did not set out with the intention of conquering the world. Even after winning Italy and Carthage, they waited a century before subduing the Orient, which lay at their feet. They conquered, it seems, without a predetermined plan, simply because they all had an interest in conquest. The magistrates who led the armies saw conquest as a means of securing the honors of triumph and the surest instrument for gaining popularity. The most powerful statesmen in Rome, Papirius, Fabius, the two Scipios, Cato, Marius, Sulla, Pompey, Caesar, and Crassus, were victorious generals. The nobles who made up the Senate benefited from the increase in Roman subjects, and they allied themselves with these subjects as governors to receive their homage and gifts. For the knights, that is, the bankers, merchants, and contractors, every new conquest was a new land to exploit. The people themselves profited from the spoils taken from the enemy. After the treasure of the king of Macedon was deposited in the public chest, taxes were finally abolished. As for the soldiers, as soon as war was waged in wealthy lands, they received immense sums from their generals, not to mention what they took from the defeated. The Romans conquered the world less for glory than for the profits of war.

The Roman Conquest and Its Effects

The Roman Empire was a vast dominion that extended from Spain to Asia Minor, encompassing all the lands around the Mediterranean. However, the conquered territories were not annexed, nor did their inhabitants become citizens of Rome. They were merely subjects under the domination of the Roman people, much like the Hindus are subjects of England today. When a people surrendered to Rome, they were expected to say, "We surrender to you the people, the town, the fields, the waters, the gods of the boundaries, and movable property; all things which belonged to the gods and to men we deliver to the power of the Roman people." This act made the Roman people the proprietor of everything the vanquished possessed, including their persons. Sometimes, the inhabitants were sold into slavery, as Aemilius Paullus did with 150,000 Epeirots who surrendered to him. However, Rome usually left the conquered people with their liberty, but their territory became part of the domain of the Roman people. The land was divided into three equal parts. One part was returned to the people, but they had to pay a tribute in money or grain, and Rome reserved the right to recall the land at will. The fields and pastures were farmed out to publicans. Finally, part of the uncultivated land was given to the first occupant, and every Roman citizen had the right to settle there and cultivate it. Thus, the Roman Conquest had a profound impact on the conquered peoples, who were forced to acknowledge the power of Rome and submit to its rule. However, it also brought about significant changes in land ownership and agriculture, which had lasting effects on the region.

The agrarian laws of Rome caused great turmoil as they dealt with the public land. No Roman had the right to evict the current occupants, as the boundaries of these lands were considered sacred and could not be disturbed. The agrarian laws allowed the people to reclaim the lands of the public domain and distribute them as property to citizens. This was legally within their rights, as all of the lands belonged to the people. However, some citizens had been allowed to occupy these lands for centuries and had come to regard them as their own. They bought, sold, and bequeathed them, and taking them away would cause great harm to many people. In Italy, for example, the result would be the expulsion of all the people of a city. Augustus took away the land of the inhabitants of Mantua, including that of Vergil, who was able to regain his property through his poetic skills. The lands that were recovered were sometimes given to poor Roman citizens, but more often to old soldiers. Sulla gave land to 120,000 veterans at the expense of the people of Etruria. The agrarian laws posed a threat to all the subjects of Rome, and it was a benefit of the emperors that they were abolished.

Chapter 21

The Peoples of the Conquered Lands

The people of conquered lands were not granted Roman citizenship, but were instead considered strangers or peregrini, who remained subjects of the Roman Empire. They were required to pay tribute, including a tithe of their crops, a silver tax, and a capitation tax. They were also required to obey Romans of every rank. However, since the Roman people could not manage the provinces themselves, they sent a magistrate to govern in their stead. The area governed by a magistrate was known as a province, which means "mission." By the end of the republic, there were seventeen provinces: ten in Europe, five in Asia, and two in Africa. Many of these provinces were quite large, with Gaul being divided into only four provinces and Spain into only two. Cicero once said, "The provinces are the domains of the Roman people." However, if the Roman people made all these peoples subjects, it was not for their benefit, but for their own. Their goal was not to govern, but to exploit. The Proconsuls. To govern a province, the Roman people always appointed a magistrate, such as a consul or a praetor, who was finishing his term in office and whose authority was extended. Like a consul, a proconsul had absolute power and could exercise it as he pleased. He was the sole authority in his province, with no other magistrates to challenge his power, no tribunes of the people to veto his actions, and no senate to oversee him. He commanded the troops, led them into battle, and stationed them wherever he saw fit. He sat in his tribunal or praetorium, imposing fines, imprisonment, or death. He issued decrees that had the force of law. He was the embodiment of the Roman people and had complete authority over himself. Tyranny and Oppression of the Proconsuls. This governor, who faced no resistance, was a true despot. He arrested, imprisoned, beat, or executed anyone who displeased him. One Roman orator tells the story of a governor's whim: "At last the consul came to Termini, where his wife took a fancy to bathe in the men's bath. All the men who were bathing there were driven out. The wife of the consul complained that it had not been done quickly enough and that the baths were not well prepared. The consul had a post set up in a public place, brought to it one of the most eminent men of the city, stripped him of his garments, and had him beaten with rods."

The governor of the province took as much money as he pleased, treating it as his personal property. He had plenty of ways to exploit it. He looted the treasuries of the cities, took statues and jewels from the temples, and demanded money or grain from the wealthy inhabitants. Because he could station troops wherever he pleased, the cities paid him money to keep the soldiers away. He could condemn people to death at will, so individuals paid him security money. If he demanded art or money, who would dare to refuse him? His entourage followed his lead, pillaging in his name and even under his protection. The governor was in a hurry to accumulate his wealth, as he had to make his fortune in one year. After he left for Rome, another governor arrived and started the process all over again. There was a law that prohibited governors from accepting gifts, and a tribunal, since 149, specifically for the crime of extortion. However, this tribunal was made up of nobles and Roman knights who would not condemn their fellow citizens. According to Cicero, the main result of this system was to force the governor to take even more plunder from the province to bribe the judges of the tribunal. It is no surprise that the term "proconsul" became a synonym for despot. The most infamous of these appointed brigands was Verres, the propraetor of Sicily. Cicero spoke out against him for political reasons, delivering seven famous speeches. But many other governors were likely just as bad as Verres.

The Tax Collectors

In every province of the Roman Empire, the people of Rome enjoyed significant revenues from various sources, such as customs, mines, imposts, grain lands, and pastures. These revenues were leased out to groups of contractors known as publicans. The publicans purchased the right to collect taxes from a specific location on behalf of the Roman government, and the people of the province were obligated to obey them as representatives of Rome. Consequently, in every province, there were numerous companies of publicans, each with a retinue of clerks and collectors. These men acted as masters, extorting more money than was due, forcing debtors into poverty, and even selling them into slavery. In Asia, they went so far as to exile inhabitants without any justification. When Marius demanded soldiers from the king of Bithynia, the king replied, that thanks to the publicans, he had only women, children, and old people left as citizens. The Romans were well aware of these excesses. Cicero wrote to his brother, who was then a governor, "If you find a way to satisfy the publicans without destroying the provincials, it is because you possess the qualities of a god." However, the publicans were judged in tribunals, and even the proconsuls obeyed them. Scaurus, the proconsul of Asia and a man of unyielding integrity, tried to prevent them from plundering his province. Upon his return to Rome however, he was accused and convicted by the publicans. The publicans even oppressed the peaceful and obedient inhabitants of the East. At the command of Mithridates, 100,000 Romans were massacred in a single night. A century later, during the time of Christ, the term "publican" was synonymous with thief.

The Bankers

The Romans had amassed a great deal of silver from the lands they conquered, leaving Rome with an abundance of silver and the provinces with almost nothing. Borrowing rates in Rome were four or five percent, while in the provinces, the rates were no less than twelve percent. The bankers would borrow money in Rome and loan it in the provinces, particularly to kings or cities. When the people were unable to repay the principal and interest, the bankers followed the example of the publicans. In 84 A.D., the cities of Asia borrowed money to pay a massive war levy, and fourteen years later, the interest alone had increased the debt to six times the original amount. The bankers forced the cities to sell their art objects, and parents even sold their children. A few years later, one of the most highly regarded Romans of his time, Brutus the Stoic, loaned the city of Salamis in Cyprus a sum of money at forty-eight percent interest or four percent per month. Scaptius, his business manager, demanded the sum with interest, but the city was unable to pay. Scaptius then went to the proconsul Appius, secured a squadron of cavalry, and went to Salamis to blockade the Senate in its hall of assembly. Five senators died of starvation. No defense for the Provincials. The provincials had no recourse against these tyrants. The governor supported the publicans, and the Roman army and people supported the governor. Even if a Roman citizen could sue the plunderers of the provinces, a governor was inviolable and could not be accused until he had given up his office. While he was in office, there was nothing to do but watch him plunder. If he were accused upon his return to Rome, he appeared before a tribunal of nobles and publicans who were more interested in supporting him than in rendering justice to the provincials. If, by chance, the tribunal condemned him, exile exempted him from further penalty, and he went to a city in Italy to enjoy his plunder. This punishment meant nothing to him and was not even a loss. Consequently, the provincials preferred to appease their governor by submitting to him. They treated him like a king, flattered him, sent gifts, and erected statues of him. In Asia, they often built altars and temples for him and adored him as a god.

Slavery existed since ancient times, and the Romans were no strangers to it. Whenever they won a war, they claimed every prisoner of war and every inhabitant of a captured city as their own. If they weren't killed, they were enslaved. This was their right, and they exercised it to the fullest. The captives were considered part of the loot and were either sold to slave merchants who followed the army or auctioned off if taken to Rome. Thousands of captives, both men and women and children born to slave mothers were sold as slaves after every war. The conquered peoples were the primary source of the slave supply for the Romans. The slaves were regarded as property and not people.

They had no rights, could not be citizens, could not own property, and could not be husbands or fathers. Slave marriages were considered taboo, and the masters had complete control over their slaves. They could send them anywhere, make them work beyond their strength, ill-treat them, beat them, torture them, and even kill them without being held accountable. The slaves had to submit to their master's whims, and the Romans believed that they had no conscience and were only meant to obey blindly. If a slave resisted or fled, the state would assist the master in subduing or recovering them. Anyone who gave refuge to a fugitive slave was liable to be charged with theft. Slaves outnumbered free men by a considerable margin. Wealthy citizens owned between 10,000 to 20,000 slaves, and some had enough to constitute a real army. Caecilius Claudius Isidorius, who was once a slave, came to possess more than 4,000 slaves. Horace, who had seven slaves, considered it a modest patrimony. In Rome, having only three slaves was considered a mark of poverty.

Urban Slaves

The Roman aristocrats, much like modern-day Orientals, took pleasure in surrounding themselves with a multitude of servants. In a grand Roman household, hundreds of slaves lived, each organized for specific services. There were slaves to tend to the furniture, silverware, and art objects; slaves for the wardrobe, valets, chambermaids, cooks, bath attendants, and the master of the house and his assistants. There were also slaves to escort the master and mistress on the street, litter-bearers, coachmen, grooms, secretaries, readers, copyists, physicians, teachers, actors, musicians, and artisans of all kinds. In every great house, grain was ground, flax was spun, and garments were woven. Others worked in workshops, manufacturing objects that the master sold for profit. Some were hired out as masons or sailors; Crassus even had 500 carpenter slaves. These classes of slaves were known as "slaves of the city." Rural Slaves. Every large estate was cultivated by a group of slaves. They were the laborers, shepherds, vine dressers, gardeners, and fishermen, grouped in squads of ten. An overseer, himself a slave, supervised them. The proprietor made it his mission to produce everything on his lands: "He buys nothing; everything that he consumes he raises at home," is the compliment paid to the wealthy. Therefore, the Romans kept a large number of country slaves, known as such. A Roman estate bore a strong resemblance to a village; in fact, it was called a "villa." The name has been preserved: what the French call "ville" since the Middle Ages is only the old Roman estate increased in size.

Treatment of Slaves

The treatment of slaves varied greatly depending on the character of their masters. Some masters, such as Cicero, Seneca, and Pliny, were enlightened and humane. They fed their slaves well, conversed with them, and even allowed them to sit at the table with them. These masters also permitted their slaves to have families and accumulate small fortunes, known as the peculium. However, there were some who treated their slaves as if they were animals. They punished them cruelly and even put them to death for the slightest whim. Vedius Pollio, a freedman of Augustus, was known to keep lampreys in his fish pond. When one of his slaves carelessly broke a vase, Pollio had him thrown into the fish pond to be devoured by the lampreys. Philosopher Seneca described the violent cruelty of these masters, saying, "If a slave coughs or sneezes during a meal, if he pursues the flies too slowly, if he lets a key fall noisily to the floor, we fall into a great rage. If he replies with too much spirit, if his countenance shows ill humor, have we any right to have him flogged? Often we strike too hard and shatter a limb or break a tooth." Even philosopher Epictetus, who was a slave himself, had his ankle fractured by his master in this way. Women were no more humane than men when it came to the treatment of slaves. Ovid once paid a compliment to a woman, saying, "Many times she had her hair dressed in my presence, but never did she thrust her needle into the arm of the serving woman." Public opinion did not condemn these cruelties. Juvenal wrote about a woman who was angry at one of her slaves. "Crucify him," she said. "By what crime has the slave merited this punishment? Blockhead! Is a slave, then, a man? It may be that he has done nothing. I wish it, I order it, my will is reason enough."

The law was as harsh as custom. Even in the first century A.D., if a master was killed in his own home, all of his slaves were put to death. When some people wanted to abolish this law, Thraseas, a highly respected philosopher, stood up in the Senate and demanded that the law be upheld. One of the most dreaded places for a slave was the ergastulum, an underground prison with narrow windows too high to reach. Slaves who had angered their masters were forced to spend the night there, and during the day they were sent to work with heavy iron chains. Many were even branded with a red-hot iron. In ancient times, there were no mills run by machines. Instead, slaves were forced to grind grain by hand, as a form of punishment. The mill was like a prison for convicts. "There," says Plautus, "moan the wicked slaves who are fed on polenta; there resound the noise of whips and the clanking of chains." Three centuries later, in the second century, Apuleius the novelist, describes the interior of a mill as follows: "Gods! what poor shrunken-up men! With white skin striped with blows of the whip, they wear only the shreds of a tunic; bent forward, head shaved, the feet held in a chain, the body deformed by the heat of the fire, the eyelids eaten away by the fumes, everything covered with grain-dust."

The character of the slaves was shaped by their brutal existence, either toiling under the lash or languishing in idleness. Some became melancholy and savage, while others were lazy and subservient. The most energetic among them even chose to end their own lives. As Cato the Elder observed, the slave's life was reduced to working or sleeping. Many lost all sense of honor, and their actions were deemed "servile," or like those of a slave. The slaves themselves did not leave behind written accounts of their thoughts and feelings about their masters. However, the masters were acutely aware of the hatred that surrounded them. Pliny the Younger once remarked that the assassination of a master by his slaves at the bath was a constant danger. Another writer noted that more Romans had fallen victim to the hate of their slaves than to the tyranny of rulers. Slave revolts, known as the servile wars, erupted at various times, particularly in Sicily and southern Italy where slaves were armed to guard herds. The most famous of these uprisings was led by Spartacus. A group of seventy gladiators escaped from Capua, seized a chariot loaded with weapons, and established themselves as a force to be reckoned with. Other slaves flocked to their banner, and soon they had an army. The slaves defeated three Roman armies sent against them, but Spartacus had a grander vision. He wanted to lead his followers across the entire Italian peninsula and return to his homeland of Thrace, where he had been captured and enslaved. However, the undisciplined ranks of the rebels were no match for the forces of Crassus, and they were ultimately crushed. All the revolutionaries were put to death. Rome responded by prohibiting slaves from carrying weapons ever again and even went so far as to execute a shepherd for killing a boar with a spear.

The Path to Citizenship

Rome was no stranger to cruelty, especially towards its subjects and slaves. However, unlike the Greek cities, Rome did not expel them. Instead, the alien could become a Roman citizen through the will of the Roman people. This favor was often granted, and sometimes even bestowed upon whole peoples at once. The Latins were made citizens in one fell swoop, followed by the Italians in 89, and the people of Cisalpine Gaul in 46. With these actions, all of Italy's inhabitants became the equals of the Romans. Slaves, too, could be granted freedom by their masters and soon became citizens themselves. This is why the Roman people, gradually wearing themselves thin, were able to renew themselves through accessions from subjects and slaves. The number of citizens grew with each census, rising from 250,000 to 700,000. Unlike Sparta, the Roman city did not empty but rather replenished itself little by little with all those it had conquered.

Chapter 22

Greek and Oriental Influence

The Romans gained a clearer understanding of the Greeks and Orientals after their conquests. Thousands of foreigners were brought to Rome as slaves or came to make their fortune, establishing themselves as physicians, professors, diviners, or actors. Generals, officers, and soldiers lived in the midst of Asia, and the Romans gradually adopted the customs and new beliefs. This transformation began with the first Macedonian War in about 200 B.C. and continued until the end of the empire. Changes in Religion. The Roman gods had only a slight resemblance to the Greek gods, even in name. However, in the majority of the divinities of Rome, the Greeks recognized or believed they recognized their own. The Roman gods had neither precise form nor history, making confusion easier. Every Roman god was represented in the form of a Greek god, and a history was made of the adventures of this god. The Latin Jupiter was confused with the Greek Zeus, Juno with Hera, Minerva, the goddess of memory, with Pallas, the goddess of wisdom, and Diana, the female counterpart of Janus, united with Artemis, the brilliant huntress. Hercules, the god of the enclosure, was assimilated to Herakles, the victor over monsters. Greek mythology insinuated itself under Latin names, and the gods of Rome found themselves transformed into Greek gods. The fusion was so complete that we have preserved the custom of designating the Greek gods by their Latin names. We still call Artemis Diana and Pallas Minerva. The Greeks had adopted an oriental god, Bacchus, the god of the vintage, and the Romans began to adore him as well. The worshippers of Bacchus celebrated his cult at night and in secret. Only the initiated were admitted to the mysteries of the Bacchanals, who swore not to reveal any of the ceremonies. However, a woman dared to denounce the Bacchanalian ceremonies that occurred in Rome in 186 to the Senate. The Senate made an inquiry, discovered 7,000 persons, men and women, who had participated in the mysteries, and had them put to death.

In ancient Rome, the gods and goddesses of foreign lands were not only welcomed but also revered. Oriental superstitions were rampant, and the Senate itself sought out the goddess Cybele during the war with Hannibal in 205. Her priests, dressed in oriental fashion, followed her through the streets, playing fifes and cymbals and begging for alms. Chaldean sorcerers also found their way to Italy, and even the great generals of Rome consulted them. Martha, a prophetess from Syria, offered victory over the barbarians to the Senate during the Cimbri invasion of 104. Although they drove her out, the Roman women brought her to the camp, and Marius, the general-in-chief, kept her by his side until the end of the war. Sulla, too, was guided by the goddess of Cappadocia on his journey to Italy. Despite the prevalence of such beliefs, there were also skeptics who scoffed at the old religion. Carneades, an Athenian ambassador, spoke publicly in Rome, drawing crowds of curious youth. The Senate eventually ordered him to leave the city, but philosophers continued to teach in Athens and Rhodes, attracting Roman students seeking knowledge. In fact, in the third century B.C., a Greek named Euhemerus wrote a book to prove that the gods were merely deified ancient men, and Jupiter himself had been a king of Crete. This book was successful and even translated into Latin by the poet Ennius. The nobles of Rome often mocked their gods, yet still maintained the cult of the old religion. Thus, Roman society was both superstitious and skeptical for over a century.

The ancient Romans were known for their diligence in farming, fighting, and religious practices. They held the ideal of the "grave" man, exemplified by figures such as Cincinnatus, who was offered the dictatorship while plowing his fields, and Fabricius, who owned only a silver cup and salt cellar. Curius Dentatus, conqueror of the Samnites, famously refused a bribe, stating that he preferred commanding those who had gold to having it himself. These anecdotes, whether true or not, represented the values of the ancient Romans. As customs began to change, one man stood out for his adherence to the "customs of the fathers": Cato the Elder. Born in 232 in the village of Tusculum, Cato worked as a laborer in his youth before joining the army at age seventeen to fight in the campaigns against Hannibal. Despite his lack of noble birth, Cato became popular for his energy, honesty, and austerity. He rose through the political ranks, serving as quaestor, aedile, praetor, consul, and censor. Like the old Romans, he was known for his stern and honest demeanor. As quaestor, he even challenged the expenses of the consul, Scipio, who replied that he had no need for such an exacting quaestor. As a praetor in Sardinia, Cato refused money offered to him by the province for entertainment expenses.

As consul, he spoke with great fervor in support of the Oppian law, which forbade Roman women from wearing expensive clothing. The women eventually complied, and the law was repealed. Cato was then sent to lead the army in Spain, where he conquered 400 towns and amassed a great fortune, which he deposited in the public treasury. Before leaving, he even sold his horse to save on transportation costs. As censor, Cato removed many prominent individuals from the senate list due to their extravagant spending. He also levied high taxes on women's clothing, jewelry, and transportation, taxing them at ten times their value. After being granted a triumph, Cato returned to the army in Macedonia as a regular officer. Throughout his life, Cato battled against the new type of noble, who were extravagant and refined. He particularly criticized the Scipio family, accusing them of misusing state funds. In return, he was sued in court forty-four times but was always acquitted. At his farm, Cato worked alongside his slaves, ate with them, and even punished them with his own hand when necessary. In his book on Agriculture, written for his son, he recorded all the traditional sayings of the Roman peasantry. He believed it was his duty to become wealthy, stating that "a widow can decrease her property, but a man ought to increase his. He who gains more than he inherits is worthy of fame and blessed by the gods." When he found that agriculture was not profitable enough, Cato invested in merchant ships. He joined forces with fifty others and together they built fifty commercial ships, sharing the risks and profits equally. Cato was a hard worker, a skilled soldier, and an opponent of luxury, always eager to increase his wealth. He was the epitome of the old-fashioned Roman.

The New Ways

In contrast to their ancestors, many Romans, particularly the nobles, were fascinated by and emulated foreigners. Leading the way were the generals who had firsthand experience of Greece and the Orient: Scipio, who defeated the king of Syria; Flamininus and Aemilius Paullus, who conquered the kings of Macedon; and later, Lucullus, who defeated the king of Armenia. They were appalled by the crude and vulgar lifestyle of their forebears and adopted a more luxurious and pleasurable way of life. Gradually, all the nobles and the wealthy followed their lead. One hundred and fifty years later, in Italy, all the great lived in Greek or Oriental fashion. Oriental Extravagance. In the East, the Romans found inspiration in the royal successors of Alexander, who possessed vast wealth. All the treasure that was not used to pay mercenaries was squandered by the court. These Oriental kings indulged their vanity by flaunting gleaming robes, precious stones, silver furniture, and golden plates, and by surrounding themselves with a multitude of useless servants, throwing money to the people who gathered to admire them. The Romans, who were very vain and had a taste for art but lacked refinement, enjoyed this type of luxury. They cared little for beauty or comfort and only thought of ostentation. They built houses with vast gardens adorned with statues and sumptuous villas that projected into the sea amidst enormous gardens. They surrounded themselves with troops of slaves. They and their wives wore garments made of gauze, silk, and gold instead of linen. At their banquets, they spread embroidered carpets, purple coverings, and gold and silver plates. Sulla had one hundred and fifty silver dishes, and Marcus Drusus's plates weighed 10,000 pounds. While the common people continued to sit at the table according to old Italian custom, the rich adopted the Oriental custom of reclining on couches at their meals. At the same time, the affected and expensive cuisine of the East was introduced, featuring exotic fish, peacock brains, and bird tongues.

From the second century A.D., the extravagance was such that a consul who died in 152 A.D. could say in his will: "As true glory does not consist in vain pomp but in the merits of the dead and of one's ancestors, I bid my children not to spend on my funeral ceremonies more than a million as". Greek Humanity. In Greece, the Romans saw the monuments, the statues, and the pictures which had crowded their cities for centuries; they came to know their learned people and the philosophers. Some of the Romans acquired a taste for the beautiful and for the life of the spirit. The Scipios surrounded themselves with cultivated Greeks. Aemilius Paullus asked from all the booty taken by him from Macedon only the library of King Perseus; he had his children taught by Greek preceptors. It was then the fashion in Rome to speak, and even to write in Greek. The nobles desired to appear as connoisseurs in painting and sculpture; they imported statues by the thousand, the famous bronzes of Corinth, and they heaped these up in their houses. Thus Verres possessed a whole gallery of objects of art that he had stolen in Sicily. Gradually the Romans assumed a gloss of Greek art and literature. This new culture was called "humanity," as opposed to the "rusticity" of the old Roman peasants. It was little else than gloss; the Romans had realized, but slightly, that beauty and truth were to be sought for their own sakes; art and science always remained objects of luxury and parade. Even in the time of Cicero the soldier, the peasant, the politician, the man of affairs, and the advocate were alone regarded as truly occupied. Writing, composing, contributing to science, philosophy, or criticism-all this was called "being at leisure." Artists and scholars were never regarded in Rome as the equals of the rich merchant. Lucian, a Greek writer, said, "If you would be a Pheidias, if you would make a thousand masterpieces, nobody will care to imitate you, for as skillful as you are, you will always pass for an artisan, a man who lives by the work of his hands."

Lucullus, a shining example of the new Roman, was born in 145 to a noble and wealthy family, which allowed him to easily rise through the ranks of politics. Even in his earliest campaigns, he was known for his generosity towards the defeated. As consul, he led the army against Mithridates and discovered that the people of Asia were furious with the banditry and brutality of the tax collectors. Lucullus made it his mission to put an end to these abuses and even forbade his soldiers from looting conquered cities. This won him the love of the Asians and the enmity of the tax collectors and soldiers who plotted to have him recalled. Despite this, he defeated Mithridates and was pursuing him with the help of the king of Armenia when his command was taken away and given to Pompey, the favorite of the tax collectors. Lucullus then retired to enjoy the wealth he had accumulated in Asia. He had celebrated gardens near Rome, a villa in Naples partially built in the sea, and a summer palace in Tusculum filled with a museum of art objects. During the beautiful season, he spent his time in Tusculum surrounded by friends, scholars, and men of letters, reading Greek authors and discussing literature and philosophy. Numerous stories are told of Lucullus' extravagance. Once, when dining alone, he found his table to be too simple and reprimanded the cook, who explained that there were no guests. "Don't you know," responded Lucullus, "that Lucullus is dining with Lucullus today?" On another occasion, he invited Caesar and Cicero to dine with him but agreed to their condition that he does not change his usual arrangements. Lucullus simply instructed a slave to prepare dinner in the Hall of Apollo. A sumptuous feast was laid out, and the guests were amazed. Lucullus explained that he had given no specific orders and that the cost of his dinners was determined by the hall in which they were held. Dinners in the Hall of Apollo were not to cost less than 10,000 dollars. When a praetor asked Lucullus if he could borrow one hundred purple robes for a grand spectacle, Lucullus offered him two hundred instead.

Lucullus was the embodiment of modernity, while Cato represented the customs of old. To the ancients, Cato was the epitome of Roman virtue, while Lucullus was seen as a degenerate. Lucullus had abandoned the ways of his forefathers, and in doing so, he had gained a more expansive, elevated, and refined spirit, as well as a greater sense of humanity towards his slaves and subjects. In the days of Polybius, the old Romans taught their children only how to read.

However, the new Romans hired Greek instructors to teach their children a broader range of subjects. Greek schools of poetry, rhetoric, and music were established in Rome, and the great families took sides on whether to embrace the old or new ways. Nevertheless, there remained a bias against music and dance, as they were seen as being fit only for the stage and not for people of good breeding. Scipio Aemilianus, the champion of the Greeks, was outraged by the existence of a dancing school that was attended by freeborn children and young girls. He could not fathom why nobles would allow their children to be taught such things. When he visited the school, he saw more than 500 boys and girls, including a twelve-year-old boy who was the son of a candidate, dancing to the sound of castanets. Sallust, when speaking of a Roman woman of questionable character, remarked that she played the lyre and danced better than was appropriate for a woman of good reputation.

The Changing Role of Women

In ancient Rome, women were deeply involved in the religious and luxurious practices of the East. They eagerly participated in the Bacchanals and the mysteries of Isis, often in large groups. Despite attempts to limit their extravagance through sumptuary laws, women were eventually allowed to follow the lead of men and indulge in opulent lifestyles. This led to noble women abandoning their homes and taking part in public life, attending the theater, circus, baths, and other gatherings with great fanfare. Unfortunately, many of these women were idle and ignorant and quickly became corrupt. While there were still some women of fine character among the nobility, they were the exception rather than the rule. The traditional family structure began to break down, and although Roman law still gave husbands power over their wives, a new form of marriage emerged that left women under the authority of their fathers and gave husbands no control. In fact, to make their daughters even more independent, parents often provided them with a dower. Overall, the status of women in ancient Rome underwent significant changes, with women becoming more visible and active in public life, but also losing some of the protections and discipline of traditional family structures.

Divorce was not uncommon in ancient Rome. It was a practice that was exercised by both the husband and the wife, but it was the husband who usually had the right to repudiate his wife. However, it was customary for this right to be exercised only in the gravest of circumstances. The wife also gained the right to leave her husband, and this made it very easy to break a marriage. There was no need for a judgment or even a motive. It was enough for the discontented husband or wife to say to the other, "Take what belongs to you, and return what is mine." After the divorce, either party could marry again. In the aristocracy, marriage was viewed as a passing union. Sulla had five wives, Caesar four, Pompey five, and Antony four. Even the daughter of Cicero had three husbands. Hortensius divorced his wife to give her to a friend. "There are noble women," says Seneca, "who count their age not by the years of the consuls, but by the husbands they have had; they divorce to marry again, they marry to divorce again." But this corruption affected only the nobles of Rome and the upstarts. In the families of Italy and the provinces, the more serious manners of the old times still prevailed. However, the discipline of the family gradually slackened, and the woman slowly freed herself from the despotism of her husband.

Chapter 23

The Peasants

The ancient Roman people were made up of small landowners who worked their land. These hardworking and sturdy peasants served as both the army and the assembly of the people. While they were still numerous in 221 B.C. during the Second Punic War, by 133 B.C., they had all but disappeared. Many had undoubtedly perished in foreign wars, but the main reason for their disappearance was that they could no longer survive. The peasants survived by growing grain. When Rome began importing grain from Sicily and Africa, the price of Italian grain fell so low that laborers could not grow enough to support their families and pay the military tax. They were forced to sell their land which was then bought by a wealthy neighbor. The neighbor combined many small fields into one large estate and used the land for grazing. To protect his herds or cultivate the land, he sent shepherds and slaves to work the fields. At that time, Italy only had large landowners and troops of slaves. "Great estates," as Pliny the Elder said, "are the ruin of Italy." It was the large estates that drove the free peasants out of the countryside. The old landowner who sold his land could no longer be a farmer; he had to give way to slaves, and he himself wandered without work. "The majority of these heads of families," said Varro in his treatise on agriculture, "have slipped within our walls, leaving the scythe and the plow; they prefer clapping their hands at the circus to working in their fields and vineyards." Tiberius Gracchus, a tribune of the plebs, exclaimed in a moment of indignation, "The wild beasts of Italy have at least their lairs, but the men who offer their blood for Italy have only the light and the air that they breathe; they wander about without shelter, without a dwelling, with their wives and their children. Those generals do but mock them who exhort them to fight for their tombs and their temples. Is there one of them who still possesses the sacred altar of his house and the tomb of his ancestors? They are called the masters of the world while they have not for themselves a single foot of earth."

The City Plebs

As the farms were drained, Rome was flooded with a new population. They were the descendants of the ruined peasants, driven to the city by misery. In addition to them, there were the freedmen and their children. They came from all corners of the world: Greeks, Syrians, Egyptians, Asians, Africans, Spaniards, and Gauls, torn from their homes and sold as slaves. Later freed by their masters and made citizens, they massed themselves in the city. It was an entirely new people that bore the name Roman. One day, Scipio, the conqueror of Carthage and Numantia, was haranguing the people in the forum when he was interrupted by the cries of the mob. "Silence, false sons of Italy!" he cried. "Do as you like; those whom I brought to Rome in chains will never frighten me, even if they are no longer slaves." The populace preserved quiet, but these "false sons of Italy," the sons of the vanquished, had already taken the place of the old Romans. This new plebeian order could not make a livelihood for itself, and so the state had to provide food for it. A beginning was made in 123 with furnishing corn at half price to all citizens, and this grain was imported from Sicily and Africa. Since the year 63, corn was distributed gratuitously, and oil was also provided. There were registers and an administration expressly for these distributions, a special service for furnishing provisions or the Annona. In 46, Caesar found 320,000 citizens enrolled for these distributions. Electoral Corruption. This miserable and lazy populace filled the forum on election days and made the laws and the magistrates. The candidates sought to win their favors by giving shows and public feasts and by dispensing provisions. They even bought votes. This sale took place on a large scale and in broad daylight. Money was given to distributors who divided it among the voters. Once, the Senate attempted to stop this trade, but when Piso, the consul, proposed a law to prohibit the sale of suffrages, the distributors excited a riot and drove the consul from the forum. In the time of Cicero, no magistrate could be elected without enormous expenditures.

The corruption of the Senate was a result of poverty among the populace and luxury among the old families who made up the Senate. The nobles believed that the state was their property and therefore divided the functions of the state among themselves, excluding the rest of the citizens. Cicero, the first "new man" to enter the succession of offices, was elected magistrate and held the position for thirty years. Some of the senators, accustomed to wielding power, believed that they were above the law. Scipio, who was accused of embezzlement, refused to exonerate himself and instead said to the Romans, "It was on this day that I conquered Hannibal and the Carthaginians. Follow me to the Capitol to render thanks to the gods and to beseech them always to provide generals like myself." To support their lavish lifestyles, majority of the nobles required a large amount of money. Many used their power to obtain it for themselves. Some governors plundered the subjects of Rome, while others forced foreign or hostile kings to pay for peace or even for allowing their armies to be defeated. Jugurtha, for example, bribed a Roman general and escaped trial for murder by buying off a tribune who forbade him to speak. As he left Rome, he reportedly said, "O city for sale, if thou only couldst find a purchaser!" The corruption of the army began when Marius admitted poor citizens to the legions who enrolled themselves for the purpose of making money from their campaigns. Soon, the whole army was full of adventurers who went to war not to perform their service but to enrich themselves from the vanquished. Being a soldier was no longer a sense of duty but a profession.

The soldiers enlisted for twenty years, and upon completion of their service, they re-enlisted themselves at higher pay to become veterans. These people knew nothing of the Senate or the laws; their loyalty was only to their general. To gain their loyalty, the general distributed the spoils of war among them. During the war against Mithridates, Sulla housed his men with the wealthy residents of Asia, where they lived as they pleased, receiving sixteen drachmas a day. These first generals, Marius and Sulla, were still Roman magistrates. However, wealthy individuals like Pompey and Crassus soon began to pay the soldiers. By 78 B.C., at the death of Sulla, there were four armies, raised entirely by and commanded by ordinary citizens. From that time, there were no more legions of Rome; there were only the legions of Pompey or Caesar. THE REVOLUTION. The Need for Revolution. The Roman people had become an impoverished and lazy mass, and the army had become a gathering of adventurers. Neither the assembly nor the legions obeyed the Senate, as the corrupt nobles had lost all moral authority. Thus, there remained only one real power-the army. There were no influential men other than the generals, and the generals no longer had any desire to obey. The government by the Senate was no longer practical, and the government of the general took its place. The Civil Wars. The revolution was inevitable, but it did not happen overnight; it took more than a century to accomplish. The Senate resisted, but it was too weak to govern and strong enough to prevent domination by another power. The generals fought among themselves to determine who would remain in power. For a century, the Romans and their subjects lived in the midst of chaos and civil war.

The Gracchi brothers, Tiberius and Gaius, hailed from one of the most esteemed families in Rome. However, they sought to overthrow the Senate and take control of the government by becoming tribunes of the plebs. At that time, there was a large group of citizens in Rome and Italy who desired a revolution, including many poor citizens and even the majority of the rich knights who felt left out of the government. Tiberius Gracchus became tribune of the plebs and proposed an agrarian law that would resume all lands of the public domain occupied by individuals, except for 500 acres per person. These lands would then be redistributed in small lots to poor citizens. The law was passed, but it caused widespread confusion regarding property ownership since most lands in the empire were considered part of the public domain, yet had been occupied for a long time by people who saw themselves as rightful owners. Additionally, the Romans had no land registry, making it difficult to determine whether a domain was private or public property. To oversee these operations, Tiberius appointed three commissioners, including his brother and father-in-law, who were granted absolute authority by the people. It was unclear whether Tiberius had acted in the interest of the people or simply to gain power. For a year, he ruled Rome, but when he sought to be re-elected tribune of the plebs for the following year, his opponents protested, leading to a riot. Tiberius and his supporters took refuge at the Capitol but were pursued and killed by the Senate's partisans and their slaves, armed with clubs and fragments of benches in the year 133.

Ten years after the death of Tiberius Gracchus, his younger brother Gaius Gracchus was elected tribune of the plebs in 123 B.C. He revived the agrarian law and established distributions of corn to poor citizens. To weaken the power of the nobles, he secured a decree that the judges should be taken from among the knights. For two years, Gaius dominated the government, but when he was absent from the city conducting a colony of Roman citizens to Carthage, the people abandoned him. On his return, he could not be re-elected. The consul armed the partisans of the Senate and marched against Gaius and his friends who had fled to the Aventine Hill. Gaius had himself killed by a slave, and his followers were massacred or executed in prison. Their houses were razed, and their property was confiscated. The riots in the streets of Rome between the Gracchi and the Senate were just the beginning. The strife that followed was a series of real wars between regular armies, wars in Italy, and wars in all the provinces. From this time, the party chiefs were no other than the generals. The first to use his army to secure obedience in Rome was Marius. He was born in Arpinum, a little town in the mountains, and was not of noble descent. He had attained reputation as an officer in the army and had been elected tribune of the plebs, then praetor, with the help of the nobles. He turned against them and was elected consul and commissioned with the war against Jugurtha, king of Numidia, who had already fought several Roman armies. It was then that Marius enrolled poor citizens for whom military service became a profession. With his army, Marius conquered Jugurtha and the barbarians, the Cimbri, and Teutones, who had invaded the empire. He then returned to Rome, where he had himself elected consul for the sixth time and now exercised absolute power.

Two parties now took form in Rome who called themselves the party of the people or the party of Marius and the party of the nobles meaning that of the Senate.

The partisans of Marius committed so many acts of violence that they ended up making him unpopular. Sulla, a nobleman from the great family of the Cornelii, took advantage of this circumstance to challenge Marius' power. Sulla was also a general. When the Italians rose against Rome to secure the right of citizenship and raised great armies that marched almost to the gates of the city, it was Sulla who saved Rome by fighting the Italians. He became consul and was tasked with the war against Mithridates, the king of Pontus, who had invaded Asia Minor and massacred all the Romans in 88. Marius, out of jealousy, incited a riot in the city. Sulla departed and joined his army, which was waiting for him in southern Italy, and then returned to Rome. Roman religion prohibited soldiers from entering the city under arms. The consul had to lay aside his mantle of war and assume the toga even before passing the gates. Sulla was the first general who dared to violate this restriction. Marius took flight. But when Sulla left for Asia, Marius came with an army of adventurers and forcibly entered Rome in 87. Then the proscriptions began. The principal partisans of Sulla were outlawed, and orders were given to kill them wherever they were found and to confiscate their goods. Marius died some months later, but his main supporter, Cinna, continued to govern Rome and put to death whomever he pleased.

During this period, Sulla had conquered Mithridates and secured the loyalty of his soldiers by granting them the spoils of Asia. He returned to Italy with his army in the year 83. His adversaries opposed him with five armies, but they were either defeated or deserted. Sulla entered Rome, executed his prisoners, and overthrew the supporters of Marius. After several days of carnage, he began to proceed systematically. He posted three lists of those he wished to be killed. "I have now posted all those whom I can remember; I have forgotten many, but their names will be added to the list as they come to me." Every proscribed individual, meaning anyone whose name was on the list, was marked for death, and the person who brought their head was rewarded. The property of the proscribed was confiscated. Proscription was not the outcome of any trial but the general's whim, and without any warning. Sulla thus massacred not only his adversaries but also the wealthy whose property he desired. It is said that a citizen who was not accustomed to politics glanced at the list of proscriptions and saw his name at the top of the list. "Oh no!" he exclaimed, "my Alban house has been the cause of my death!" Sulla is believed to have proscribed 1,800 knights. After eliminating his opponents, he attempted to establish a government in which the Senate held all power. He appointed himself as Dictator, an old title previously given to generals in times of danger, which granted absolute power. Sulla used the position to enact laws that altered the entire constitution. From that point on, all judges were to be selected from the Senate, no law could be debated before it was accepted by the Senate, and the right to propose laws was taken away from the tribunes of the plebs. After these reforms, Sulla resigned from his position and retired to private life in the year 79. He knew he had nothing to fear because he had stationed 100,000 of his soldiers in Italy.

Pompey and Caesar

The Senate had regained its power thanks to Sulla, but it lacked the strength to keep it if a general wished to seize it again. Nevertheless, the Senate's rule appeared to last for over thirty years because several generals prevented any one rival from gaining all power. After Sulla's death, four armies emerged. Two were led by generals who supported the Senate, Crassus and Pompey, while the other two followed generals who were against the Senate, Lepidus in Italy and Sertorius in Spain. It's noteworthy that none of these armies were regular, and none of the generals were magistrates with the right to command troops. Until then, generals had been consuls, but now they were private individuals, and their soldiers joined them not to serve the state but to profit at the expense of the inhabitants. The armies of the Senate's enemies were destroyed, and Crassus and Pompey were left to control affairs. They were elected consuls and Pompey was given command of two wars. He went to Asia with a devoted army and ruled Rome for several years. However, as he held more offices than power, he changed nothing in the government. It was during this time that Caesar, a young noble, became popular. Pompey, Crassus, and Caesar joined forces to divide the power between themselves. Crassus received command of the army sent to Asia against the Parthians and was killed in 53. Pompey remained in Rome while Caesar went to Gaul, where he stayed for eight years, subduing the country and building an army for himself.

Pompey and Caesar were now the only players in the game. Both wanted to be the master. Pompey had the upper hand as he was in Rome and had control over the Senate. On the other hand, Caesar had his army which was disciplined through eight years of expeditions. Pompey got the Senate to pass a decree that Caesar should give up his army and return to Rome. Caesar, in turn, decided to cross the boundary of his province, the river Rubicon, and march on Rome. Pompey had no army in Italy to defend himself, so he and the majority of the senators fled to the other side of the Adriatic. Pompey had several armies in Spain, Greece, and Africa. Caesar defeated them one by one, starting with Spain in 49, then Greece at Pharsalus in 48, and finally Africa in 46. Pompey, defeated at Pharsalus, fled to Egypt where the king had him assassinated. After returning to Rome, Caesar was appointed dictator for ten years and exercised absolute power. The Senate even paid him divine honors, and it is possible that Caesar desired the title of king. However, he was assassinated by some of his favorites who aimed to reestablish the sovereignty of the Senate in 44. The people of Rome, who loved Caesar, forced Brutus and Cassius, the leaders of the assassins, to flee. They went to the East where they raised a large army. The West remained under the control of Antony, who governed Rome despotically with the support of Caesar's army. In his will, Caesar had adopted his sister's son, an eighteen-year-old boy named Octavian, who then assumed the name of his adoptive father, Julius Caesar Octavianus, according to Roman tradition. Octavian rallied the soldiers of Caesar to his side and was tasked by the Senate with waging war against Antony. However, after defeating him, he chose to join forces with him for a division of power. They brought Lepidus into the fold, and all three returned to Rome, securing absolute power for five years under the title of triumvirs for organizing public affairs.

They started by condemning their enemies and personal foes. Antony ensured the death of Cicero in 43 B.C. Then they traveled to the East to vanquish the conspirators' army. Once they had split the empire among themselves, it was impossible to maintain harmony, and war broke out in Italy. The soldiers forced them to negotiate peace. They made a new division: Antony took the East, and Octavian took the West in 39 B.C. For some years, peace reigned. Antony lived like an oriental monarch with Cleopatra, the queen of Egypt. Octavian had to fight against Pompey's sons. Eventually, the two leaders had a falling out, and the final civil war erupted. This was a conflict between the East and the West. It was decided by the naval battle of Actium. Antony fled to Egypt and committed suicide after being deserted by Cleopatra's fleet. Octavian was left alone and became the absolute ruler of the empire. The Senate's government came to an end. The Need for Peace. Everyone had suffered from these wars. The soldiers looted, tormented, and massacred the inhabitants of the provinces. Each of the opposing generals forced them to take sides, and the winner punished them for supporting the loser. The generals promised land to the old soldiers and then expelled all the city's inhabitants to make room for the veterans. The wealthy Romans risked their lives and property. When their faction was defeated, they were at the mercy of the victor. Sulla had set the precedent for organized massacres in 81 B.C. Forty years later, Octavian and Antony drew up lists of condemnation again in 43 B.C. The common people suffered. The grain on which they depended no longer arrived in Rome with regularity because of pirates or an enemy fleet.

After a century of this way of life, all the Romans and provincials, whether rich or poor, had one common desire-peace. It was during this time that the heir of Caesar, Octavian, who was one of the triumvirs and his nephew, presented himself to the people who were tired of the civil discord. He had defeated his two colleagues and drew to himself all the powers of the people, the Senate, and the magistrates. For twelve years, he ruled as an emperor without having the title. No one dared to resist him. He had brought peace to the world by closing the temple of Janus, and this was what everyone wished for. The government of the republic by the Senate only represented pillage and civil war. A strong master was needed to stop the wars and revolutions. Thus, the Roman Empire was founded.

Chapter 24

The Emperors

The Emperor was the one man who held absolute power in the new regime. He was known as the Imperator, or the commander. He alone exercised all the functions of the ancient magistrates. He presided over the Senate, commanded all the armies, levied taxes, and was the supreme judge. He was even the pontifex maximus and had the power of the tribunes. To show that he was a superhuman being, he was given the religious surname Augustus, meaning the venerable. The empire was not established through a radical revolution. The name of the republic was not suppressed, and for over three centuries, the standards of the soldiers continued to bear the initials S.P.Q.R. The emperor's power was granted to him for life, unlike the old magistrates who had it for one year. The emperor was the only lifelong magistrate of the republic, and in him, the Roman people were incarnate, which is why he was absolute. As long as the emperor lived, he was the sole master of the empire, as the Roman people had conveyed all its power to him. But upon his death, the Senate reviewed his life and passed judgment upon it in the name of the people. If he were condemned, all his acts were nullified, his statues thrown down, and his name effaced from the monuments. However, if his acts were ratified, which almost always occurred, the Senate decreed that the deceased emperor should be elevated to the rank of the gods. The majority of the emperors became gods after their death, and temples were raised to them, with priests appointed to render their worship. Throughout the empire, there were temples dedicated to the god Augustus and the goddess Roma. Persons are known who performed the functions of flamen, or priest, of the divine Claudius or the divine Vespasian.

This practice of deifying the dead emperor was called Apotheosis, a Greek word. The custom probably came from the Greeks of the Orient.

The Senate and the People

The Roman Senate remained what it had always been, the assembly of the wealthiest and most distinguished individuals of the empire. To be a senator was still a highly coveted honor; when referring to a prominent family, one would say "a senatorial family." However, while the Senate was respected, it had lost its power as the emperor could easily dismiss it. Although it remained the most prestigious body in the state, it was no longer in control of the government. The emperor would often pretend to seek its advice, but was not obligated to follow it. The people had lost all their power since the assemblies or the Comitia, were abolished during the reign of Tiberius. The population of two million residents in Rome consisted of only a few thousand wealthy lords with their slaves and a throng of paupers. The state had already taken on the responsibility of feeding the latter, with the emperors continuing to distribute grain and provide money or the congiarium. Augustus donated 140 dollars each in nine different distributions, while Nero gave 50 dollars in three. Additionally, shows were presented to entertain the populace. Under the republic, the number of days regularly appointed for shows was 66 per year. In a century and a half, under Marcus Aurelius, it had increased to 135, and in the fourth century to 175 not including supplementary days. These spectacles continued from sunrise to sunset each day, with the spectators eating lunch in their seats. The emperors used this as a means of occupying the crowd. "It is for your advantage, Caesar," said an actor to Augustus, "that the people engage themselves with us." It was also a way of gaining popularity. The worst emperors were among the most popular; Nero was adored for his magnificent spectacles, and the people refused to believe that he was dead, waiting for his return for thirty years.

The city of Rome, once a great power, had become a place of amusement and sustenance. As Juvenal put it, the people only required "bread and the games of the circus" or food and entertainment. The Praetorians, a group of about 10,000 soldiers, were the emperor's personal military escort. They were recruited from veterans, paid well, and given frequent bonuses. With the Praetorians on his side, the emperor had nothing to fear from dissidents in Rome. However, the real danger came from the Praetorians themselves. They believed that their power gave them free rein, and their leader, the Praetorian prefect, was sometimes even stronger than the emperor. Since the monarchy had replaced the republic, the emperor was the only magistrate. With an empire of 80 million people to govern, the emperor needed assistants. He found them among the slaves, whom he trusted more than the men of great families. The emperor's secretaries, trusted men, and ministers were all freedmen, mostly from Greece or the Orient. They were pliant people, skilled in flattery, inventiveness, and loquacity. Sometimes, when the emperor was tired of serious matters, he left the government in their hands. In absolute monarchies, the freedmen often supplemented their master instead of aiding him. Claudius's freedmen, Pallas and Narcissus, distributed offices and pronounced judgments. Helius, Nero's freedman, even executed knights and senators without consulting his master. Of all the freedmen, Pallas was the most powerful, richest, and insolent. He gave orders to his underlings only by signs or in writing. This outraged the old noble families of Rome. As a Roman writer put it, "The princes are the masters of citizens and the slaves of their freedmen." One of the gravest scandals with which the emperors were reproached was governing Roman citizens by former slaves.

Despotism and Disorder

In ancient Rome, the rulers had two major flaws that plagued their regime: 1. Despotism. The emperor held an unlimited, extravagant, and almost inconceivable power for life. They could dispose of people and their property, condemn, confiscate, and execute without any restraint. The emperor's will was not fettered by any institution or law. The jurisconsults themselves said, "The decree of the emperor has the force of law." The Roman Empire recognized the unlimited despotism that the tyrants had exercised in the Greek cities. While some honorable tyrants presented themselves in Greece, some wise and honest monarchs like Augustus, Vespasian, and Titus appeared in Rome. However, few men had a headstrong enough to resist vertigo when they saw themselves so elevated above other men. The majority of the emperors profited from their tremendous power only to make their names proverbial: Tiberius, Nero, Domitian by their cruelty, Vitellius by his gluttony, and Claudius by his imbecility. One of them, Caligula, was a veritable fool; he had his horse made consul and himself worshipped as a god. The emperors persecuted the nobles, especially to keep them from conspiring against them, and the rich to confiscate their goods. 2. Disorder. This overweening authority was, moreover, very ill-regulated, residing entirely in the person of the emperor. When the emperor died, everything was in question. It was well known that the world could not continue without a master, but no law or usage determined who was to be this master. The Senate alone had the right of nominating the emperor, but almost always it would elect under pressure the one whom the preceding emperor had designated or the man who was pleasing to the soldiers.

After the death of Caligula, some Praetorians who were looting the palace found a terrified, poor man hiding behind a tapestry. He turned out to be a relative of Caligula, and the Praetorians made him emperor. This man was Claudius. Following Nero's death, the Senate elected Galba as emperor. However, the Praetorians did not find him liberal enough and massacred him to put Otho, a favorite of Nero, in his place. The soldiers on the frontier also wanted to make an emperor, and the legions of the Rhine entered Italy to overthrow the Praetorians at Bedriac near Cremona. The battle lasted all night, and the soldiers compelled the Senate to elect their general, Vitellius, as emperor. Meanwhile, the army of Syria had elected Vespasian as their chief. Vespasian defeated Vitellius and was named emperor in his place. Thus, in two years, three emperors were created and three were overthrown by the soldiers. The new emperor often undid what his predecessor had done, and imperial despotism was not even stable. The regime of oppression interrupted by violence lasted for more than a century, from 31 B.C. to 96 A.D. The twelve emperors who came to the throne during this time are known as the Twelve Caesars, although only the first six were from the family of Augustus. It is difficult to judge them fairly. Almost all of them persecuted the noble families of Rome, whom they feared, and it is the writers of these families who have made their reputation. However, it is possible that their government was mild and just in the provinces, superior to that of the senators of the republic. This period is known as the Century of the Antonines, named after the four emperors who ruled during this time: Nerva, Trajan, Hadrian, and Antoninus Pius. They were known for their wisdom, justice, and benevolence, and their reigns were marked by peace and prosperity. However, their successors were not as successful, and the empire began to decline.

The Antonines, five emperors who succeeded the twelve Caesars, Nerva, Trajan, Hadrian, Antoninus, and Marcus Aurelius from 96 until 180, were renowned for their justice and wisdom. Although the name Antonines properly belongs only to the last two, they have all left a lasting legacy. Unlike the old families of Rome, Trajan and Hadrian were Spaniards, and Antoninus was born in Nimes, Gaul. They were not princes of imperial families, destined from birth to rule. Four emperors ascended the throne without sons, so the empire could not be inherited. Instead, the prince chose the man most capable of succeeding him from among his generals and governors, adopted him as his son, and sought confirmation from the Senate. Thus, only experienced men came to the empire, who without confusion assumed the throne of their adoptive fathers. During this century of the Antonines, the ancient world experienced unprecedented calm. Wars were relegated to the empire's frontier, and military seditions, tyranny, and arbitrary condemnations were still present in the interior. However, the Antonines held the army in check, organized a council of state of jurisconsults, established tribunals, and replaced the freedmen who had so long irritated the Romans under the twelve Caesars with regular functionaries taken from among the men of the second class, the knights. The emperor was no longer a tyrant served by the soldiers, but truly the first magistrate of the republic, using his authority only for the good of the citizens. The last two Antonines, Antoninus and

Marcus Aurelius, honored the empire with their integrity. Both lived simply, like ordinary men, although they were very rich, without anything that resembled a court or a palace, never giving the impression that they were masters. Marcus Aurelius consulted the Senate on all state business and regularly attended its sessions. Marcus Aurelius, in particular, has been termed the Philosopher on the Throne. He governed from a sense of duty against his disposition, for he loved solitude. Yet, he spent his life in administration and the command of armies. His private journal, his "Thoughts," exhibits the character of the Stoic, virtuous, austere, separated from the world, and yet mild and good. "The best form of vengeance on the wicked is not to imitate them; the gods themselves do good to evil men; it is your privilege to act like the gods."

In the days of the Antonine emperors, the Roman Empire continued its path of conquest. The first-century emperors had already subdued the Britons in England, and the Germans on the left bank of the Rhine, and had taken control of several countries that had previously retained their own kings, such as Mauretania, Thrace, and Cappadocia. The empire's borders were marked by the Rhine, the Danube, and the Euphrates. The second-century emperors were mostly generals, and they had ample opportunity to wage wars against hostile peoples attempting to invade the empire. The enemies were particularly concentrated in two areas: 1. The Dacians, a barbarous people who lived in the mountainous and forested region now known as Transylvania, were located on the Danube. 2. The Parthians, a great military monarchy with its capital at Ctesiphon near the ruins of Babylon, extended over all of Persia and were located on the Euphrates. Trajan, one of the Antonine emperors, launched several expeditions against the Dacians. He crossed the Danube and won three significant battles, ultimately taking the Dacians' capital from 101 to 102. He offered them peace, but when they reopened the war, he decided to end the conflict once and for all. He had a stone bridge built over the Danube and invaded Dacia, reducing it to a Roman province in 106. Colonies were established there, cities were constructed, and Dacia became a Roman province where Latin was spoken and Roman customs were assimilated. Even after the Roman armies withdrew at the end of the third century, the Latin language remained and persisted throughout the Middle Ages, despite invasions by the barbarian Slavs. The peoples who now inhabit the plains to the north of the Danube came from Transylvania or ancient Dacia, from the twelfth to the fourteenth century. It has preserved the name of Rome or Roumania and speaks a language derived from Latin, similar to French or Spanish. Trajan also waged war on the Parthians. He crossed the Euphrates, took Ctesiphon, the capital, and advanced into Persia, even reaching Susa, from which he took the massive gold throne of the kings of Persia. He constructed a fleet on the Tigris, sailed down the river to its mouth, and sailed into the Persian Gulf. He would have been thrilled, like Alexander, to conquer India. He took control of the country between the Euphrates and the Tigris, including Assyria and Mesopotamia, and established two Roman provinces there.

To honor his victories, Trajan built monuments that still stand today. The Column of Trajan, located in the Roman Forum, is a towering structure adorned with bas-reliefs depicting the war against the Dacians. Meanwhile, the arch of triumph in Benevento serves as a reminder of the triumphs over the Parthians. However, of these two conquests, only one proved to be permanent: that of Dacia. The provinces taken from the Parthians rebelled after the Roman army's departure. Emperor Hadrian chose to keep Dacia but returned the provinces to the Parthians, once again making the Euphrates the eastern boundary of the Roman Empire. To avoid further conflict with the Scottish highlanders, Hadrian built a wall in the north of England, known as the Wall of Hadrian, which spanned the entire island. The only remaining conflict was against the rebellious Jews, whom the Romans defeated and expelled from Jerusalem, renaming the city to erase the memory of the old Jewish kingdom. The last of the Antonines, Marcus Aurelius, faced an invasion from several barbaric Germanic tribes that had crossed the Danube on the ice and made their way as far as Aquileia in northern Italy. To assemble a sufficient army, Marcus had to enlist slaves and barbarians. The Germans eventually retreated, but while Marcus was dealing with a general uprising in Syria, they launched another attack on the empire. The emperor died on the banks of the Danube in 180, marking the end of the conquest.

In the second century, the Roman emperors were not particularly interested in conquest. However, they continued to conquer barbarian peoples for over a century to keep their army occupied and secure easily defensible frontiers. After Trajan, the course of conquest was finally halted, and the empire extended over the south of Europe, the north of Africa, and the west of Asia. The empire was limited by natural frontiers, including the ocean to the west, the mountains of Scotland, the Rhine, the Danube, and the Caucasus to the north, the deserts of the Euphrates and Arabia to the east, and the cataracts of the Nile and the great desert to the south. The empire included the territories that now make up England, Spain, Italy, France, Belgium, Switzerland, Bavaria, Austria, Hungary, European Turkey, Morocco, Algiers, Tunis, Egypt, Syria, Palestine, and Asiatic Turkey. This empire was more than twice the size of Alexander's empire. This vast territory was divided into forty-eight provinces of unequal size, but most of them were quite large. For example, Gaul from the Pyrenees to the Rhine, was divided into only seven provinces. In the provinces of the interior, there was no Roman army because the peoples of the empire had no desire to revolt. However, on the frontier, the empire had enemies, including foreigners who were always ready to invade. Behind the Rhine and the Danube were the barbarian Germans, behind the sands of Africa were the nomads of the desert, and behind the Euphrates was the Persian army. On this constantly threatened frontier, it was necessary to have soldiers always ready. Augustus understood this and created a permanent army. The soldiers of the empire were no longer proprietors transferred from their fields to serve during a few campaigns, but poor men who made war their profession. They enlisted for sixteen or twenty years and often reenlisted. There were thirty legions of citizens, which means there were 180,000 legionaries, and according to Roman usage, a slightly larger number of auxiliaries, making a total of about 400,000 men. This number was small for such a vast territory.

In the early days of the Roman Empire, each frontier province had its own little army, stationed in a permanent camp that resembled a fortress. As merchants came to establish themselves in the area, the camp slowly transformed into a city. However, the soldiers remained encamped in the face of the enemy, preserving their valor and discipline. For three centuries, there were severe wars, especially on the banks of the Rhine and Danube rivers, where Roman soldiers fought fiercely against barbarians in a swampy, uncultivated land covered with forests and bogs. Despite the obscurity of these wars, the imperial army exhibited as much bravery and energy as the ancient Romans did during the conquest of the world. All the provinces belonged to the emperor, who represented the Roman people. As such, he was the general of all soldiers, master of all persons, and proprietor of all lands. However, since the emperor couldn't be everywhere at once, he appointed deputies to represent him. Each province had a lieutenant, called a deputy of Augustus with the function of praetor, who governed the country, commanded the army, and traveled throughout the province to judge important cases. Like the emperor, the praetor had the right of life and death. The emperor also sent a financial agent, called the procurator of Augustus, to levy taxes and return the money to the imperial chest. These two men represented the emperor, governing his subjects, commanding his soldiers, and exploiting his domain. The emperor always chose them from the two nobilities of Rome: the praetors from the senators and the procurators from the knights. They held a succession of offices, passing from one province to another, from one end of the empire to the other, from Syria to Spain, and from Britain to Africa. The epitaphs of officials from this time carefully inscribed all the posts they had occupied, and inscriptions on their tombs were sufficient to construct their biographies.

Municipal Life

Beneath the all-powerful representatives of the emperor, the smaller subject peoples continued to govern themselves. The emperor had the right to interfere in their local affairs but typically chose not to exercise this right. Instead, he simply demanded that they maintain peace, pay their taxes regularly, and appear before the governor's tribunal. In every province, there were several of these little subordinate governments, called "cities" or "municipalities," just as the Roman state was called at other times. The provincial cities were modeled after Rome, with their own assembly of the people, magistrates elected for a year and grouped into colleges of two members, and a senate, called a curia, made up of the great proprietors, wealthy people of old family. As in Rome, the assembly of the people was little more than a formality; it was the nobility, or senate, that truly governed. The center of the provincial city was always a town, a miniature Rome, complete with temples, triumphal arches, public baths, fountains, theaters, and arenas for combats. The life led there was that of Rome on a small scale: distributions of grain and money, public banquets, grand religious ceremonies, and bloody spectacles. However, in the municipalities, it was the nobility itself that defrayed the costs of government and festivities, rather than the money of the provinces paying the expenses, as was the case in Rome. The tax levied for the treasury of the emperor went entirely to the imperial chest, so the rich of the city had to celebrate the games, heat the baths, pave the streets, and construct the bridges, aqueducts, and circuses at their own expense. They did so generously for more than two centuries, as monuments scattered throughout the empire and thousands of inscriptions attest.

The Imperial Regime

After the conquest, three or four hundred families of the nobility of Rome reigned over and exploited the rest of the world. The emperor stripped them of their power and subjected them to his tyranny. Roman writers lamented their lost liberty, but the inhabitants of the provinces had nothing to mourn. Instead of several hundred masters, constantly replaced and determined to enrich themselves, they now had a single ruler, the emperor, who had an interest in sparing them. Tiberius summed up the imperial policy when he said, "A good shepherd shears his sheep, but does not flay them." For over two centuries, the emperors contented themselves with shearing the people of the empire. They took much of their money but protected them from external enemies and even from their own officials. If the provincials had any grievances due to the violence or robbery of their governor, they could appeal to the emperor and receive justice. The emperor was known to receive complaints against his subordinates, which was enough to scare bad governors and reassure subjects. Some emperors, like Marcus Aurelius, realized that they had duties to their subjects. The other emperors at least allowed their subjects to govern themselves when they had no interest in preventing it. The imperial regime was a loss for the Romans, but a deliverance for their subjects. It humbled the conquerors and elevated the conquered, reconciling them and preparing them for assimilation into the empire.

Social Life During the Roman Empire

Moral decay continued to plague Rome during the reign of the Caesars, as depicted in the letters of Seneca and the satires of Juvenal. The corruption of the time was so notorious that it has become proverbial. The disorders that plagued the republic, such as the extravagance of the rich, the cruelty of masters towards their slaves, and the frivolity of women, persisted under the imperial regime. These evils were not caused by the empire itself, but rather by the excessive accumulation of wealth in the hands of a few thousand nobles and upstarts. Meanwhile, hundreds of free men lived in poverty, and millions of slaves were subjected to unrestrained oppression. Each of these wealthy proprietors lived like a petty prince, surrounded by their slaves. Their homes in Rome were like palaces, and every morning, the hall of honor, or the atrium, was filled with clients who came to greet the master and escort him in the street for a meager salary. Fashion demanded that a rich man should never appear in public without a crowd of followers. Horace even ridiculed a praetor who traversed the streets of Tibur with only five slaves in his entourage. Outside of Rome, the wealthy owned magnificent villas at the seashore or in the mountains, but they went from one to the other, idle and bored. These great families were rapidly dying out, and Augustus had made laws to encourage marriage and punish celibacy.

However, his laws did not remedy the problem. So many rich men had not married that it had become a lucrative trade to flatter them in order to be mentioned in their will. By having no children, one could surround himself with a crowd of flatterers. "In the city," says a Roman storyteller, "all men divide themselves into two classes, those who fish, and those who are angled for." Losing one's children increased one's influence.

The Spectacles

In the life of the idle people of Rome, the spectacles held a place that we can hardly conceive of today. They were, like in Greece, games that were also religious ceremonies. These games went on throughout the day and the following day, and sometimes even for a week. The amphitheater was the gathering place for the entire free population, and it was there that they showed themselves. In 196, during the civil wars, all the spectators cried out with one voice, "Peace!" The spectacle was the passion of the time. Three emperors even appeared in public: Caligula as a driver, Nero as an actor, and Commodus as a gladiator. The Theatre. There were three types of spectacles: the theatre, the circus, and the amphitheater. The theatre was organized based on Greek models. The actors were masked and presented plays imitated from the Greek. The Romans had little taste for this recreation, which was too delicate for them. They preferred the mimes, comedies of a coarse character, and especially the pantomimes, in which the actor expressed the sentiments of the character through his attitude without speaking. The Circus. Between the two hills of the Aventine and the Palatine extended a field filled with race courses surrounded by arcades and tiers of seats rising above them. This was the Circus Maximus. After Nero enlarged it, it could accommodate 250,000 spectators. In the fourth century, its size was increased to provide seating for 385,000 people. Here was presented the favorite spectacle of the Roman people: the four-horse chariot race or quadrigae. In each race, the chariot made a triple circuit of the circus, and there were twenty-five races in a single day. The drivers belonged to rival companies whose colors they wore. There were initially four of these colors, but they were later reduced to two: the Blue and the Green, notorious in the history of riots. At Rome, there was the same passion for chariot races that there is now for horse races. Women and even children talked about them. Often the emperor participated, and the quarrel between the Blues and the Greens became an affair of state.

The Amphitheater stands at the gates of Rome, a grand edifice constructed by Emperor Vespasian. Its two stories can hold up to 87,000 spectators, who come to witness the circus surrounding the arena where hunts and combats take place. During the hunts, the arena transforms into a forest where wild beasts are released to fight against men armed with spears. The spectacle aims to entertain the audience by employing the rarest animals, including lions, panthers, elephants, bears, buffaloes, rhinoceroses, giraffes, tigers, and crocodiles. Some emperors even maintain a large menagerie to showcase these animals. However, instead of armed men, sometimes the beasts are let loose on naked and bound men, which proves to be more dramatic. This custom spreads throughout the empire, compelling those condemned to death to furnish this form of entertainment for the people. Thousands of people of all ages and sexes, including Christian martyrs, are devoured by beasts under the eyes of the multitude. The national spectacle of the Romans is the fight of gladiators, men armed with swords. Armed men descend into the arena and fight a duel to the death. From the time of Caesar, as many as 320 pairs of gladiators fought at once. Augustus fought 10,000 of them in his lifetime, and Trajan had the same number in four months. The vanquished is slain on the field unless the people wish to show him mercy. The condemned are sometimes compelled to fight, but more often slaves and prisoners of war are forced into the arena. Each victory brings bands of barbarians to the amphitheater who exterminate one another for the delight of the spectators. Gladiators are furnished by all countries, including Gauls, Germans, and Thracians. These peoples fight with various weapons, usually with their national arms. The Romans love to behold these battles in miniature.

In the midst of the circus contestants, there were those who fought not because they were slaves, but because they chose to. These were free men who craved the thrill of danger and willingly subjected themselves to the brutal discipline of the gladiator. They pledged to their leader that they would endure being beaten with rods, burned with hot iron, and even killed. Some senators even joined these bands of adventurers, and one emperor, Commodus, even descended into the arena. These bloody games were not limited to Rome but were also practiced in all the cities of Italy, Gaul, and Africa. The Greeks, however, always opposed their adoption. In the small city of Minturnae, an inscription on a statue of one of the notables reads, "He presented in four days eleven pairs of gladiators who ceased to fight only when half of them had fallen in the arena. He gave a hunt of ten terrible bears. Treasure this in memory, noble fellow citizens." The people had a passion for blood, which is still evident in Spain's bullfights. The emperor, like the modern king of Spain, was expected to attend these barbaric spectacles. Marcus Aurelius, however, became unpopular in Rome because he showed his weariness at the amphitheater's games by reading, speaking, or giving audiences instead of watching the games. When he enlisted gladiators to serve against the barbarians who invaded Italy, the populace was on the verge of revolt. "He would deprive us of our amusements," cried one, "to compel us to become philosophers."

The Roman Empire was more than just the city of Rome. To truly understand the empire, one must look at events in the provinces. The Romans had conquered and subdued all peoples, which led to the suppression of war within the empire. This established what the Greeks called the Roman Peace. It was a time when anyone could go anywhere without fear, and the land was safe for all. The earth was common to everyone, as Homer had said. For the first time, people in the West could build their homes and cultivate their fields without fear of being robbed, massacred, or enslaved. This security was something we take for granted today, but it was a luxury for people in ancient times. With peace came easy travel. The Romans built roads in every direction, making it easy for people to travel from one end of the empire to the other. Artisans, traders, rhetors, and philosophers traveled throughout Europe, giving lectures and spreading their knowledge. People from remote provinces could be found in every province, bringing with them their customs, arts, and religion. They mingled and transported these things, slowly adapting to the language of the Romans. By the third century, Latin had become the common language of the West, just as Greek had been the language of the Orient since the time of Alexander the Great. This led to the development of a common civilization, which has been called Roman, even though it was more than just that. It was the civilization of the ancient world united under the emperor's authority.

Superstitions were woven into the fabric of ancient religious beliefs. With no concept of a single deity, it was simple for them to accept new gods. Each people had their own religion, but instead of rejecting the beliefs of others, they embraced the gods of their neighbors and merged them with their own. The Romans were the pioneers of this practice, constructing the Pantheon, a temple dedicated to "all the gods," where each deity had their own sanctuary. Credulity was rampant, and people believed in the divinity of deceased emperors. It was said that Vespasian had miraculously healed a blind man and a paralytic in Egypt. During the war with the Dacians, the Roman army was dying of thirst. Suddenly, rain began to pour down, and the sudden storm was seen as a miracle. Some claimed that an Egyptian magician had conjured Hermes, while others believed that Jupiter had taken pity on the soldiers. On the column of Marcus Aurelius, Jupiter was depicted with a thunderbolt in hand, sending the rain that the soldiers caught in their shields.

When Barnabas and Paul, two apostles, arrived in the city of Lystra in Asia Minor, the locals mistook them for the gods Jupiter and Mercury, respectively. The people even held a procession, with priests leading a bull for sacrifice. Despite their education, the people of that time were still superstitious. Even the Stoic philosophers believed in omens, and the emperor Augustus considered it a bad sign if he put on the wrong shoe. Suetonius once asked Pliny the Younger to postpone their meeting due to a dream he had, and Pliny himself believed in ghosts. Strangely enough, instead of fragmenting, different religions merged into a single, dominant religion that was a mix of Greek, Roman, Egyptian, and Asian influences. This religion was so pervasive that Christians referred to it as the "religion of the nations," and until the fourth century, they called the non-Christians "gentiles" or "men of the nations." The common law of the time was also known as the Law of Nations.

Chapter 25

Greek Influence on Roman Art

The Romans were not naturally inclined towards art. It wasn't until they began imitating the Greeks that they became artists. They borrowed from the Greeks their models of tragedy, comedy, epic, ode, didactic poem, pastoral poetry, and history. Some writers limited themselves to translating a Greek original freely, such as Horace in his Odes. But they brought their qualities of patience and vigor into this work of adaptation, and many achieved true originality. The Golden Age of Augustus. The fifty years of Augustus' reign are widely regarded as the most brilliant period in Latin literature. It was the time of Vergil, Horace, Ovid, Tibullus, Propertius, and Livy. The emperor, or rather his friend Maecenas, personally patronized some of these poets, especially Horace and Vergil, who sang the glory of Augustus and his time. But this Augustan Age was preceded and followed by two centuries that perhaps equaled it. In the first century BC, the most original Roman poet, Caesar, appeared, along with the most elegant prose writer, and the greatest orator, Cicero. In the following age, Seneca, Lucan, Tacitus, Pliny, and Juvenal wrote. Between Lucretius and Tacitus, there were many great writers in Rome for three centuries. One might also add another century by going back to the time of Plautus, the second century B.C. Of these great authors, a few came from Roman families, but the majority were Italians. Many came from the provinces, such as Vergil from Mantua, Livy from Padua in Cisalpine Gaul, while Seneca was Spaniard. Orators and Rhetors. The true national art in Rome was eloquence. Like modern Italians, the Romans loved to speak in public. In the forum, where they held assemblies of the people, was the rostrum, the platform for addressing the people, so named from the prows of captured ships that ornamented it like trophies of war. There, in the last epoch of the republic, the orators came to declaim and gesticulate before a tumultuous crowd. The tribunals, often composed of a hundred judges, furnished another occasion for eloquent advocates. Roman law permitted the accused to have an advocate speak in his place.

From the second century, Rome was home to orators. Like Athens, the early orators, including Cato and the Gracchi, spoke plainly, which Cicero found unsatisfactory. In the first century, orators learned from Greek rhetors, adopting long, pompous speeches. Cicero was the greatest of them all, and his speeches are the only ones that have survived in full. However, we have them as he wrote them, not as he delivered them. After the fall of the republic, political trials and assemblies ceased, and eloquence died out. The rhetors proliferated, teaching the art of speaking well. Some of these teachers had their pupils compose pleas on imaginary rhetorical subjects. Seneca, a rhetor, left us with many of these oratorical themes, which covered topics such as stolen children, brigands, and romantic adventures. Public lectures became fashionable, with Pollio, a favorite of Augustus, setting the example. For a century, people read poems, panegyrics, and even tragedies before an audience of friends who applauded them. The taste for eloquence that once produced great orators only produced finished declaimers in later centuries. Latin literature benefited from Rome's conquests, with the Romans taking their language and literature to their barbarian subjects in the West. All the peoples of Italy, Gaul, Spain, Africa, and the Danubian lands discarded their languages and adopted Latin. Having no national literature, they adopted that of their masters. The empire was thus divided between the two languages of the two great peoples of antiquity: the Orient continued to speak Greek, while almost the entire Occident acquired Latin. Latin was not only the official language of state functionaries and great men, like English in India today, but the people themselves spoke it with greater or lesser correctness. Today, five languages of Europe are derived from Latin: Italian, Spanish, Portuguese, French, and Romanian.

In the West, Latin literature spread with the Latin language. In the fifth century, only Latin poets and orators were studied in the schools of Bordeaux and Autun. Even after the barbarians arrived, bishops and monks continued to write in Latin and spread this practice to the peoples of England and Germany who still spoke their native languages. Throughout the medieval period, acts, laws, histories, and books of science were written in Latin. In the convents and schools, only works written in Latin were read, copied, and appreciated. Besides books of piety, only Latin authors were known, such as Vergil, Horace, Cicero, and Pliny the Younger. The Renaissance of the fifteenth and sixteenth centuries partly consisted of reviving forgotten Latin writers. More than ever, it was fashionable to know and imitate them. As the Romans constructed a literature in imitation of the Greeks, the moderns have taken the Latin writers as their models. Whether this is good or bad, who would venture to say? But the fact is indisputable. Our romance languages are daughters of Latin, and our literatures are full of the ideas and literary methods of the Romans. The whole Western world is impregnated with Latin literature. The arts of sculpture and painting have also been influenced by the Romans. Many Roman statues and bas-reliefs from the time of the empire have been discovered. Some are reproductions, and almost all are imitations of Greek works, but less elegant and delicate than the models. The most original productions of this form of art are the bas-reliefs and busts. Bas-reliefs adorned monuments such as temples, columns, and triumphal arches, as well as tombs and sarcophagi. They represent real scenes with scrupulous fidelity, such as processions, sacrifices, combats, and funeral ceremonies, and thus provide us with information about ancient life. The bas-reliefs surrounding the columns of Trajan and Marcus Aurelius bring us into the presence of the great scenes of their wars. We can see the soldiers fighting against the barbarians, besieging their fortresses, leading away the captives, the solemn sacrifices, and the emperor haranguing the troops.

The busts of the emperors, their wives, and their children are found in abundance throughout the empire. The great museums of Europe house collections of these imperial busts, which are real portraits that likely bear a striking resemblance to their subjects. Each emperor had a unique and often unattractive physiognomy that was accurately captured by the artists who created these busts. Roman sculpture is known for its realistic representation of its subjects, more so than Greek sculpture. The Roman artist was less concerned with beauty and more focused on accuracy. Roman painting is mostly lost to history, with only frescoes from Pompeii and the house of Livy in Rome remaining. It is possible that these frescoes were the work of Greek painters, as they share a similar simple and elegant grace to the paintings found on Greek vases. The true Roman art form was architecture, which was driven by practical needs. Roman architecture borrowed the column from the Greeks but also employed the arch, a technique of arranging cut stones in the arc of a circle to support one another. This allowed the Romans to construct larger and more varied buildings than the Greeks.

In the ancient world, the Romans were known for their impressive monuments. Here are some of the main types: 1. The Temple was a grand structure that sometimes resembled a Greek temple, but could also be larger and topped with a dome. One famous example is the Pantheon, which was built in Rome during the reign of Augustus. 2. The Basilica was a long, low building with a roof and porticos. It was used as a marketplace and a courtroom, where judges and traders would gather. Later on, Christians used basilicas for their religious assemblies, and many early churches were modeled after them. 3. The Amphitheatre and the Circus were massive structures with multiple levels of arches surrounding an arena. They were used for public spectacles and entertainment, such as gladiatorial contests and chariot races. Famous examples include the Colosseum in Rome and the arenas in Arles and Nimes. 4. The Arch of Triumph was a grand gateway that could accommodate a chariot passing through. It was decorated with columns and sculptures and served as a symbol of victory or honor. The Arch of Titus is a well-known example. 5. The Sepulchral Vault was an arched building with many niches, each containing the ashes of a deceased person. It was called a Columbarium because of its pigeonhole-like shape. 6. The Thermae were bathing complexes with heated rooms and pools. They were popular gathering places for the idle and wealthy and often included gardens and exercise halls. The Baths of Caracalla were particularly large and impressive. 7. The Bridge and the Aqueduct were structures that spanned rivers and valleys, supported by rows of arches. They were essential for transportation and water supply. Examples include the Alcantara Bridge and the Pont du Gard. 8. The House of a wealthy Roman was a masterpiece of design and decoration. Unlike modern houses, the focus was on the interior, with plain walls facing the street. These houses often had courtyards, gardens, and elaborate mosaics and frescoes.

The chambers were small, poorly furnished, and dimly lit, with light only filtering through the atrium. In the center stood the grand hall of honor, or atrium, where statues of ancestors were erected and visitors were received. The room was illuminated by an opening in the roof. Behind the atrium was the peristyle, a garden surrounded by colonnades, where the dining halls were located. These halls were richly ornamented and provided with couches, as guests reclined on them during banquets, much like the Asiatic Greeks. The pavement was often made of mosaic. The Romans, unlike the Greeks, did not always build in marble. Instead, they used the stone found in the country, bound together with an indestructible mortar that has resisted dampness for eighteen hundred years. Their monuments lacked the grace of the Greek monuments, but they were large, strong, and solid, much like the Roman power. The empire's soil is still covered with their debris, and monuments almost intact can be found in remote areas such as the deserts of Africa. Repairing a Roman aqueduct was all that was needed to furnish a water system for the city of Tunis. During the time of the emperors, Rome was home to two million inhabitants. These people lived in poorly built, crowded houses of five or six stories. The populous quarters were a labyrinth of tortuous paths, steep and ill-paved. Juvenal, who frequented these areas, painted a picture of them that was unattractive. In Pompeii, a city of luxury, the narrow streets of a Roman city can be seen. Despite the hovels, hundreds of monuments were erected, with Augustus boasting of restoring more than eighty temples. He said, "I found a city of bricks; I leave a city of marble." His successors also worked to embellish Rome. The Forum was where the monuments accumulated, with the Capitol and its temple of Jupiter becoming almost like the Acropolis in Athens. The most notable monumental areas were constructed in the same quarter, including the forum of Caesar, Augustus, Nerva, and the most brilliant of all, the forum of Trajan. Two villas, surrounded by a park, were situated in the middle of the city, with the Golden House, built for Nero, being the most famous.

The Law

In the early days, the Romans had no written laws. They simply followed the customs of their ancestors, doing things the same way each generation as the one before. But in 450 B.C., ten magistrates known as the decemvirs were elected to create a set of laws. They wrote these laws on twelve tables made of stone, and thus the Law of the Twelve Tables was born. The laws were written in short, blunt, and powerful sentences, reflecting the rough and barbaric nature of the people for whom they were created. The Law of the Twelve Tables punished those who used magic to harm their neighbors' crops, and it dealt harshly with debtors who could not pay what they owed. If a debtor failed to pay, he would be brought before a court. If he was too sick or too old to appear, he would be given a horse to ride but no litter. He would have thirty days to pay his debt, and if he failed to do so, his creditor could bind him with straps or chains weighing fifteen pounds. If he still could not pay after sixty days, he could be sold beyond the Tiber. If there were many creditors, they could cut him into pieces, and there would be no legal repercussions for doing so. As Cicero said, the Law of the Twelve Tables was the foundation of all Roman law. Even four centuries after it was written, children were required to learn it in school.

The Symbolic Process

In ancient Roman law, it was not enough to simply intend to buy, sell, or inherit. To receive justice in the Roman tribunal, one had to use specific words and gestures, in addition to presenting the case. For example, when purchasing something, the buyer would place a piece of brass, representing the price, in a balance held by a sixth citizen while five others represented an assembly. If the item sold was an animal or slave, the purchaser would touch it and say, "This is mine by the law of the Romans. I have bought it with this brass, duly weighed." In the tribunal, every process was a pantomime. To reclaim an object, one would seize it with their hand. To protest a neighbor who erected a wall, one would throw a stone against it. When two men claimed proprietorship of a field, they would grasp hands and appear to fight. Then they would separate and each declares, "I declare this field is mine by the law of the Romans. I cite you before the tribunal of the praetor to debate our right at the place in question." The judge would order them to go to the place and say, "Before these witnesses here present, this is your road to the place. Go!" The litigants would take a few steps as if to go there, symbolizing the journey. A witness would then say, "Return," and the journey would be regarded as completed. Each of the two would present a clod of earth, symbolizing the field. This would commence the trial, and then the judge would hear the case alone. Like all primitive peoples, the Romans only comprehended what they saw. Material acts served to represent the right that could not be seen.

The Formalism of Roman Law

The Romans were meticulous in their adherence to ancient forms. They followed the letter of the law in both justice and religion, disregarding its sense. Every form was sacred and had to be strictly applied. In court cases, their maxim was "What has already been pronounced ought to be the law." If an advocate made a mistake in even one word while reciting the formula, his case was lost. For instance, a man sued his neighbor for cutting down his vines, but he lost the case because he used the word "vinea" instead of "arbor" in the formula he recited. This absolute reverence for the form allowed the Romans to make some strange accommodations. According to the law, if a father sold his son three times, the son would be freed from the father's power. When a Roman wanted to emancipate his son, he sold him three times in succession, and this comedy of sale sufficed to emancipate him. The law required that before beginning war, a herald should be sent to declare it at the enemy's frontier. When Rome wanted to make war on Pyrrhus, the king of Epirus, who had his kingdom on the other side of the Adriatic, they were embarrassed to execute this formality. They came up with a solution: a subject of Pyrrhus, perhaps a deserter, bought a field in Rome. They then assumed that this territory had become Epirus's territory, and the herald threw his javelin on this land and made his solemn declaration. Like all other immature peoples, the Romans believed that consecrated formulas had a magical virtue. Jurisprudence. The Law of the Twelve Tables and the laws made after them were brief and incomplete. However, many questions arose that had no law for their solution. In these embarrassing cases, it was customary in Rome to consult certain individuals who were highly respected for their knowledge of legal questions. These were often old consuls or pontiffs. They gave their advice in writing, and their replies were called the Responses of the Wise. Usually, these responses were authoritative according to the respect given to the sages. Emperor Augustus went further and named some of them whose responses should have the force of law. Thus, Law began to be a science, and the men versed in law formulated new rules that became obligatory. This was Jurisprudence.

The Praetor's Edict was a crucial aspect of Roman law, requiring a supreme magistrate to apply the sacred rules of justice. Only a consul or a praetor held the power to direct a tribunal and, as the Romans put it, "say the law." Consuls, who were primarily concerned with military matters, typically left this responsibility to the praetors. In Rome, there were always at least two praetors serving as judges. One adjudicated disputes between citizens and was known as the praetor of the city or praetor urbanus. The other presided over cases involving citizens and aliens and was called the praetor of the aliens or praetor peregrinus, or more specifically, the praetor between aliens and citizens. At least two tribunals were necessary since aliens were not allowed to participate in the tribunal of the citizens. Thanks to their absolute power, the praetors were able to settle cases based on their own sense of fairness. The praetor of the aliens was not bound by

Roman law, which was only applicable to Roman citizens. Nevertheless, when each praetor assumed office for a year, they promulgated a decree outlining the rules they intended to follow in their tribunal. This was known as the Praetor's Edict. Once the praetor's term ended, their ordinance was no longer valid, and their successor had the right to create an entirely new one. Over time, it became customary for each praetor to preserve the edicts of their predecessors, making a few changes and additions. Thus, the ordinances of the magistrates accumulated for centuries. In the second century, Emperor Hadrian codified the Praetorian Edict and gave it the force of law. This ensured that the Praetor's Edict would continue to shape Roman law for generations to come.

In the days of old, there existed two distinct tribunals, each with its own set of regulations and laws. The Civil Law, which pertained to the affairs of citizens, was governed by the praetor of the city. Meanwhile, the Law of Nations, which concerned the dealings of peoples who were alien to Rome, was overseen by the praetor of aliens. It became apparent that the Law of Nations was the more humane, sensible, and straightforward of the two laws. The Law of Citizens, derived from the strict and superstitious rules of the ancient Romans, had retained troublesome formulas and barbarous regulations from its rough beginnings. In contrast, the Law of Nations was founded on the experiences of merchants and people who had settled in Rome. These dealings were free from any national prejudices or formulas and were gradually developed and tested over several centuries. It was clear that the ancient law was contrary to reason, as the Roman proverb goes, "Strict law is the highest injustice." The praetors of the city began to correct the ancient law and judge according to equity or justice. They gradually applied the same rules that the praetor of aliens followed in his tribunal to citizens as well. For example, the Roman law stipulated that only male relatives could be heirs, but the praetor summoned female relatives to participate in the succession as well. The old law required a man to perform a complicated ceremony of sale to become a proprietor, but the praetor recognized that it was sufficient to have paid the price of the sale and to be in possession of the property. Thus, the Law of Nations gradually superseded the Civil Law.

Under the reign of the emperors, the Roman law underwent a transformation. The Antonines issued numerous edicts and letters in response to those who sought their counsel. These emperors were aided by jurisconsults who helped them implement reforms. Even during the third century, when both good and bad emperors ruled, new rules were established and old ones were corrected. Among the most renowned lawyers of this time were Papinian, Ulpian, Modestinus, and Paullus, whose works ultimately established the Roman law. The law of the third century differed greatly from the old Roman law, which was harsh towards the weak. The jurisconsults adopted the ideas of Greek philosophers, particularly the Stoics. They believed that all men were entitled to liberty and that slavery was unnatural. They even allowed slaves to seek justice against their masters and demanded that masters who killed their slaves be punished as murderers. They also protected children from the tyranny of their fathers. This new law was later known as Written Reason, as it was a philosophical law that could be applied to all men. The strict and crude law of the Twelve Tables had been completely replaced. The Roman law that governed Europe for centuries and is still partially preserved in the laws of some European countries today is not the law of the old Romans. Instead, it is a combination of the customs of various ancient peoples and the principles of Greek philosophers, which were fused and codified over time by Roman magistrates and jurisconsults.

Chapter 26

The Appearance of Jesus

The Christ appeared in Galilee, a small province in the North, hardly regarded as Jewish, and born into a humble family of carpenters. He was called Jesus, but his Greek disciples called him the Christ, meaning the king consecrated by holy oil. He was also known as the Master, the Lord, and the Saviour. The religion he founded is the one we now possess. We all know his life, which serves as the model for every Christian, and we know his instructions by heart, as they form our moral law. It is enough to indicate the new doctrines he disseminated in the world. First and foremost, Christ commended love. "Thou shalt love the Lord thy God with all thy heart and with all thy mind and thy neighbor as thyself. On these two commandments hang all the law and the prophets." The first duty is to love others and to benefit them. When God judges men, he will set on his right hand those who have fed the hungry, given drink to those who were thirsty, and clothed those that were naked. To those who would follow him, the Christ said at the beginning: "Go, sell all that ye have and give to the poor." For the ancients, the good man was the noble, the rich, and the brave. Since the time of Christ, the word has changed its sense: the good man is he who loves others. Doing good is loving others and seeking to be of service to them. Charity, the Latin name for love, has become the cardinal virtue. Charitable has become synonymous with beneficent. To the old doctrine of vengeance, the Christ formally opposes his doctrine of charity. "Ye have heard that it was said, An eye for an eye and a tooth for a tooth; but I say unto you, whosoever shall smite thee on thy right cheek, turn to him the other also. Ye have heard that it hath been said, Thou shalt love thy neighbor and hate thine enemy; but I say unto you love your enemies, do good to them that hate you, and pray for them that persecute you, that ye may be the children of your Father who is in heaven, who maketh his sun to rise on the evil and the good, and sendeth rain on the just and the unjust." He himself, on the cross, prayed for his executioners, "Father, forgive them, for they know not what they do."

Equality is a fundamental tenet of Christianity. Christ loved all people and died for the salvation of all humanity, not just one group. He treated everyone equally, without distinction. This was a radical departure from ancient religions, including Judaism, which were often exclusive and kept secret from outsiders. Christ instructed his disciples to spread his message to all nations, and the apostle Paul emphasized the importance of equality in his teachings. He said that there is no difference between Greeks and Jews, circumcised or uncircumcised, barbarians, slaves, or free people. Two centuries later, Tertullian, a Christian writer, declared that the world is a republic, a common land for all human beings. Poverty and humility are also central to Christian beliefs. Unlike the ancient world, which valued wealth and pride, Christ taught that the poor are blessed and that the kingdom of heaven belongs to them. He urged his followers to renounce all their possessions and to trust in God's providence. He himself lived a simple life, owning nothing, and relied on the generosity of others. Christ also emphasized the importance of humility and service. He taught that the greatest among his followers should be their servant and that those who exalt themselves will be humbled, while those who humble themselves will be exalted. This message has resonated throughout Christian history, and even today, the Pope, the successor of Saint Peter, calls himself the "Servant of the servants of God." Christ also showed compassion for the weak and vulnerable, including the poor, the sick, women, and children. He chose his disciples from among the common people and urged them to be meek and humble of heart.

The establishment of the Kingdom of God was the purpose of Christ's arrival on Earth. However, his enemies falsely believed he sought to become a king, as evidenced by the inscription on his cross: "Jesus of Nazareth, king of the Jews." This was a grave error. Christ had explicitly stated, "My kingdom is not of this world." He did not intend to overthrow governments or reform society. When asked about paying Roman taxes, he replied, "Render unto Caesar the things that are Caesar's, and to God the things that are God's." Christians accepted the established order and worked to perfect it, rather than attempting to reshape society. True worship, according to Christ, did not require sacrifices or strict adherence to formulas. "True worshippers shall worship the Father in spirit and truth." The moral law was summed up in Christ's words: "Be ye therefore perfect even as your Father which is in heaven is perfect." The twelve disciples who followed Christ were given the mission to spread his teachings to all nations and thus became known as Apostles. Most of them remained in Jerusalem and preached in Judaea, where the earliest Christians were Jews. However, it was Saul, who later changed his name to Paul, that carried Christianity to the Gentiles in the East. Paul spent his life traveling to Greek cities in Asia, Greece, and Macedonia, inviting both Jews and Gentiles to embrace the new religion. "You were once without Christ," he told them, "strangers to the covenant and to the promises; but you have been brought nigh by the blood of Christ, for it is he who of two peoples hath made both one." This marked a significant shift, as it was no longer necessary to be a Jew to become a Christian. Through Christ's law, the other nations that had been ignored by the law of Moses were brought closer to God. This unification of different peoples was the work of St. Paul, who became known as the Apostle to the Gentiles.

The religion of Christ spread slowly, just as he prophesied: "The kingdom of heaven is like a tiny mustard seed which is the smallest of all seeds; but when it has grown, it is the largest of the garden plants and the birds of the air come and nest in its branches." The Church was formed in every city where Christians gathered to pray, sing praises to God, and partake in the Lord's Supper. Their meetings were called Ecclesia, or assembly. The Christians of the same assembly saw themselves as brothers and sisters, and they shared their property to support the widows, the poor, and the sick. The most prominent members directed the community and led the religious ceremonies. They were called Priests, which meant "elders." Others were responsible for managing the community's goods and were known as Deacons or servants. In each city there was a supreme leader, the Bishop or overseer. As time passed, the Church's functions became more demanding, and the body of Christians was divided into two groups: the clergy who were the officials of the community, and the rest, the faithful, who were called the laity. Each city had its independent church, such as the church of Antioch, Corinth, or Rome. However, they all formed one church, the church of Christ, in which everyone was united in one faith. The universal or Catholic faith was considered the only correct belief system, and all conflicting opinions, or heresies, were condemned as errors.

The Sacred Books hold a special place in the hearts of many. For the Jews, the Old Testament is a sacred scripture. For the Christians, the Old Testament remains sacred, but they also have other sacred books that the church has brought together into one structure, known as the New Testament. The four Gospels tell the story of Christ's life and the "good news" of salvation that he brought. The Acts of the Apostles describes how the gospel was spread throughout the world. The Epistles are letters written by the apostles to the Christians of the first century. The Apocalypse, also known as Revelation, is the revelation made through Saint John to the seven churches of Asia. Many other books were considered sacred by some Christians, but the church has rejected these and labeled them as apocryphal. The Christian religion has faced persecution since its inception. The Jews were the first to oppose it, forcing the Roman governor of Judaea to crucify Christ. They also stoned Saint Stephen, the first martyr, and nearly killed Saint Paul. Later, the Pagans persecuted the Christians. The Romans tolerated all the religions of the East because the followers of Osiris, Mithra, and the Good Goddess recognized the Roman gods. However, the Christians, who worshipped the living God, rejected the petty divinities of antiquity. Worse yet, they refused to worship the emperor as a god and to burn incense on the altar of the goddess Roma. Several emperors issued edicts against the Christians, ordering governors to arrest and execute them. A letter from Pliny the Younger, a governor in Asia, to the emperor Trajan shows the procedure used against them. Pliny asked suspected Christians if they were Christians. If they confessed, he asked them two more times, threatening them with death. When they persisted, he had them executed, believing that their disobedience and obstinacy deserved punishment.

Many who have been accused of not being Christians have denied the allegations. They have repeated a prayer that I pronounced before them, have offered wine and incense to your statue, which I had set forth for this purpose together with the statues of the gods, and have even reviled the name of Christ. All these are things that no true Christian would do. Others have confessed that they were Christians, but they claim that their only crime was assembling on certain days before sunrise to worship Christ as God, to sing together in his honor, and to bind themselves by oath to commit no crime, to perpetrate no theft, murder, adultery, nor to violate their word. In order to secure the truth, I have believed it necessary to put two female slaves whom they called deaconesses to the torture, but I have discovered only an absurd and exaggerated superstition. The Roman government was a persecutor, but the populace was even more severe. They could not tolerate these people who worshipped a different god than theirs and disrespected their deities. Whenever famine or epidemic occurred, the well-known cry was heard, "To the lions with the Christians!" The people forced the magistrates to hunt and persecute the Christians. The Martyrs endured persecution for two and a half centuries throughout the empire, with thousands of victims of every age, sex, and condition. Roman citizens, like Saint Paul, were beheaded, and the others were crucified, burned, and most often sent to the beasts in the amphitheater. If they were allowed to escape with their lives, they were set to forced labor in the mines. Sometimes torture was aggravated by every sort of invention. In the great execution at Lyons in 177, the Christians, after being tortured and confined in narrow prison quarters, were brought to the arena. The beasts mutilated them without killing them. They were then seated in iron chairs heated red by fire. Blandina, a young slave, who survived all these torments, was bound with cords and exposed to the fury of a bull. The Christians joyfully suffered these persecutions, which gave them entrance to heaven. The occasion presented an opportunity for rendering public testimony to Christ. And so they did not call themselves victims, but martyrs meaning witnesses; their torture was a testimony. They compared it to the combat of the Olympian games; like the victor in the athletic contests, they spoke of the palm or the crown. Even now, the festal day of a martyr is the day of their death.

Frequently, a Christian who witnessed the persecution would pen a written account of the martyrdom. They would recount the arrest, the interrogation, the torture, and the death. These accounts, filled with uplifting details, were known as The Acts of the Martyrs. They were circulated throughout even the most remote communities. From one end of the empire to the other, they extolled the glory of the martyrs and stirred a desire to emulate them. Thousands of the faithful, seized by a thirst for martyrdom, eagerly stepped forward to incriminate themselves and demand condemnation. On one occasion, a governor of Asia had ordered the persecution of some Christians. All the Christians in the city presented themselves in his court and requested to be persecuted. The governor, infuriated, had some of them executed and sent the rest away. "Begone, you wretches! If you are so eager for death, you can find cliffs and ropes." Some of the faithful, to ensure torture, entered the temples and toppled the idols of the gods. It was necessary for the church to intervene and prohibit the solicitation of martyrdom. The ancient practice of cremation was repugnant to the Christians. Like the Jews, they buried their dead wrapped in a shroud in a sarcophagus. Cemeteries were therefore necessary. In Rome, where land was exceedingly expensive, the Christians went underground. In the fragile tufa on which Rome was built, one can see long passageways and subterranean chambers. There, in niches carved along the corridors, they placed the bodies of their dead. As each generation dug new passageways, a subterranean city was formed, known as the Catacombs or "to the tombs". Similar catacombs existed in several cities, such as Naples, Milan, and Alexandria, but the most renowned were those in Rome. In modern times, these catacombs have been explored, and thousands of Christian tombs and inscriptions have been discovered. The revelation of this subterranean world gave rise to a new field of historical science: Christian Epigraphy and Archaeology.

The catacombs' sepulchral halls are stark and austere, unlike those of the Egyptians or Etruscans. The Christians knew that corpses had no physical needs, so they refrained from embellishing the tombs. The most significant halls feature simple adornments and paintings, typically depicting the same scenes. The most common subjects include the faithful in prayer and the Good Shepherd, symbolizing Christ. Some halls even resembled chapels, where the bodies of holy martyrs and faithful were interred. Christians would visit these halls annually to celebrate the mysteries. During the third century's persecutions, Roman Christians often sought refuge in these underground chambers to worship or escape pursuit. The Christians felt secure in the labyrinth of galleries, whose entrance was often marked by a pagan tomb.

The Monks of the Third Century
The Solitaries

Christians, particularly in the East, believed that one could not become a perfect Christian by remaining among other people. Christ himself said, "If any man come to me and hate not his father, and mother, and wife, and children, and brethren, and sisters he cannot be my disciple." Therefore, faithful men and women who withdrew from the world to secure their salvation were called Anchorites, the man who is set apart or Monks meaning solitary. This practice began in the East during the mid-third century. The first anchorites settled in the deserts and ruins of Thebes in Upper Egypt, which remained the solitaries' holy land.

In the desert of Egypt, there lived a monk named Paul who reached the ripe old age of ninety. He resided in a grotto near a spring and a palm tree that provided him with sustenance and clothing. The monks modeled themselves after Saint Anthony, and Paul was the eldest among them. At the age of twenty, Paul heard the gospel being read, and it spoke to him. The text read, "If thou wilt be perfect, sell all thy goods and give to the poor." Paul was a handsome and wealthy man who inherited his riches from his parents. He sold all his possessions, gave the proceeds to the needy, and disappeared into the Egyptian desert. Paul first sought refuge in an empty tomb, and then he moved to the ruins of a fortress. He wore a hair shirt and ate only bread, which was brought to him every six months. He fasted, starved himself, and prayed day and night. Often, he prayed until sunrise, and then he cried out, "O sun, why hast thou risen and prevented my contemplating the true light?" Demons surrounded him, trying to distract him from his religious thoughts. As Paul aged, he became revered throughout Egypt. He returned to Alexandria for a day to preach against the Arian heretics, but he soon returned to the desert. When asked to stay in the city, he replied, "The fishes die on land, the monks waste away in the city; we return to our mountains like the fish to the water." Women also became solitaries, such as Alexandra, who lived in an empty tomb for ten years without seeing anyone. The monks believed that everything that came from the world turned the soul from God and endangered salvation. They thought that Christians should belong entirely to God and forget everything behind them. Saint Nilus warned, "Do you not know that it is a trap of Satan to be too much attached to one's family?" The monk Poemen and his brothers withdrew to the desert, and when their mother came to visit, they refused to appear. They only spoke to her when they were concealed and told her that she would see them in the other world.

But danger for the monk lurks not only in the world. Each man carries within himself an enemy from whom he cannot deliver himself as he has delivered himself from the world, his own body. The body prevents the soul from rising to God and draws it to worldly pleasures that come from the devil. And so, the solitaries applied themselves to overcoming the body by denying it everything that it loved. They subsisted only on bread and water; many ate but twice a week, some went to the mountains to cut herbs which they ate raw. They dwelt in grottoes, ruins, and tombs, lying on the earth or on a mat of rushes. The most zealous of them added other tortures to mortify, or kill, the body. Saint Pachomius for fifteen years slept only in an erect position, leaning against a wall. Macarius remained six months in a morass, the prey of mosquitoes "whose stings would have penetrated the hide of a wild boar." The most noted of these monks was Saint Simeon, surnamed Stylites or the man of the column. For forty years, he lived in the desert of Arabia on the summit of a column, exposed to the sun and the rain, compelling himself to stay in one position for a whole day. The faithful flocked from afar to behold him; he gave them audience from the top of his column, bidding creditors free their debtors, and masters liberate their slaves. He even sent reproaches to ministers and counselors of the emperor. This form of life was called Asceticism. The solitaries who lived in the same desert drew together and adopted a common life for the practice of their austerities. About Saint Anthony were already assembled many anchorites who gave him their obedience. Saint Pachomius in this way assembled 3,000. Their establishment was at Tabenna, near the first cataract of the Nile. He founded many other similar communities, either of men or women. In 256, a traveler said he had seen in a single city of Egypt 10,000 monks and 20,000 vowed to a religious life. There were more of them in Syria, in Palestine, in all the Orient. The monks thus united in communities and became Cenobites or people who live in common. They chose a chief, the abbot, a word that signifies "father" in Syriac, and they implicitly obeyed him. Cassian relates that in one community in Egypt, he had seen the abbot before the whole refectory give a cenobite a violent blow on the head to test his obedience.

In the early days of the monastic movement, the monks were a simple folk who gave up all worldly possessions and family ties. The cenobites, on the other hand, went even further and relinquished their own will. Upon entering the community, they vowed to own nothing, remain celibate, and submit to authority. Saint Basil described the monks as living a spiritual life akin to that of angels. The first cenobites banded together to construct houses in close proximity to one another. Eventually, each community built a grand monastery where every monk had his own cell. A Christian might liken these cells to a hive of bees, where each monk had the wax of work in his hands and the honey of psalms and prayers on his lips. These great houses required a written constitution which came to be known as the Monastic Rule. Saint Pachomius was the first to draft one, and Saint Basil later wrote another that was embraced by nearly all of the monasteries in the East.

Chapter 27

The Conclusion: The Fall

After the reigns of the Antonines, the empire was plunged into civil wars. There were several great armies stationed in Rome, on the Rhine, on the Danube, in the East, and in England, each aiming to make its general emperor. Typically, the rivals fought until only one was left, who then governed for a few years before being assassinated. If he was lucky enough to pass on his power to his son, the soldiers would revolt against the son, and the war would start all over again. In 193, the Praetorians massacred Emperor Pertinax, and the army decided to auction off the empire. Two buyers presented themselves: Sulpicius, offering each soldier 1,000 dollars, and Didius, offering more than 1,200 dollars. The Praetorians brought Didius to the Senate and had him named emperor. Later, when he did not pay them, they murdered him. At the same time, the great armies of Britain, Illyricum, and Syria each proclaimed their own general as emperor, and the three rivals marched on Rome. The Illyrian legions arrived first, and their general, Septimius Severus, was named emperor by the Senate. Then began two bloody wars, one against the legions of Syria and the other against the legions of Britain. After two years, Severus emerged as the victor. For a century, there was no other form of government than the will of the soldiers. They killed the emperors who displeased them and replaced them with their favorites. Strange emperors occupied the throne, such as Elagabalus, a Syrian priest who dressed like a woman and had his mother assemble a senate of women, and Maximin, a soldier of fortune, a rough and bloodthirsty giant who ate thirty pounds of food and drank twenty-one quarts of wine a day. At one point, there were twenty emperors at the same time, each in a corner of the empire from 260 to 278. These have been called the Thirty Tyrants.

In this century of war, superstitions abound. The gods of the Orient, such as Isis, Osiris, and the Great Mother, have followers throughout the empire. But above all others, Mithra, a Persian deity, becomes the universal god of the empire. Mithra is none other than the sun. Monuments in his honor are found throughout the empire, depicting him slaughtering a bull with the inscription, "To the unconquerable sun, to the god Mithra." His cult is complex, sometimes resembling Christian worship, with baptism, sacred feasts, anointing, penance, and chapels. To be admitted, one must pass through an initiatory ceremony, fasting, and certain fearful tests. By the end of the third century, the religion of Mithra is the official religion of the empire. The Invincible God is the god of the emperors, with chapels in the form of grottoes, altars, and bas-reliefs everywhere, including a magnificent temple in Rome erected by Emperor Aurelian. One of the most pressing needs of the time is reconciliation with the deity, leading to the invention of purification ceremonies. The most striking of these is the Taurobolia. The worshipper, adorned in a white robe with gold ornaments, takes their place at the bottom of a ditch covered by a platform pierced with holes. A bull is led over the platform, and the priest kills it, allowing its blood to run through the holes onto the garments, face, and hair of the worshipper. It is believed that this "baptism of blood" purifies one of all sins. The recipient emerges from the ditch hideous to look upon, but happy and envied, born into a new life.

The Jumbled Faiths of Antiquity

In the time before Christianity's triumph, the world's religions were a jumbled mess. The sun was worshipped under many monikers, such as Sol, Helios, Baal, Elagabal, and Mithra. All the cults imitated one another and sometimes even mimicked Christian practices. Even the life of Christ was replicated. The Asiatic philosopher Apollonius of Tyana, who lived in the first century, became a legendary figure, a sort of prophet and son of a god, who traveled with his disciples, casting out demons, healing the sick, and raising the dead. It was said he had come to reform the teachings of Pythagoras and Plato. In the third century, an empress had Apollonius of Tyana's life story written, as if it were a Pythagorean gospel that opposed the gospel of Christ. The most notable example of this religious confusion was given by Alexander Severus, a pious and conscientious emperor who had a chapel in his palace where he worshipped the benefactors of humanity: Abraham, Orpheus, Jesus, and Apollonius of Tyana.

The Reforms of Diocletian and Constantine

After a century of civil wars, emperors emerged who were capable of halting the anarchy. They were common men, rough and active, soldiers of fortune who rose from one rank to another until they became generals-in-chief and then emperors. Almost all of them came from the semi-barbarous provinces of the Danube and Illyria. Some had been shepherds or peasants in their youth. They had the simple manners of the old Roman generals. When the envoys of the king of Persia asked to see Emperor Probus, they found a bald old man dressed in a linen cassock, lying on the ground, eating peas and bacon. It was the story of Curius Dentatus repeated after five centuries.

With a firm hand, these emperors enforced discipline among their soldiers, thus restoring order to the empire. However, change was necessary. The vast territory required more than one man to govern and defend it. Each emperor chose two or three collaborators from among his relatives or friends, each tasked with governing a portion of the empire. They were known as Caesars, and sometimes there were two equal emperors, both holding the title of Augustus. Upon the emperor's death, one of the Caesars succeeded him. It was no longer possible for the army to create emperors. The provinces were too vast, and Diocletian divided them. To replace the dangerous Praetorian Guard of Rome, Diocletian established two legions. The Western part of the empire was in ruins and depopulated, making the Eastern part more important. Therefore, Diocletian abandoned Rome and made his capital at Nicomedia in Asia Minor. Constantine went further and founded a new Rome in the East, which he named

Constantinople. Constantinople was founded on a promontory where Europe and Asia were separated only by the narrow channel of the Bosporus. The Greek colonists had founded the town of Byzantium in a country of vineyards and rich harvests, under a beautiful sky. The hills surrounding the area made it easily defensible. Its port, the Golden Horn, was one of the best in the world, capable of sheltering 1,200 ships. A chain 820 feet in length was all that was necessary to exclude a hostile fleet. This was the perfect location for Constantine's new city, Constantinople, which means "the city of Constantine."

Walls of great strength encircled the city, while two public squares adorned with porticos were built. A palace, circus, theaters, aqueducts, baths, temples, and even a Christian church were erected to further beautify the city. Constantine, in his desire to adorn the city, brought in the most celebrated statues and bas-reliefs from other cities. To populate the city, he compelled people from neighboring towns to move there and offered rewards and honors to the great families who would make their homes there. As in Rome, distributions of grain, wine, and oil were established, and a continuous round of shows was provided. This was one of those rapid transformations, almost fantastic, in which the Orient delights. The task began on November the fourth, 326, and on May the eleventh, 330, the city was dedicated. It was a permanent creation. For ten centuries, Constantinople resisted invasions, preserving its rank as the capital of the empire. Today, it still stands as the first city of the East. The emperors who resided in the East adopted the customs of the Orient, wearing delicate garments of silk and gold and a diadem of pearls as a headdress. They secluded themselves in the depths of their palace, sitting on a throne of gold, surrounded by ministers and separated from the world by a crowd of courtiers, servants, functionaries, and military guards. One must prostrate oneself before them with face to the earth, as a token of adoration. They were called Lord and Majesty and were treated as gods. Everything that touched their person was sacred, and so men spoke of the sacred palace, the sacred bed-chamber, the sacred Council of State, and even the sacred treasury. The period of this regime has been termed the Later Empire, distinguished from the Early Empire of the preceding three centuries.

THE ECHO OF ANCIENT CIVILIZATIONS

In the days of the Early Empire, an emperor's life was one of both magistrate and general. However, as time passed and the Later Empire came into being, the emperor's palace became more akin to the court of a Persian king. The officials of the empire were plentiful, with Diocletian finding the provinces too large to manage effectively. To combat this, he divided them into smaller sections. For example, Lugdunensis, the province surrounding Lyons, was split into four, while Aquitaine was split into three. This resulted in a total of 117 officials, up from the previous 46. As the number of officials grew, so did their duties. In addition to governors and deputies in the provinces, there were military commanders in the border provinces, known as dukes and counts. The emperor himself had a select group of bodyguards, chamberlains, assistants, domestics, and a council of state. There were also bailiffs, messengers, and a whole host of secretaries organized into four bureaus. These officials no longer received their orders directly from the emperor. Instead, they communicated with him through their superior officers. The governors answered to the two praetorian prefects, while the officials of public works were subordinate to the two prefects of the city. The collectors of taxes answered to the Count of the Sacred Largesses, and the deputies to the Count of the Domains. All palace officers answered to the Master of the Offices, while the court's domestics answered to the Chamberlain. These heads of departments were akin to ministers in their character.

This particular system is not a difficult one for us to understand. We are used to seeing officials, judges, generals, collectors, and engineers organized into distinct departments, each with their own specific duties, and all subordinated to the commands of a chief of the service. We even have more ministers than there were in Constantinople. However, this administrative machine, which has become so familiar to us because we have been acquainted with it from our infancy, is nonetheless complicated and unnatural. It is the Later Empire that gave us the first model of this. The Byzantine Empire preserved it, and since that time, all absolute governments have been forced to imitate it because it has made the work of government easier for those who have it to do. Society in the Later

Empire. The Later Empire is a decisive moment in the history of civilization. The absolute power of the Roman magistrate is united with the pompous ceremonial of the eastern kings to create a power unknown before in history. This new imperial majesty crushes everything beneath it. The inhabitants of the empire cease to be citizens and, from the fourth century, are called "subjects" in Latin and "slaves" in Greek. In reality, all are slaves of the emperor, but there are different grades of servitude. There are various degrees of nobility that the master confers on them, which they transmit to their posterity.

In this series, we have the Nobilissimi, or the very noble, who are the imperial family. Following them are the Illustres, or the notable, who are the chief ministers of departments. The Spectabiles, or the eminent, are the high dignitaries, while the Clarissimi, or most renowned, are the great officials, sometimes referred to as senators. Finally, we have the Perfectissimi, or the very perfect. Each important man has his rank, title, and functions. The only men who matter are the courtiers and officials. It's a regime of titles and etiquette, a clear example of absolute power combined with a mania for titles and the desire to regulate everything. The Later Empire exemplifies a society reduced to a machine and a government absorbed by a court. It achieved the ideal that today's supporters of absolute power propose, and for a long time, champions of liberty must combat the traditions that the Later Empire left behind.

The Triumph of Christianity

In the early years of the first two centuries, Christians were a small minority in the empire. They were mostly from the lower classes, including workmen, freedmen, and slaves, who lived in obscurity within the great cities. The aristocracy paid little attention to them, and even Suetonius, in his "Lives of the Twelve Caesars," only mentions a certain Chrestus who caused trouble among the people of Rome. The rich and educated only took an interest in Christianity to ridicule it as a religion for the poor and ignorant. However, Christianity's promise of compensation in the afterlife for the poor of this world made it an attractive option for many. Persecution only made it stronger. "The blood of the martyrs," the faithful said, "is the seed of the church." Throughout the third century, conversions continued, not only among the poor but also among the aristocracy. By the beginning of the fourth century, Christianity had spread throughout the East. Helena, the mother of Constantine, was a Christian and has since been canonized by the church. When Constantine marched against his rival, he carried a standard or labarum, bearing the cross and the monogram of Christ. His victory was the victory of the Christians. He allowed them to freely perform their religious rites by edict in 313, and later openly favored them. Despite this, Constantine did not completely break with the ancient religion. While he presided over the assembly of Christian bishops, he continued to hold the title of Pontifex Maximus. He also carried a nail from the true cross in his helmet and depicted the sun god on his coins. In Constantinople, he built both a Christian church and a temple to Victory. For fifty years, it was unclear what the official religion of the empire was.

The Christians, even in the midst of persecution, never entertained the idea of toppling the empire. Once the persecution ended, the bishops joined forces with the emperors. This marked the definitive organization of the Christian church, which was modeled after the Later Empire and remains in that form to this day. Each city had a bishop who resided within the city and governed the people of the surrounding area. This area, subject to the bishop's authority, was called a Diocese. In the Later Empire, there were as many bishops and dioceses as there were cities in any given country. This is why the bishops were so numerous and the dioceses so plentiful in the East and Italy, where cities were abundant. In Gaul, however, there were only 120 dioceses between the Rhine and the Pyrenees, and most of these, except in the south, were similar in size to a modern French department. Each province became an ecclesiastical province, with the bishop of the capital or metropolis, becoming the metropolitan, or archbishop, as he was later called. In this century, the councils, great assemblies of the church, began. Local councils had already taken place, where bishops and priests from a single province were present. In 324, Constantine called for a

General Assembly of the World, in Nicaea, Asia Minor, with 318 ecclesiastics in attendance. They discussed theological questions and created the Nicene Creed, the Catholic confession of faith. The emperor then wrote to all the churches, commanding them to "conform to the will of God as expressed by the council." This was the first ecumenical council, and there were three more before the arrival of the barbarians made it impossible to assemble the entire church. The decisions made by these councils had the power of law for all Christians and were called Canons, or rules. The collection of these regulations formed the Canon Law.

The Heretics From the second century, there were Christians who held opinions that were contrary to those of the majority of the church. These individuals were known as heretics. Often, the bishops of a country would gather to declare the new teachings as false, to force the author to renounce them, and if they refused, to separate them from the communion of Christians. However, the author of the heresy often had supporters who believed in the truth of their teachings and refused to submit, causing hatred and violent strife between them and the faithful who adhered to the church's orthodox creed. As long as Christians were weak and persecuted by the state, their disagreements were limited to words and books. But when society became entirely Christian, the conflicts against the heretics turned into persecutions and sometimes even civil wars. Most of the heresies of this time arose among the Greeks of Asia or Egypt, peoples who were subtle, sophistical, and disputatious. These heresies were usually attempts to explain the mysteries of the Trinity and the Incarnation. The most significant of these heresies was that of Arius, who taught that Christ was created by God the Father and was not equal to him. The Council of Nicaea condemned this view, but his doctrine, called Arianism, spread throughout the East. For two centuries, Catholics and Arians fought to see who should have supremacy in the church. The stronger party anathematized, exiled, imprisoned, and sometimes killed the leaders of the opposition. For a long time, the Arians had the advantage. Several emperors took their side, and as the barbarians entered the empire, they were converted to Arianism and received by Arian bishops. It took more than two centuries before the Catholics overcame this heresy.

Paganism, the ancient religion of the Gentiles, did not vanish in a single moment. While the Orient converted quickly, in the Occident, few Christians existed outside of the cities. Even there, many continued to worship idols. The first Christian emperors did not wish to sever ties with the ancient imperial religion. They protected both the bishops of the Christians and the priests of the gods. They presided over councils and remained pontifex maximus. Julian, also known as the Apostate, openly returned to the ancient religion. In 384, Emperor Gratian was the first to refuse the insignia of the pontifex maximus. However, as intolerance was widespread in this century, as soon as the Roman religion ceased to be official, people began to persecute it. The sacred fire of Rome, which had burned for eleven centuries, was extinguished. The Vestals were removed, and the Olympian games were celebrated for the last time in 394. Then, the monks of Egypt emerged from their deserts to destroy the altars of the false gods and establish relics in the temples of Anubis and Serapis. Marcellus, a bishop of Syria, at the head of a band of soldiers and gladiators, sacked the temple of Jupiter at Aparna and set out to scour the country for the destruction of the sanctuaries. He was killed by the peasants and raised by the church to the honor of a saint. Soon, idolatry persisted only in the rural districts where it escaped detection. The idolaters were peasants who continued to adore sacred trees and fountains and assemble in proscribed sanctuaries. The Christians began to refer to these peasants as "pagans," a name that has stuck with them to this day. Paganism thus led an obscure existence in Italy, Gaul, and Spain until the end of the sixth century.

The incursions of the Germanic peoples into the empire continued for two centuries until the Huns, a people of Tartar horsemen, came from the steppes of Asia and threw themselves on the Germans who occupied the country to the north of the Danube. In that country, there was already a great German kingdom, that of the Goths, who had been converted to Christianity by Ulfilas, an Arian. To escape the Huns, a part of this people, the West Goths or Visigoths, fled into Roman territory, defeated the Roman armies, and overran the country all the way to Greece. Valens, the emperor of the East, had perished in the defeat of Adrianople in 378. Gratian, the emperor of the West, took as a colleague a noble Spaniard, Theodosius by name, and gave him the title of Augustus of the East in 379. Theodosius was able to rehabilitate his army by avoiding a great battle with the Visigoths and by making a war of skirmishes against them; this led to a treaty. They accepted service under the empire and land was given to them in the country to the south of the Danube. They were charged with preventing the enemies of the empire from crossing the river. Theodosius, having reestablished peace in the East, came to the West where Gratian had been killed by order of the usurper Maximus. This Maximus who was the commander of the Roman army of Britain and had crossed into Gaul with his army, abandoning the Roman provinces of Britain to the ravages of the highland Scots. Here, he defeated Gratian, and invaded Italy. He was the master of the West, Theodosius of the East. The contest between them was not only one between persons but a battle between two religions. Theodosius was Catholic and had assembled a council at Constantinople to condemn the heresy of Arius whereas Maximus was ill-disposed toward the church. The engagement occurred on the banks of the Save and Maximus was defeated, taken, and executed.

In the days of Theodosius, Valentinian the Second, son of Gratian, was established in the West, and Theodosius returned to the East. However, a barbarian Frank named Arbogast, who was the general of Valentinian's troops, had Valentinian killed. Arbogast did not proclaim himself emperor, as he was not Roman, but instead had his Roman secretary Eugenius made emperor. This was a religious war, as Arbogast had taken the side of the pagans. Theodosius emerged victorious, had Eugenius executed, and remained the sole emperor. His victory was that of the Catholic Church. In 391, Theodosius issued the Edict of Milan, which prohibited the practice of the ancient religion. Anyone who offered a sacrifice, adored an idol, or entered a temple would be condemned to death as a state criminal, and their goods would be confiscated to the profit of the informer. All pagan temples were either destroyed or converted into Christian churches. Theodosius was praised by ecclesiastical writers as a model for emperors. Theodosius demonstrated a rare example of submission to the church. The inhabitants of Thessalonica had risen in riot, killed their governor, and overthrown the statues of the emperor. In response, Theodosius ordered the people to be massacred, resulting in the death of 7,000 individuals. Later, when Theodosius presented himself to enter the cathedral of Milan, Bishop Ambrose charged him with his crime before all the people. The bishop declared that he could not give entrance to the church to a man defiled with so many murders. Theodosius confessed his sin, accepted the public penance imposed upon him by the bishop, and remained at the door of the church for eight months, concluding the last chapter of the dawn of civilization.

THE END.

Thank You!

This concludes "*The Echo of Ancient Civilizations*" by Doug Richardson. Narrated by H.K. Marks.

We thank you.

You could have picked from dozens of other books, but you took a chance and chose this one.

So THANK YOU for getting this book and for making it all the way to the end.

Before you go, I wanted to ask you for one small favor. **Could you please consider posting a review on the platform? Posting a review is the best and easiest way to support the work of independent publishers.**

Your feedback will help us to keep publishing the kind of books you love to read.

>> **Leave a review on Amazon US** <<

>> **Leave a review on Amazon UK** <<

Printed in Great Britain
by Amazon